THE PROBLEM WITH I
Tarek El Diwany

2nd *Edition*
Published by Kreatoc Ltd., London

Published in 2003 by Kreatoc Ltd.
72 New Bond Street, London, W1S 1RR, United Kingdom
ISBN 0-9544974-0-6

Website: www.theproblemwithinterest.com

First edition published in 1997 by Ta-Ha Publishers Ltd.
1 Wynne Road, London, SW9 0BB, United Kingdom
ISBN 1 897940 64 5 Paperback
ISBN 1 897940 65 3 Hardback

Copyright © Tarek El Diwany 1997-2003

All rights reserved. No part of this publication may be reproduced, stored in any retrieval system, or transmitted in any form or by any means, electronic or otherwise, without the written permission of the publisher.

Tarek El Diwany has asserted his right under the Copyright, Designs and Patents Act 1988 to be identified as the author of this work

A CIP catalogue record for this book is available from the British Library

Printed by Partners In Print, Birmingham, United Kingdom

CONTENTS

FOREWORD		**VII**
PREFACE		**IX**
1	*Interest and the physical system*	1
2	*The production of money*	35
3	*The currency game*	75
4	*Wealth creation and wealth transfer*	99
5	*Value judgements*	119
6	*Trade or interest?*	135
7	*Banking and money under Islam*	175
IN CONCLUSION		**193**
BIBLIOGRAPHY		**197**
INDEX		**205**

ACKNOWLEDGEMENTS

BISMILLAHI RAHMANI RAHIM

for my friend and teacher, Mohamed Ghanem;

and to the following with many thanks for their kind help and advice over the years:

Dr. Sheikh Ghazali Abod

Dr. Usama Hassan

Christopher Jack

Sheikh Muhammad Kholwadia

Dr. Purnendu Nath

Afsar Siddiqui

Richard Webb

Shaharuddin Zainuddin

Mohammed Junaid Ahmed Zakir

FOREWORD

One of the fundamental goals of human intuition is to perceive what the purpose of life is, and to answer the ultimate question of how that purpose can be achieved. In spite of a vast amount of knowledge accumulated through the ages, that has enabled humans to exploit the properties of matter to highly complex ends, uncertainty on this simple yet vital issue remains.

Sometimes one encounters the speculative assumption that the capacity of the human intellect is unlimited but, in the case at hand, the kind of knowledge required for certainty lies beyond the ability of mankind to discover. It is a kind of knowledge that can only be provided by the same Authority which creates life in the first instance. Without this knowledge the whole of creation would be meaningless, a huge mechanical structure with no purpose, contradicting the perfection in nature which science can only confirm.

Muslims believe that Islam provides that knowledge which is beyond the human capacity to discover, in order and in sum. It furnishes us with concepts and facts in the realms of morality and ethics, and in the physical world too, which cannot be negated by any standard of scientific logic or scientific discovery. It is a knowledge based upon a voluntary belief in an absolute and transcendent truth, namely that 'There is no God but Allah and that Muhammad is His final Prophet and Messenger'. This significant single truth and the message that was carried with it was revealed letter by letter, word by word, and verse by verse by Allah, the only God, in the Arabic language to the Prophet Muhammad sal'Allahu alaihi wassalam (s.a.w.), and was collected in the Qur'an nearly fourteen hundred years ago. It has been protected from all forms of distortion since and is available now, exactly as it was revealed, for anyone who wishes to read it.

Within the words of the Qur'an is a thorough constitution for human activity, as practised by the Prophet s.a.w. himself, his family and disciples. All of its injunctions, in both the positive and negative forms of 'do' and 'do not', form a guidance that allows humanity to live according to the single truth. God is the only Creator, He alone decides the purpose of His creation, and the way of achieving that purpose. It is a purpose that is simply and clearly stated within the Qur'an:

For no other reason have I created Jinns and humans but to worship me alone. No sustenance do I require of them, nor do I require that they should feed me.
Qur'an 51: 56 & 57

So to fulfil the purpose of life is to worship God. This can only be achieved by applying His constitution as described in the Qur'an and as practised by His final Prophet s.a.w. in all fields of human endeavour including the social, the economic and the political. The intention to follow God's rules must be purely for His worship. The final result is human freedom, dignity and justice.

Throughout history there have always been some humans who fell into the temptation of hijacking the Divine legislation, who violated its conditions under false claims, who were ignorant and arrogant, and who secularised human society in both ideology and institution. It is a phenomenon that is common throughout the world today. The way to uncover the falseness of their claims is to educate people about the Qur'an and the tradition of the last Prophet s.a.w., and to explain to them the meaning of the single truth. Economics has now become the latest challenge in this process, and I am sure that the content of this book will be a good contribution towards meeting it.

Mohamed A. Ghanem
July 1997

PREFACE

For patients suffering from 'illnesses of indiscretion', European physicians once prescribed mercury. At their disposal for the treatment of other illnesses were remedies that included the leech, confinement to bed in an unventilated room and the soaking of sores with urine. Meanwhile, the syphilis remained and the teeth turned black, the fever worsened, the invalid developed bed sores and the skin stank of urea. A panoply of problems made worse by a panoply of quacks. The physicians' explanation of their failures invoked a science with which few laymen dared argue and, in this manner, the orthodox treatments were perpetuated. Having suggested the use of clean bandages in the wards, Pasteur found himself mocked by an intellectually arrogant establishment. The press published cartoons in which he was portrayed spraying the air with disinfectant. When Copernicus and Galileo attacked the science of their time, they too suffered at the hands of established opinion. Whilst demanding a retraction of their heresy, the Church conveniently ignored the growing gulf between evidence and its own pet theories. But the Earth became increasingly round and drifted ever further from the centre of the universe.

Orthodox views have often proved all-pervasive and wrong. Even in the light of facts that state otherwise, established assumptions have an uncanny knack of surviving. It is my contention that such is the case in the field of western economic debate today. Where once the student asked 'does raising the interest rate reduce inflation?', he now asks, 'by how much must we raise the interest rate in order to reduce inflation?'. These are the complacent assumptions of the new 'consensus economics'.

Many developing nations now reach for the medicines that consensus recommends. But treatments involving 'shock-therapy' and IMF austerity packages are uncomfortably reminiscent of the remedies of the quacks: extreme in their side effects and of ambiguous benefit. Sometimes, there appears the assertion that things would be worse under any other economic regime. Of course, the assertion is untestable because one can never relive the past to know the difference. Meanwhile, consensus economics extends its grasp, and society is increasingly coming to accept pollution, the business cycle, inflation and gross inequalities in wealth as the unavoidable facts of economic life.

The focus of this work is upon interest and its impact on humanity. It is an impact that reaches beyond the debtor-creditor relationship and one which cannot be expressed in terms of monetary units alone. In the pages that follow I shall argue that our world has become beholden to interest, enslaved by those who profit from it, and misled by those who justify it. My work shall not add to the existing stockpile of facts on the topic of interest. That stockpile already requires more than a lifetime to read. What is needed now is not more fact, but more understanding of the facts that we already know.

One problem that confronts the modern economist is the sheer complexity of the system that he seeks to describe. This complexity makes any attempt to model the system extremely difficult, and without some kind of model no scientific attempt at forecasting can be undertaken. In building an economic model, the econometrician must identify the precise starting values of every variable in the economic process and describe the exact nature of those processes and their inter-relationships. Meteorologists know how complex a task this is. Yet where the meteorologist works with precise and measurable physical laws, economists deal in uncertainty and unquantifiable propositions, and where meteorologists hesitate to predict weather patterns more than one week ahead, the bold economist may stretch his own horizons over several years. Though economic forecasts over short time periods are sometimes broadly accurate, over longer periods they are usually inaccurate.

The chaotic system is simply too complex for the economist to understand let alone to model on a computer. It would be quite an achievement if forecasters could reliably predict the direction of change, never mind its amount. Whilst physicists, doctors and chemists can predict the events of their own domain with some success, there are no economists whose modelling efforts are as reliable. I do not wish to belittle economic forecasters for many are extremely able. I shall simply wish them good luck in their endeavours and proceed in my own direction.

So often we hear that religion should not interfere with science. I maintain that science should not interfere with religion. If God says that interest is prohibited, who are we to disagree? And it is hardly plausible to argue that Muslims should not interfere with modern economics, since men of other religions have most clearly done so already. It's just that people don't refer to Ricardo, Marx, Keynes and Friedman as Jewish economists. Instead they speak of Classicism, Marxism, Keynesianism and Monetarism. Islamic economics is not like this. In the very name of our discipline we announce who we are, and in our work we set out clearly what we are trying to do for the world.

Nevertheless, others may not maintain as I do. Hence, in the first four chapters of this work I have adopted a largely 'positive' approach to economics. The final three chapters are devoted to a 'normative' discussion from the perspective of Islam. It is a basic principle in Islam that where the foundations of our economic and social life are just, so too will be the results of their interaction. Of course, we may not be *content* with those results but, according to this philosophy, they will at least be better than the alternatives. Where they are given, my recommendations for economic change assume likewise.

To my mind, the economics embodied in the religion of Islam probably constitutes the last remaining serious challenge to free market capitalism. However, because the Muslim world is not yet in a position to lecture the West on how to attain economic success, I hope that I strike a sufficiently modest note in offering my insights.

Tarek El Diwany

Chapter one
INTEREST AND THE PHYSICAL SYSTEM

> *Entropy is a word that is used to describe the amount of disorder in a physical system. A feature of the world around us is that physical systems decay, in other words that they experience increasing entropy. Fruit rots and buildings become dilapidated, unless energy is expended in order to maintain them. Left to itself, the physical world follows the path of compound decrement towards, but never quite reaching, zero. Meanwhile, loans at interest are often structured so as to follow the path of compound increment towards infinity. This chapter contrasts interest and entropy and highlights the contradiction between the laws of interest and the laws of nature. It is proposed that 'short-termism', pollution and resource depletion can be encouraged by the use of interest in the financing of industry.*

The Importance of Entropy

When physicists say that 'entropy is increasing' they are describing the tendency of all physical systems towards greater disorder. This principle of physics, underlying the laws of thermodynamics, was applied to the physical dimension of wealth as early as 1926 by Frederick Soddy in *Wealth, Virtual Wealth and Debt* and developed in detail by others, notably Nicolas Georgescu-Roegen in *The Entropy Law and the Economic Process* (1971). These analyses have many implications for economics.

The first law of thermodynamics states that the total energy of a thermodynamic system remains constant although it may be transformed from one form to another. Here is the principle of the conservation of energy. The second law of thermodynamics states that heat can never spontaneously pass from a body at a lower temperature to one at a higher temperature. Taken together, these two (of the three) laws of thermodynamics say that as time passes a closed system incurs a constant total of energy, but that the distribution of this energy becomes more even. Here is the entropy process in a nutshell.

A simple example has a metallic container at room temperature into which a block of metal at 100 degrees Celsius is placed. If insulated from the outside environment, it will be found upon later examination that the *average* temperature of the container and its content remains at the initial level but that the *difference* in temperature between the two components has narrowed. Ultimately, any difference in temperature will disappear entirely. Where once the block was hot enough to boil water, it is now no longer able to do so. The ability to perform work has therefore diminished even though the total amount of energy in the system has not. This loss of ability to perform work is a key feature of the entropy process.

Within the constraints imposed by the laws of thermodynamics, there is great freedom as to the path followed by an entropic process. Although entropy is increasing, it may do so in a variety of ways. The entropic process is thus said to be *indeterminate*. The ultimate fact though is that entropy must increase from one time period to the next. It is an irrevocable and qualitative process that represents decay.

To say that entropy increases irrevocably is not however the same as saying that the effects of the entropy process cannot be reversed. An open physical system may in fact experience decreasing entropy over a given time period. For example, the plant, an open physical system, consumes energy and nutrients from the external physical system that is the environment. In this manner the plant creates a highly ordered structure called fruit. Similarly, the repair men consume energy and materials in maintaining the building. However, precisely because of the consumption of external matter and energy in these processes, entropy in that external physical system will increase. The entropy law tells us that, external and internal systems combined, the net amount of entropy must continue to increase. In this way the entropy law remains valid.

Though entropy is always increasing, its rate of increase varies from one system to the next. Fruit and vegetables on a market stall display a higher rate of increase in entropy than for example buildings, which in turn display a higher rate of increase in entropy than minerals in the Earth's crust. The fruit decays within a few days once picked, the buildings decay within a matter of years if unattended and minerals in the Earth's crust remain for millennia with little sign of deterioration.

It was Schrodinger who first proposed that life bearing structures maintain themselves by consuming low entropy from the environment and transforming it into higher entropy. Given that average entropy in a physical system is always increasing at a natural rate, it must be true that man's activity in establishing lower degrees of entropy in some components of his physical environment inevitably accelerates the increase of entropy in other components. The *Guardian* leader page from 25 March 1995 comments :
Global warming is, above all, an index of the rate at which the world squanders its resources and of the resulting disturbance to natural ecological balances maintained for millions of years. No one can seriously deny that energy is now being consumed on a scale never achieved by humanity before. The only question - and it is the critical one - is whether it can be stopped and how.

Georgescu-Roegen informs us that the entropy process dominates almost every facet of the economic process. If we are then to ignore it in our economic analysis, we are doomed to failure before we begin. We must first accept that our economic activity does not take place in a closed system. Even on a global scale we receive low entropy energy from the Sun daily, and free of charge. This very fact makes our land valuable and productive and allows humans to live, but rarely does it appear in econometric models.

Early classical models of physics, developed by Newton and applied so successfully to the world of machines and mechanical processes, inspired economists to seek similar mechanical descriptions within their own field of endeavour. However, mechanical processes are by nature revocable. A ball can be picked up if dropped. Today, these mechanical ideas are prominent in economic analysis. Meanwhile, the entropy law, when applied to the economic process, involves an irrevocable flow from low entropy resource to high entropy waste. This 'one way flow' concept opposes the idea of revocability in economic processes, and contrasts strikingly with such models as the 'circular flow of funds' that are used by some modern economists. The modern approach tends to view the economic system in a mechanical way that assumes change to be revocable, or in some formula bound way that assumes a determinate process. In criticism of this approach Georgescu-Roegen reminds us of Alfred Marshall's comment, in his *Principles of Economics*, that biology rather than mechanics "is the true Mecca of the economist".

In Europe, the concepts of thermodynamics probably sprang from Carnot's memoir on the efficiency of steam engines in 1824. Given that this was the mechanical age, it is not surprising to find that within a few years theorists were tempted to interpret the new ideas of thermodynamics with the aid of existing mechanical theories, this time in the form of statistics. Georgescu-Roegen is once again critical of this approach and its progenitor, Ludwig Boltzman. Boltzman's 'statistical thermodynamics' focused on entropy at the microscopic level. When a system reaches a condition in which no change in entropy occurs that system is said to be 'isentropic' and such a stage represents an equilibrium. It is the state with the greatest amount of disorder and, for Boltzman at least, is the state which displays the distribution of molecules that has the greatest probability of occurring.

If probability is involved in the entropy process, then at each point in time there must be some degree of probability that entropy will decrease. In this way Boltzman explains the increases in order that we see in the world around us. According to this view, the actions of living organisms to grow and reproduce, indeed to exist in the first place, arise out of pure chance and despite the prevailing trend towards decreasing order. In other words, if order is to increase, it does so according to the law of probability and nothing else.

But is it not an observable fact that living things act in a purposeful manner to increase order in their environment? Is it by chance that human beings build comfortable homes in which to live? In his discussions of entropy, Georgescu-Roegen comments that :
... statistical thermodynamics completely denies the possibility of any purposive activity because it claims that everything is completely determined by the laws of mechanics.
Georgescu-Roegen, N., *The Entropy Law and the Economic Process* (1971) p. 194

Since purpose clearly does exist among life bearing structures to maintain or increase order through the consumption of energy, it is natural to ask how such a purpose could have originated. It seems unlikely that increases in order could arise in some way out of an entropy law that demands decreasing order in general. For many who are dissatisfied with the circular proposition that life exists in order to reproduce itself, God becomes the ultimate answer in the search for purpose. Meanwhile, Georgescu-Roegen proposes that on a worldly level, man's purpose is simply the creation of structures that allow him to enjoy life. These are the structures that we commonly refer to as wealth, structures that may be stored until increasing entropy devalues them. (In contrast, the benefit derived from stored wealth cannot itself be stored. Thus, whilst warm water can be stored in a tank, the pleasure of a warm shower cannot be stored, except perhaps in one's memory).

Many forms of wealth may be synthesised by mankind from the low entropy resources available to him. But Georgescu-Roegen argues that there is often a most unwelcome cost attached to the consumption of these resources. Put simply, low entropy resources are transformed through man's economic activity into high entropy waste plus the enjoyment of life. By extending this line of reasoning, the true nature of the environmental choice facing modern man can be uncovered.

Consider the impact of sunlight upon the Earth as being similar to the input of energy into a physical system as discussed earlier. On a simple level, it is the free energy of the Sun that must in some form or other be consumed in order to allow the enjoyment of life to proceed. For example, it is the sunlight of past millennia that allows man to increase his enjoyment of life through the burning of coal. It is the sunlight of the present that allows him to grow crops and experience the seasons. If society aims for higher levels of enjoyment, it may do so by consuming greater amounts of past sunlight, or by catching present sunlight in a more efficient way. Whichever approach is adopted, entropy will continue to increase, but the effects of that increased entropy are to be seen in different places. Few on Earth care for the higher entropy that results in the Sun as it converts hydrogen into helium. Far more of us care for global warming as coal is burnt to fire our power stations. Here then is the environmental choice that faces us. It is a choice that pits sustainable development against unsustainable development, renewable resource against non-renewable resource.

Much effort has been devoted in recent times to finding some kind of free market solution that allows economic activity to continue with due regard for the environment. For example, tradable pollution permits have been issued in the United States. These were designed to encourage industry to account adequately for the costs of the environmental damage that it causes. (Economists use the word 'externalities' to describe the adverse side effects of an economic system that is driven by profitability only). In essence, the price of a permit is supposed to reflect the cost of the pollution that it allows the buyer to cause. It is however something of a problem to know how much should be charged for such a permit. How does one put a price on fresh air or a beautiful view?

A debate as to why some essential forms of wealth are free in monetary terms can easily enter into this kind of discussion but for our purpose let us note only that there is some kind of discrepancy between 'use value' and 'price'. The value enjoyed by one who 'uses' a beautiful view is often very great, but its price is often zero. The difference between the price of two similar houses, one with a beautiful view and one with no view, might give an economist some idea of the amount of money that individuals are prepared to pay for beautiful views in general. Yet this type of analysis is highly subjective and therefore rather inconsistent. Hence it has been argued that a market with competing buyers and sellers is the only proper means of pricing the permits that allow polluters to pollute.

As mankind's consumption of natural resources increasingly threatens his existence, the proper means of valuing externalities may become a topic for public debate. In having this debate, society at large would recognise that some forms of wealth have not always had a price, and have not therefore been accounted for in our conventional measures of wealth.

I contend that fresh air, clean rivers and a stable climate have quite a high priority in society's hierarchy of needs, but that society may not fully appreciate their value until they have been lost for ever. If such a gloomy outcome does materialise it will be in part due to the striving of mankind to supplement a flow of sunlight energy that is now deemed insufficient to meet his requirements for the enjoyment of life. As decades pass, the entropic consequences of this new avarice grow ever clearer. Some may argue that it has been unleashed by a technological innovation that just happens to have occurred in the nineteenth and twentieth centuries. However, technology can itself be used to combat the Earth-borne entropy that our activities encourage. Energy, for example, need not come from stocks of past sunlight alone, for the energy of present sunlight can be harnessed in ever more efficient ways. If a way can be found to price in the costs of Earth-borne entropy that arise from, say, coal burning power stations, then perhaps solar or wind or geothermal energy may stand a chance in the competitive market place for energy. But so long as Earth-borne entropy is not accounted for, we shall continue to undervalue the environment of our collective home.

These points aside, I shall now move to the main body of the argument and propose that the structure of our present financial system contradicts the nature of the entropy process. In contrast to the entropy law, the laws of modern financial theory that we now turn to are entirely of man's own creation.

Interest and Entropy

In a simple barter economy, an individual would hold his surplus wealth in the form of physical assets. In holding this surplus wealth he would perhaps incur some kind of storage cost. A further cost might also arise over time since the quality of the stored assets would be subject to the fact that entropy is increasing. Hence, depending upon the nature of the asset, the one who held wealth would often encounter unavoidable costs in so doing.

Of course the individual may instead decide to lend his physical wealth. The question now is what happens to the costs associated with the holding of that wealth when such a loan is made? The thought may not immediately occur to the one who borrows an ox to plough a field, and thereby make a profit. But for our purpose it is important to know exactly what kind of ox the borrower must repay. Should it be the same ox that was borrowed, or should it be an ox equal in age and health to the one that first left the lender's farm?

In a modern interest-based economy, £100 borrowed must be repaid to the sum of £100 plus interest. In so structuring our financial conventions we are effectively saying that an ox equal in age and health to the original must be repaid, plus interest. One notable feature of this convention is that the lender of the ox passes on, to the borrower, costs which he himself would otherwise have had to bear. £100 of money lent at interest does not obey the same law as the £100 of physical assets that the money must buy in order to fund the interest charge. In the application of compound interest, a given monetary value can merrily march the path of geometric increment towards infinity. In contrast, as Frederick Soddy puts it, it is due to increasing entropy that physical wealth follows the path of compound decrement toward, but never quite reaching, zero. The parallel within our barter economy is that whilst our financier may store his assets and find upon later inspection that they have deteriorated, in a loan transaction those very assets exist for him as a non-depreciating entry on a loan document.

Soddy comments:
... the ruling passion of the age is to convert wealth into debt in order to derive a permanent future income from it - to convert wealth that perishes into debt that endures, debt that does not rot, costs nothing to maintain, and brings in perennial interest.
Soddy, F., *Money versus Man* (1933), quoted by Daly H., in Kaufman, G.B., (1986)

If the stipulations of a compound interest money loan applied to a loan of physical capital, then physical capital would remain undegraded throughout the life of a loan whilst at the same time generating new wealth. This new wealth in turn would not depreciate and would itself be expected to yield further wealth in the familiar compound process. Such a state of affairs would be wonderful were it attainable but, due to the entropy principle, it isn't. Perpetual wealth creation from a single stock of non-depreciating capital will remain impossible so long as the laws of thermodynamics hold true.

Of the many types of interest convention applied in modern finance, a distinction is often made between 'simple interest' and 'compound interest'. The former convention applies to the charging of interest on the principal of a loan only. The latter involves a charging of interest on both principal and interest, a process that requires interest amounts payable to be 'compounded' into the principal at stated intervals.

To see compound interest at work, let us follow the example of Soddy and imagine that a man living in the year 20 AD makes a loan of one hundred loaves of bread to a borrower. Our lender trusts that the borrower (or his successors) will honour the repayment terms, which are 5% interest compounded once per year. The total amount due for repayment after one year, the year 21 AD, would be the original loan amount of one hundred loaves plus five loaves of interest. If the loan is not at this stage repaid, then the interest charge of five loaves will be compounded into the original principal of one hundred loaves, to give a new principal amount of one hundred and five loaves. Interest will then be charged on this new principal amount at the rate of 5% during the following year. By the year 22 AD the total amount due for repayment will then be one hundred and ten and one-quarter loaves of bread.

In contrast, the amount of the loan outstanding at the end of the second year under simple interest would be only one hundred and ten loaves of bread since the first year's interest of five loaves would not itself earn interest during the second year. In other words, no compounding would have occurred under the simple interest convention.

$$F = P(1 + r\,t)$$
$$= 100(1 + .05\,0.2)$$
$$= 110$$

REPAYMENT AMOUNT UNDER SIMPLE INTEREST

$$F = P(1 + r)^t$$
$$= 100(1 + .05)^2$$
$$= 110.25$$

REPAYMENT AMOUNT UNDER COMPOUND INTEREST

Where, for both simple and compound formulae;

- F = repayment amount
- P = amount loaned
- r = interest rate as a fraction, per period
- t = number of periods of loan

The above formulae are the basis of the financial mathematics described in the example with loaves of bread. P is often said to be the 'present value' of the amount F, and F the 'future value' of P. Hence, if interest rates are five per cent per year, an individual who is offered £110.25 to be received in two years' time would put a present value on that amount of only £100, when using the compound interest convention. Under the same circumstances, an individual who is offered £100 now would put a two year future value on that amount of £110.25. In both cases, the individual would be indifferent to receiving £100 now or £110.25 in two years' time.

The indifference arises because £100 received now could be lent at five per cent interest, producing £110.25 in two years' time. Hence, an individual could borrow £100 at 5% interest per year for two years and repay the loan by using the £110.25 that is to be received in two years' time. By borrowing or lending, the individual can create either one of the cash-flows out of the other. So it doesn't actually matter which cash-flow he is offered, the £100 now or the £110.25 later.

In accordance with this mathematics there arises the 'forward price', this being the price agreed under a transaction where payment is delayed until a date at some point in the future. Let us say that an ounce of gold can be purchased for delivery today for $400, this being the 'spot price'. Should one prefer to arrange that the payment and delivery of that ounce of gold occurs in one year's time, then the 'one year forward price' will be largely determined by the rate of interest over the period. In determining the fair forward price to charge the buyer, the one who is to sell the gold will ask himself, "how much does it cost me to buy gold today, store it for a year, and then deliver it to the buyer?" Well, if the interest rate is 5% per year and the storage cost for gold is $1 per ounce, it will cost him $400 in purchase price, $20 in interest on the money he borrows to pay that purchase price, and $1 in storage cost. In other words, the fair one year forward price is $421 per ounce. Perhaps the seller will add a little extra to this price in order to make a profit. Note that if the interest rate increases, say to 10%, then so too does the forward price, in this case to $441 per ounce.

To return to the subject of compound interest and Soddy's example, those familiar with its processes will not be surprised by the rather amusing result of extending the calculations over extremely long periods. By the year 1995 AD the total amount of the loan outstanding and now due for repayment, given by $100 (1 + 0.05)^{1975}$ for the above data, is in excess of seven hundred thousand billion billion billion billion loaves of bread. One remarkable fact regarding the size of this repayment amount, reductio ad absurdum though it may be, is that there would not be sufficient bread available to meet it, even if every person who has since lived on Earth were to have produced and successfully stored ten million loaves of bread per day for life. Repayment would in fact still be impossible even if the original lender had charged a more lenient 2.5% interest per year.

A strange phenomenon seems to be at work in the above example, and it is one that arises because the mathematics that it employs conflicts with the realities of the physical world. Bread rots, loans at interest don't. This conflict can be an extremely dangerous one for the environment.

We have seen that if man is to establish greater order in a physical system, he must reverse the entropy process in that system by inputting matter or energy from outside it. When rain, fertiliser, seed, sunlight and human effort are combined in the correct manner, greater order results in the form of bread. This decrease in entropy can only be achieved at the cost of an increase in entropy in some other part of the physical system. In this example, the greater degree of disorder manifests itself partly in those structures that have contributed to the production of bread. The farm equipment will become worn out and the land slightly less fertile. Net, the total amount of order decreases due to the entropy law.

Continuing the example of the loan of bread, we know that as the interest rate increases, the amount of bread that is required to make the repayment also increases. We can therefore say that as the interest rate increases, entropy also *tends* to increase. It is the borrower's attempt to make the required loan repayments by producing more bread that causes this to be so. The higher the interest rate, the higher the cost to the Earth's environment *may* be.

But why the italics? One crucial question relates to where increases in entropy occur. On the one hand, energy may be provided by consumption of those renewable resources powered by flows of sunlight, in which case Earth-borne entropy costs are low. On the other hand, stocks of previous sunlight may be utilised, in which case Earth-borne entropy costs are higher. The Sun will continue to shine, and its entropy increase, whether we use its light or not. But in using the Earth's oil to power our farm equipment, the Earth suffers an increase in entropy that would not otherwise occur.

This argument is not as abstract as it might at first sight seem. In terms of foreign borrowings outstanding, Brazil, Mexico and Indonesia are among the most indebted nations in the world. They are also among the world's top deforesters. On current trends the Brazilian rain forest, source of 40% of our planet's oxygen, will almost disappear within two lifetimes. For the poor and the starving, survival comes before preservation of the rainforest. The conversion of hardwood to ash, to disorder, enables survival for some. Its conversion to timber for export enables survival for others. In the meantime, the Brazilian rainforest suffers to the cost of all of us.

Country	1981 to 1990 average sq. kms. of deforestation per annum	1992 foreign debt outstanding as a percentage of GDP	1992 debt repayment as a percentage of export value
Brazil	36,710	31.3	24.4
Indonesia	12,120	67.4	32.1
Zaire	7,320	111.5	34.8
Mexico	6,780	35.2	44.4
Bolivia	6,250	83.6	39.1
Venezuela	5,990	62.5	19.5
Thailand	5,150	36.3	13.1
Sudan	4,820	220.7	n/a
Tanzania	4,380	268.4	32.5

n/a : ranking not available

DEFORESTATION AND FOREIGN DEBT
(source: Pocket World in Figures, The Economist Books, 1994)

The above table may portray coincidence only, but the work of increasing numbers of academics stands in evidence of the conflict between interest and entropy described so far. In *Time Discounting and Value* (1994), Colin Price reminds us of Miller's work in *Debt and the Environment : Converging Crises* (1991) where the depletion of natural resources is linked explicitly to the payment of interest on international debt. Is it really possible that such phenomena are in any way related to a contradiction between the financial and physical systems, between a requirement to pay off foreign creditors and the reality of an impoverished economy? Or is deforestation merely one expression of economic development? In order to answer such questions satisfactorily we must now attempt to quantify the impact of interest upon economic activity.

Discounting

The simple scenario described below is based on an idea by Michael Lipton at the University of Sussex (1992). Imagine a farmer who wishes to buy a plot of land and farm it. His purchase and operating costs are to be financed entirely on borrowed funds. The land is capable of supporting a highly intensive technique which is forecast to produce £150 per year of net profit for fifteen years, and which results in the land's desertification. An alternative production technique produces only £100 per year of net profit, but allows the land to regenerate and maintain its productive potential indefinitely.

Discounted cash-flow analysis allows the modern farmer to compare the two cash-flows and select the most profitable. For each interest rate, the present value of each set of cash-flows is calculated according to the formulae described earlier in this chapter. It is the farming approach that provides the highest total present value of those cash-flows that is then recommended. The tables displayed on the following pages show the relevant calculations where 't1' represents year 1, 't2' year 2, and so on.

These calculations show clearly that with interest rates at 5% the highest present value (£2,000) resides in the low intensity farming approach, whilst with rates at 10% the highest present value (£1,140.91) resides in the high intensity option.

Year	Profit per year	Present value of profit per year at 5% discount rate	Present value of profit per year at 10% discount rate
t1	150	142.85	136.36
t2	150	136.05	123.96
t3	150	129.57	112.69
t4	150	123.40	102.45
t5	150	117.52	93.13
t6	150	111.93	84.66
t7	150	106.59	76.96
t8	150	101.52	69.96
t9	150	96.68	63.61
t10	150	92.07	57.82
t11	150	87.69	52.56
t12	150	83.51	47.79
t13	150	79.54	43.44
t14	150	75.75	39.49
t15	150	72.15	35.91
and periods to t∞	0	0	0
Column Totals	2,250	1,556.82	1,140.79

DISCOUNTED CASH-FLOW ANALYSIS
for High Yield Farming Method
(yields £150 cash-flow per annum for fifteen years
after which land is desertified)

Year	Profit per year	Present value of profit per year at 5% discount rate	Present value of profit per year at 10% discount rate
t1	100	95.24	90.90
t2	100	90.70	82.64
t3	100	86.38	75.13
t4	100	82.27	68.30
t5	100	78.35	62.09
t6	100	74.62	56.45
t7	100	71.06	51.31
t8	100	67.68	46.65
t9	100	64.46	42.40
t10	100	61.39	38.55
t11	100	58.46	35.04
t12	100	55.68	31.86
t13	100	53.03	28.96
t14	100	50.50	26.33
t15	100	48.10	23.94
and periods to t∞	100	amounts decreasing towards zero	amounts decreasing towards zero
Column Totals	∞	2,000	1,000

DISCOUNTED CASH-FLOW ANALYSIS
for Low Yield Farming Method
(yields £100 cash-flow per annum indefinitely)

So the incentive toward intensive farming, and thus desertification, increases as the interest rate increases. This unfortunate result is entirely due to the familiar way in which the discounting process progressively reduces the present value of the land's output in future years toward zero. £100 of net profit earned in year fifty has a present value of approximately £0.85 if the interest rate is 10% per year. No wonder then that the analyst who relies on discounted cash-flow analysis has little care for what the land can produce in year fifty. Whether the land at that time is desertified or not is of little relevance, since its contribution to present value is negligible. Lipton argues that :

Dramatically rising interest rates in 1977-79, sustained ever since, have increased the incentives - to families, businesses and governments - to use up natural resources now, and to ignore the consequences later ... for third world governments that wanted to provide resources or subsidies for conservation, rising interest rates drained their ability to do so. In 1972, interest payments - at home as well as abroad - comprised 5.6% of spending, including net lending, by governments in non-oil developing nations; by 1988, they had reached 18.7%. ... Participants at Rio warned of impending famine, dearth, and depletion. The rate of interest is our spectre at their fast.

Michael Lipton, *The Spectre at the Fast* in *Financial Times* (24 June, 1992)

Despite the mathematical recommendations, one can be excused for believing that the bankrupting of land for the sake of increased short term returns does not make intuitive sense. An immortal goose that lays one golden egg per week should not have its immortality traded in for the sake of two golden eggs per week in the meantime. It appears however that some natural assets can be sacrificed at the behest of discounted cash-flow analysis. Whether such sacrifice takes the form of desertification, the extinction of a species or the immensely long-lived pollution of a nuclear power plant, the principle remains the same. Compound interest values the distant consequences of current actions at next to nothing. The problems return home for a future generation that has no say in their creation.

Colin Price insists that 'uniform negative exponential' discounting is almost always incorrect as a valuation technique in a physical world which provides a wealth of non-exponential functions:

We are prepared to go along with discounting, because abandoning it would give our own interests less importance than we would like; it threatens too uncomfortable and too uncompromising a departure from our present shameful indifference to the distant future.

Price, C., *Time Discounting and Value* (1994) p. 346

Yet, even where the distant future is not concerned, discounting can still display its encouragement for questionable consumption patterns in the present. As an example, let us use discounting in a second analysis. Here we aim to help an individual value two different holiday plans, between which he must choose. The first involves taking no holidays for the first ten years, and the enjoyment of one holiday per year every year thereafter for twenty years. The second involves taking one holiday per year for each of the first ten years and no holidays thereafter. The individual knows that each holiday currently costs one thousand pounds, and he assumes that prices will remain the same in real terms throughout the period.

The analysis for this example is shown in the next table. Those years in which no holiday is taken are shown as a zero value. The time period of the analysis extends to year thirty, and discounting is undertaken at a rate of 10% per year for each flow of holidays.

The choice indicated by discounting is to select the flow that constitutes 'holidays first' since this has the highest present value (£6,141) in preference to the flow that constitutes 'holidays later' (present value £3,282). Whether such a pattern of consumption is one that would be preferred in practice is a question of much relevance to all those who contemplate the sacrifice of current pleasure for the sake of later reward. Given the choice, how many individuals would really prefer ten holidays soon to twenty holidays of the same quality later? An individual with a high risk of death early in life might prefer to take what holidays he could as soon as possible. But for many would not the rational choice be to take a greater number of holidays later? Unfortunately, discounting does not give us a choice here. It is irrelevant whether the individual's assumptions on prices, inflation and life-span are correct or not. The point is that if the individual uses the technique of discounting, whatever his assumptions, his choice will be guided by a mathematical process that is severely biased towards the short term. As interest rates increase, the incentive to be impatient increases.

Year	No holidays taken during first ten years and one holiday per year thereafter until year 30 (£)	Present value of each holiday using 10% discount rate (£)	Holidays taken during first ten years and none thereafter (£)	Present value of each holiday using 10% discount rate (£)
t1	0	0	1000	909
t2	0	0	1000	826
t3	0	0	1000	751
t4	0	0	1000	683
t5	0	0	1000	620
t6	0	0	1000	564
t7	0	0	1000	513
t8	0	0	1000	466
t9	0	0	1000	424
t10	0	0	1000	385
t11	1000	350	0	0
t12	1000	318	0	0
t13	1000	289	0	0
and every period to t30	1000	various discounted amounts	0	0
Column Totals	20,000	3,282	10,000	6,141

DISCOUNTING ANALYSIS
for two flows of holidays

The debate on global warming provides us with the ultimate environmental example of discounting's bias toward the short term. It is widely agreed among climatologists that emissions of gases such as carbon dioxide and methane are now causing changes in Earth's atmospheric system that will increase average global temperature in the longer term. The mechanism is often referred to as the 'greenhouse effect' since the Earth's atmosphere acts rather like the glass of a greenhouse, allowing in the short wave radiation of the Sun but trapping long wave radiation reflected by the Earth.

Due to increasing emissions of 'greenhouse gases', the proposition is that greater amounts of reflected outward bound radiation will be trapped within the Earth's atmosphere than is presently the case, causing a general warming of the Earth. Furthermore, the occurrence of warming is substantially lagged from initial causation, a process that takes a number of decades to complete.

Annual output of greenhouse gases in 1990 stood at approximately six gigatonnes (billion tonnes) of 'carbon dioxide equivalent', so called because this figure also accounts for the effects of non-carbon dioxide emissions. The current atmospheric stock of carbon comprises 0.353% of atmospheric weight, having increased from 0.285% in pre-industrial times. On current trends, the atmospheric carbon equivalent will double over pre-industrial levels by the year 2025.

The central official estimate of the Intergovernmental Panel on Climate Change (IPCC) is that a doubling of carbon equivalent levels will cause a rise in average global temperature of two and a half degrees Celsius over pre-industrial levels by 2025. However, due to thermal lags, the process of global warming will not stop there. In fact, the current commitment to increases in global average temperature arising from additions to carbon equivalents already present in the atmosphere is centrally estimated at almost six degrees Celsius by 2100 and ten degrees Celsius by 2275.

One aspect of the global warming debate concerns itself with the advisability of taking pre-emptive action in order to prevent the phenomenon from occurring in the first place. In other words, is it worth spending money today, on clean air technology for example, in order to limit the output of greenhouse gases and hence combat global warming?

In order to answer this kind of question, a discounting analysis could be carried out in which the estimated costs of global warming in years to come are present-valued and compared to the amount of current investment aimed at eliminating them. In fact, just such an exercise has been undertaken.

The International Institute for Economics believes that an aggressive attempt to avoid the occurrence of global warming would cost approximately 2.5% of world GDP per year into the foreseeable future. But their research shows that, if a discount rate of 3% per year or more is used in a cost-benefit analysis stretching over the period to 2275 then, unless global warming is very severe, it is simply not worth bothering to take any action to prevent it.

The Institute's researchers recognise the difficulties inherent in discounting over the long term. Eventually, they settle upon 1.5% per year as an 'appropriate' discount rate for use in their central case estimates. Unsurprisingly, with a lower discount rate, it now becomes worth taking pre-emptive action in order to avoid global warming in many of the scenarios that they analyse. The level of the discount rate is therefore crucial in determining the results of the Institute's analysis. So how is it arrived at?

Some academics argue that a market interest rate is an unsuitable choice for use as a discount rate, particularly where very long term analysis is undertaken. The derivation of the 'social rate of time preference' (SRTP) provides an example of the tortuous theoretical route that can be followed in finding an alternative discount rate (see William Cline in *The Economics of Global Warming* (1992)).

The SRTP is a rate which, in a 'steady state economy', describes the extra amount of *future* consumption that could be achieved by foregoing a given amount of consumption *today* and investing that foregone amount instead. In other words the SRTP is related to the 'marginal productivity of capital' in this steady state economy.

In a steady state economy, each generation would allow its successors the opportunity to enjoy an unchanged standard of living. For this to happen, one generation must neither consume too much thereby sacrificing investment and hence the future capital stock, nor invest too much thereby requiring future generations to sacrifice consumption in order to maintain the stock of capital that they inherit. Importantly, the ratio of capital to labour must remain unchanged between generations under this approach. For example, if one generation found that there were fewer hospital beds per head of population then they might argue that their standard of living had decreased.

Proceeding from such reasoning, academics have proposed an SRTP of some 2.5% although, where a steady state is not a practical proposition, an SRTP as low as 0.5% has been identified. But does it matter what value theorists give to the SRTP? After all, industry borrows money at the market rate of interest, not the SRTP, and it is industry whose activities are primarily responsible for the greenhouse effect. If the money that an industrialist uses to finance a production process attracts interest at 10%, why should the industrialist choose which investment to make by using a discount rate equal to the SRTP?

In any event, even low discount rates can encourage undesirable outcomes of the varieties discussed earlier. It might therefore seem that there is a problem with discounting itself, not just the level of discount rate to be employed therein. The concerns become more marked when one finds that the discount rate needs to be massaged downwards, and the massage justified with complex arguments, in order for the results of the discounting process to make sense.

Some theorists argue that applying discounting to a very long term analysis pushes to an extreme a theory which was intended only for short term analysis. Yet what is the long term, other than a series of short terms? And is our thirty year period with two different flows of holiday really 'too long' for discounting? After all, financial market specialists seem happy to use discounting when valuing thirty year government bonds.

Cline reminds us that:
... the principle reason for discounting future consumption is that in the future people may have higher incomes than today, and a lower marginal utility of consumption...if one is pessimistic about future per capita income growth, there is an intuitive case for not discounting consumption at all.
Cline, W. R., *The Economics of Global Warming* (1992) p. 257

On inter-generational discounting, Cline quotes Mishan in *Cost Benefit Analysis : An Informal Introduction* (1975) :
... Person A would therefore have no business in evaluating the future worth of 100 by discounting it for 50 years at 10 percent when he himself is not, in any case, going to receive it ... Whenever inter-generational comparisons are involved it is as well to recognize that there is no satisfactory way of determining social worth at different points in time. In such cases a zero rate of time preference, though arbitrary, is probably more acceptable than the use today of existing individuals' rate of time preference or of a rate of interest that would arise in a market solely for consumption loans.
Cline, W. R., *The Economics of Global Warming* (1992) p. 239

Colin Price comments once more :
... where every person's income grew exponentially at a constant rate, where tastes were constant across time and where elasticity of marginal utility of income was constant across income, where the abundance of all goods and services could be confidently predicted, in every likely circumstance, to grow in proportion to the increasing demand for them, in such a world one could safely discount marginal units of consumption at a single discount rate ... The list of symptoms does not provide a recognisable portrait of the real world. And yet the prescription is the one routinely handed out.
Price, C., *Time Discounting and Value* (1994) p. 227

Appropriating 'tomorrow's value today' may have formed the philosophical underpinning to Lord Hanson's commercial activities, but we thank the likes of Sir Christopher Wren for allowing us to enjoy the values of yesterday today. With Hanson's attitude in the ascendancy, there will be fewer St. Paul's Cathedrals, fewer grand infrastructure projects for future generations to enjoy. For those who base their financing decisions on discounting, it simply isn't worth creating value for the long term future.

Justifications for Interest

It is surely a part of every decent philosophy that man should do his best to maintain the Earth for succeeding generations. But since our valuation of the rights of future generations is tied so very closely to the practice of discounting, and thus in practical terms to the institution of interest, no discussion on a society's duty to its offspring can be isolated from an examination of its position on interest.

The questioning of interest on theoretical grounds is not a recent development. Plato regarded it as a means whereby the rich could exploit the poor, and Aristotle believed that money was to be 'used in exchange and not to increase at interest'. In the *End of Economics* (1991), 'Umar Vadillo tells us that among the Romans, Seneca and Cicero argued vehemently against usury; and among the early Christians, Nysennas, Augustinus and Acquinas were similarly opposed.

Prohibitions on usury appear in the *Torah* and the *Bible*.
If you advance money to any poor man amongst my people, you are not to act like a money lender; you must not exact interest from him.
Revised English Bible, Exodus 22 : 25
You are not to exact interest on anything you lend to a fellow countryman, whether money or food or anything else on which interest can be charged.
Revised English Bible Deuteronomy 23 : 19

However, many Jews later interpreted the prohibition on usury as applying only to loans made between Jew and Jew, not between Jew and Gentile. The Biblical evidence for this has sponsored derision in some quarters. Interest is a terrible thing, but not if practised on a non-Jew?
You may exact interest on a loan to a foreigner but not on a loan to a fellow countryman, and then the Lord your God will bless you in all you undertake in the land which you are entering to occupy.
Revised English Bible Deuteronomy 23 : 20

At the Council of Nicea in 325 AD, despite compromising on some key principles under pressure from King Constantine, the Church's representatives remained united on the topic of usury. Usury among the clergy was banned. Over the centuries that followed, there developed an increasingly bitter struggle between the Church and the merchants of Europe on the subject of usury.

A variety of legal devices were invented to circumvent the Church ban on interest. Chown describes one of the later inventions, the *contractum trinius*. The investor would simultaneously enter into three contracts with an entrepreneur; to invest money as a sleeping partner; to insure himself against any loss; and to sell any profits over and above a given level back to the entrepreneur in return for a fixed amount of money per year.
All three [contracts], taken separately, bypass the usury provisions, but the overall effect is simply a loan for interest.
J. F. Chown: *A History of Money* (1994) p. 121

The major strands of the theological capitulation on usury are discussed at length by John Noonan in *The Scholastic Inquiry into Usury* (Harvard University Press, 1957). Some time before 1220, the canonist Hispanus identified a charge that would be paid by a borrower who was late in repaying a usury-free loan. This charge would compensate the lender for the loss of use of his money in between the time that repayment should have been made and the time when it was actually made. It would be called "interesse", derived from the Latin for "in between", and was to give rise to the modern term "interest". Then, during the fourteenth century CE, came the crucial innovation. It was argued that a charge could be made for a loan from the outset, not simply where a borrower was late in making repayment. The justification for this was on two counts. "Lucrum cessans" (literally "profit ceasing") was the profit that a lender had to give up in order to lend his money, and "damnum emergens" (literally "loss occurring") was an actual loss incurred by a lender as a result of having loaned his money.

Though proposing different linguistic origins, other writers also view interest as something that compensates the lender for an assumed loss in not having the use of his money.
The Latin noun *usura* means the "use" of anything, in this case the use of borrowed capital; hence, usury was the price paid for the use of money. The Latin verb intereo means "to be lost"; a substantive form *interisse* developed into the modern term "interest". Interest was not profit but loss.
S. Homer & R. Sylla : *A History of Interest Rates* (1996) p. 73

When confronted with the seemingly unstoppable spread of interest-based practices in the world of business, the Church eventually became silent on its principle. In 1545, under Henry VIII, English law permitted the charging of interest up to a maximum defined rate of 10%, although any amount in excess of this was regarded as being usury. The scholastic proposals that had for some three centuries undermined the prohibition of usury were thus confirmed. Soon, the pro-interest lobby began to find its intellectual champions in the unlikeliest of places:
The Christian reformers, both Luther and Zwingli, condemned usury, but the reformer Jean Calvin was the first to raise his voice in favour of usury; one century later his disciple Claude Saumairc [Saumaise], in his book "Concerning Usury" (1638) argued that the taking of interest was necessary to achieve salvation.
'Umar Vadillo : *The End of Economics* (1991) p. 17

Eventually, in 1917, a last formal step was taken by the Church in accepting the practice of interest. The Codex Iuris Canonici issued in that year replaced earlier statements of Canon Law, and its position on usury is quoted by Noonan as follows:

... in lending a fungible thing it is not itself illicit to contract for the payment of the profit allocated by law, unless it is clear that this is excessive, or even for a higher profit, if a just and adequate title be present
Codex Iuris Canonici, Rome, 1920, c. 1735

Scholars of Islam have always condemned interest.
O you who believe, fear God and give up what remains of your claims of usury if you are truly believers. If you do not, then take notice of war from God and His apostle.
Qur'an 2 : 278

But even here, some say that practice has diverged from theory:
The Qur'an ... prohibits the charging of interest, although various methods have been devised in order to circumvent the prohibition. For instance, a higher price may be charged for goods when payment is deferred than is charged if payment is made in advance or upon delivery.
Encyclopaedia Britannica 1996

Nowadays, injunctions against usury from religious quarters are frequently seen as little more than an embarrassing appendage of backwardness, motivated perhaps by simple-minded distaste for the money-lenders of old. Often, the religious arguments seem unscientific and weak when placed before the articulate economists of the pro-interest camp.

In contrast, a variety of seemingly scientific and well-reasoned arguments have been deployed in the effort first to justify, then to explain the level of, interest rates. In arguments of justification, expected inflation, positive time preference, anticipated risk and diminishing marginal utility feature prominently. These justifications all propose the superiority of the present over the future, and thereafter that interest exists to compensate those who give up money now in return for money later. Meanwhile, in arguments of explanation, the classical theory proposes that interest is the price of money as determined by supply and demand in the marketplace for funds. Keynes developed his alternative, arguing that money is the asset that is most readily exchangeable into all other forms of asset, in other words that it is the most *liquid* asset. He proposed that a variety of factors determine the price, in other words the rate of interest, that must be paid in order to obtain *liquidity*.

What we are interested in here are the justifications for interest rather than explanations of the mechanisms that determine its level. Some detail is required before proceeding.

The idea that an element of interest is somehow justified as a compensation for the effect of inflation is a most common one. The lender of money thus includes a certain amount of interest, commensurate with expected inflation, in order to maintain the purchasing power of his initial investment. The desire to protect ones savings from inflation is quite understandable and is not criticised here. However, the inflation argument does not attempt to explain the existence of rates of interest in excess of expected inflation. For the time being I shall focus on the 'real' rate of interest only, this being the amount by which a quoted interest rate (the 'nominal rate of interest') exceeds the expected rate of inflation for a given period. In subsequent discussions I shall question those arguments that assume inflation to be causative of interest and (in Chapter Two) argue that precisely the opposite is often true.

In his 1836 work *Outline of the Science of Political Economy*, the English economist Nassau Senior proposed that interest is charged because by lending money the lender has to abstain from consumption. Interest was the reward for the lender's abstinence. Mr. Senior's critics observed that lenders of money were usually rather wealthy people who didn't have to abstain from very much at all as a result of lending their money. Life in the country house remained much the same after the loan as before, and so the question returned ... why interest?

Alfred Marshall in due course proposed an improvement to Senior's theory. It was not the lender's abstinence that gave him the right to charge interest, rather it was the fact of 'waiting' to get one's money back. Under this theoretical improvement, the obvious lack of abstinence among the rich no longer presented a problem. Of course many individuals wait (save) when interest rates are zero, and in this regard Marshall's explanation failed to satisfy the enquiring mind.

In 1893, Eugene Böhm-Bawerk provided his answer in *Positive Theorie des Kapitalzinses*. He proposed that human beings prefer to have pleasurable experiences sooner and painful experiences later, in other words that they have positive time preference. This was widely seen as a breakthrough among justifications for interest. Money allows its holder to satisfy needs now rather than later, so money now must surely be better than money later, argued Böhm-Bawerk.

It is nevertheless apparent that in many cases individuals prefer pleasure in the future to pleasure today. For example, even an older individual would prefer one breakfast per day for the next week, rather than a week's worth of breakfasts today. In the physical sense, the preference for breakfast does not accord with assumptions about the preference for money. If an individual does not necessarily prefer current consumption to future consumption, why should he prefer the money that can finance such consumption now as opposed to later? Then, once needs are satisfied, Böhm-Bawerk argued that money now could be invested to generate profit sooner rather than later ... here we are told that money now is superior because it can produce money now!

An element of any given interest rate is usually held to act as a compensation for risk. For instance, a lender may believe that he will not be alive to enjoy repayment, hence an older person may require far more reward for delaying consumption than a younger person. Lenders also discriminate between borrowers by lending to those of higher risk at a higher rate of interest. The more uncertain the future repayment, the higher the returns demanded. Hence the 'risk premium' in consideration of higher risk loans.

Calculation of risk is the subject of much mathematical analysis of past and recent events in a given borrower's history. Is the company cash-rich? Has it ever defaulted or come close to default on a loan? On such evidence, credit rating agencies such as Standard & Poor's and Moody's make statements about a borrower's creditworthiness, assigning a 'credit rating' in each case. The interest rate charged to a borrower by lenders will reflect the credit rating. So it is that the interest rate that is said to reflect future risk is in fact largely based upon an appraisal of the past.

Despite the fact that no man knows the future, modern lenders have little hesitation in varying the risk premium by small fractions according to the borrower in question. So precise about such an unknowable thing. As Price points out, the incorporation of a *fixed* interest premium into any loan also implies an unchanging level of risk over the time horizon under consideration. It is far from clear that this is justified. For instance, over time, a given borrower may become established in the marketplace, and therefore less risky.

A discussion of risk cannot be complete without paying at least some attention to the existence of the 'risk-free rate of interest'. If it is clear that an amount of physical wealth cannot often be maintained without cost, it seems clearer still that such wealth can never be maintained without some degree of risk. Because many events can act to reduce the value of physical assets, theft and fire for example, nothing in the physical world is risk-free. Indeed, the most that a financier in a barter economy can do is to minimise the risks involved in holding his wealth. The expected net rate of return derived from a securely stored physical asset will usually be negative due to the various costs incurred in storing and, or, maintaining it. One might term this rate the risk-minimised rate of return.

In contrast, modern financial theory states that the risk-free rate of interest is a positive rate of return that an investor derives from investing in a financial asset that is free of risk. An amount of money lent to a government, and the interest amount charged, is assumed to be risk-free because it is in turn assumed that a government can tax, borrow or print further amounts of money to repay its debt. These three options are indeed available to a modern government, but because the government has no access to risk-free rates of return when investing the borrowed money, such options are merely a means of passing on the bill to others when the fact of a non-risk-free physical system eventually reasserts itself. The very existence of a risk-free interest rate does however have a pervasive effect upon the financial economy. Given that government is prepared to pay a specified rate of interest and is a risk-free borrower, lenders will inevitably have little appetite for lending at rates that are below this risk-free rate. With a few aid related exceptions, the risk-free rate becomes the lowest interest rate at which borrowers may obtain loan funding. It is a rate that, as we shall see, is often determined by the authorities often with little regard to returns available in the real economy.

An alternative, and widely applauded, justification for interest begins by proposing that the 'marginal utility' of consumption is declining, in other words that the next unit of consumption is of less use value to a consumer than the previous one. If one assumes that real incomes grow over time, then future consumption should be greater than current consumption. And if it is true that marginal utility is declining, then an extra unit of consumption in the future must be of lower utility than an extra unit of consumption in the present. Hence, interest arises as a result of the comparison between present and future utilities that can be obtained by the spending of a given amount of money.

An immediate response to the marginal utility argument is that incomes may not increase in future periods and therefore that marginal utility will not necessarily be lower in future periods. Discounting would, under these circumstances, be quite inappropriate as an analytical tool. Indeed there have been long episodes of human experience in which real income has declined. Nordhaus and Tobin's analysis of economic performance in the United States using their 'Measure of Economic Welfare', rather than the more traditional yardstick of 'Gross Domestic Product', showed real income to be declining.

Even where statistics show that real income is increasing, there are many kinds of utility that cannot necessarily be enjoyed simply by spending money. An unpolluted environment is one of them. Who is to say that an extra unit of clean environment in the future will be of less utility to a consumer than an extra unit of clean environment today? In fact, one could argue that the opposite will be the case.

Even if the assumption of continued growth in real income is valid, the marginal utility approach relies upon a proper identification of which incomes one is to analyse when calculating growth of income. Should one look at the incomes of the poor, the rich or the national average? As Price points out:
Thus a social discount rate based on mean income growth rate overemphasises income growth of the affluent, and underemphasises the changing importance of consumption by the poor. Where the rich are getting richer and the poor poorer, the social discount rate will be much too high; it may even have the wrong sign.
Price, C., *Time Discounting and Value* (1994) p. 236

Of those arguments that seek to explain the level of interest rates in a modern economy, the simplest is that which views interest as the 'price' of money. This approach portrays money as an item that can be bought and sold like other goods or services. The rate of interest is then that which equates saving with borrowing. According to the *UK Budget Red Book* of 1990 :
... interest rates are the price of money and credit. Changing the price is the best method of influencing the degree of monetary tightness.

In Chapter Two, the Red Book's view is refuted in detail. Here, we should remind ourselves of the entropy principle. Why, if money is indeed 'sold', must it then be returned to the seller at the end of the sale transaction? Of course, money is not so much sold as lent and interest cannot therefore be the price of money. Rather, most will regard interest as a 'rent' on money. Now, if interest is a rental charge, then money is unlike any other rented item since it does not depreciate through usage, and rental payments on money do not relate to the utility gained by the borrower since money borrowed might not be invested profitably. In contrast, a rented physical item, the ox of the earlier example perhaps, wears out with usage and provides a known utility in the meantime.

Keynes proposed three reasons that individuals might prefer to hold their assets in the form of money, the ultimate form of liquidity. These were the need to transact, the need to hold money as a precaution for unforeseen events, and the opportunity to speculate that money gives to the one who holds it. Keynes proposed that when a loan of money is made, liquidity is lost and that an element of interest will therefore be charged by the lender for foregoing the advantages of that liquidity. These ideas were encapsulated in the 'liquidity preference theory', a short run model for determining the rate of interest according to the supply of money in the economy and the demand to hold it.

Price questions the various liquidity arguments :
Nor is it clear, in a time preference sense, that anyone would be better off eventually for having liquidity now, if taking advantage of that liquidity (for transactions, precautionary or speculative motives) meant sacrificing equal liquidity next year. Indeed it could be argued that early liquidity simply offers early opportunities to commit funds - that is to establish early loss of liquidity. It is of course advantageous to be able to acquire resources at the most propitious time - the time of lowest price, or the time when their quality meets some particular requirement. But exercising this advantage early denies it in future periods. The liquidity premium element in rates of return does not represent the betterness of earliness.
Price, C., *Time Discounting and Value* (1994) p. 209

It is worthwhile noting that in the long run, according to Keynes, a completely different set of factors would come into play. Where the Classical theory proposed that saving would increase if interest rates increased, Keynes argued that if people's saving increased then their consumption spending would inevitably fall. With less being spent on goods and services, businessmen would lay off their staff. The total amount of income earned in the economy would therefore fall, and with it the amount saved. A rise in interest rates could therefore reduce the aggregate amount of money saved, the opposite of what the Classical theorists had proposed.

Irrespective of the level of interest rates there remain distinctions between the conventions of the money lender and the reality of the activity that he seeks to finance. For instance, revenues realised on a project financed with borrowed money will usually vary in both amount and timing during the life of the loan. But if profits are not received on a regular and predictable basis, how can the borrower have the opportunity to reinvest those profits in the regular manner assumed by the compounding process? Even if clockwork reliability to cash-flows is attainable, in assuming reinvestment of profits at a fixed rate of return, the financial mathematics assumes that there is no such thing as diminishing marginal returns on capital employed. Compound fixed interest simplifies real world processes by assuming that, throughout the life of a loan, the rate of return on those real world processes remains unchanged.

Whilst flows of cash can be reinvested, a flow of utility, the enjoyment of a hot shower for example, cannot be. If at any stage one wishes to enjoy part or all of the output of a productive process, that output must be enjoyed as a flow. Compound interest assumes the full reinvestment of yields and inevitably implies that, on the physical level, consumption of those yields cannot occur. This, as Soddy put it, is a process that forever sees bulb issuing in bulb, never in flower. What precisely is the point of such a process from the human perspective?

It was suggested earlier that compounding of interest does not accommodate a physical world in which capacity constraints exist and that, in order to meet the high real rates of interest occasionally thrust upon it, enterprise attempts to increase the rate of resource extraction or energy consumption, or both, by boosting the productivity of physical capital. If, since the Industrial revolution, advances in technology have presented this very solution to developed societies, such advances may only delay the day of reckoning with mathematical inevitability. However long this delay proves to be, and it may be a very long delay indeed, our earlier argument foretells the dire consequences that productivity increases can have upon the entropic Earth-bound system. Polluted rivers, festering rubbish tips and resource-depleted seas may be just the first instalment of the price that is paid for entering into a race with compound interest.

The conventional theorists have argued on many occasions that society's ability to widen the selection and quality of available goods for consumption defeats all attempts at reductio ad absurdum examples with loaves of bread. Bread is not the only item that man can consume and it is not the only item that he can produce. We may be unable to produce 7×10^{42} loaves of bread with which to repay a loan in the year 1995, but we can produce cars, hi-fi's and spacecraft. How many loaves of bread are equal to just one of these products of new technology? Infinite amounts, if one happens to be living in the year 22 AD.

Unfortunately, such an argument, being one that highlights 'product substitution' over time, does not address the central issue in the loaves of bread example. For 'loaves of bread' read 'physical resource'. It really does not matter whether we are addressing loaves of bread or spacecraft. The point is that, by determining production in the physical world according to the mathematics of interest, progressively greater increases in entropy are encouraged over time. Yes, one might equate the energy consumed in manufacturing one spacecraft to the energy consumed in producing a given number of loaves of bread, but we are not concerned with the use to which energy is put here. The fact is that as energy consumption increases, Earth-borne entropy also tends to increase.

In setting course for a more appealing future, we will first need to complete our description of the deficiencies of the present. In the meantime, if the arguments employed so far draw criticism, then it will most likely be on the grounds that they rely too heavily on physical reductionism. Analogy with the physical world has indeed been frequent in this section, and for this I make no apology. Finance is the servant of industry and real world processes, not their master. The theory of our financial conventions must address this fact and, unless corrected by reasoned argument, I shall continue to believe that we survive by virtue of processes in the physical world. Herman Daly, in an excellent review of Soddy's work, comments:

If debt and money are the units of measure by which we account for and keep track of the production and distribution of physical wealth, then surely the units of measure and

the reality being measured cannot be governed by different laws ... If [physical] wealth cannot grow at compound interest, then debt should not either.
H. Daly in G. B. Kaufman: *Frederick Soddy 1877-1956* (1986)

When industrialists and environmentalists complain about the attitudes of bankers, could it be that they too are motivated by a conflict between finance and the reality of the world in which they operate? Or does their motivation arise from a 'simple-minded distaste' for the activities of the money-lender? We have already seen that modern financing theory can exert a subtle influence upon the nature of economic activity. The discussion now focuses upon the structure of the financial system itself.

Chapter two

THE PRODUCTION OF MONEY

> *In this chapter, two forms of money are identified. One is the money produced by the modern state in the form of notes and coins, the other is the money that is produced by commercial banks. The technique of fractional reserve banking, whereby banks create money, is examined and the history of its development described. Banking is seen as an industry and money as its product. The consequences of allowing private firms the authority to manufacture money and lend it at interest are analysed.*

From Gold to Receipts

Money can take more than one form. At various times and in various places, the function of money has been fulfilled by items such as salt, printed paper and gold, to name a few. Although money defies any specific definition, it can generally be regarded as that which is readily accepted in exchange for goods and services. On this basis, both a five pound note and a guaranteed cheque written in the amount of five pounds can be exchanged for five pounds worth of goods or services, and both are therefore forms of money. One difference between these two forms of money is that it is the state that produces the banknotes whilst it is a commercial bank that provides us with a cheque-book and guarantee card. The distinction between 'state money' and 'bank money' will be of vital importance to the following discussion.

The roots of modern banking in England can be traced back at least as far as the mid-seventeenth century, in particular to the activities of the goldsmith. The goldsmith would take deposits from customers in the form of precious metal coins, predominantly gold coins, since these constituted state money at that time. These early banks were little more than safe-keeping houses that had secure vaults in which to keep their own valuables and, for a fee, the gold coins of depositors. Upon taking a deposit, the goldsmith would issue a 'bearer receipt' to the depositor confirming the amount of the deposit. The depositor, or any individual 'bearing' the receipt, could then present it to the goldsmith at a later date and claim back the sum deposited.

As time passed, the goldsmith bankers realised that their customers preferred to leave most of their state money on deposit most of the time. State money in the bank was regarded as being safer from theft than state money under one's bed and, in aggregate, the small amount of state money that was withdrawn from a bank by customers on any one day was generally replenished by fresh deposits of state money from other customers on that same day.

For their part, the goldsmiths' customers found that the receipts issued to them would be accepted by merchants as payment for goods and services. The goldsmiths' receipts had become bank money. Hence, instead of going to withdraw their gold coins from the goldsmith, depositors would simply pass over the required amount of bearer receipts to a merchant in payment. The merchant in turn would be able to claim back the underlying gold coins from the goldsmith but more usually would choose to use those same receipts in payment for his own purchases. In this manner, receipts would stay in circulation for some time.

The goldsmiths knew that if their receipts stayed in circulation for long periods of time then the gold in their vaults would remain largely idle. The most obvious use for these idle reserves of gold was to lend them to those of good standing who wished to borrow. However, great care would have to be taken by the goldsmiths not to lend too much of their gold coin reserves. They would need to keep sufficient quantities in reserve so as to meet requests for redemption of their receipts by customers. The proportion of coins thus kept in reserve against receipts issued came to be known as the 'cash reserve ratio', and because the net amount of receipts redeemed on any one day was usually small, only a small cash reserve ratio was required for a bank to operate safely under most circumstances.

Of course, if it did happen that heavy withdrawals occurred at short notice, then the bank would have to close its doors. The crisis of confidence caused by the failure of one bank to meet its redemption obligations would naturally lead to a crisis of confidence in other banking institutions. In this manner there occurred numerous 'bank runs', in which customers would run to their bank to withdraw their deposits of state money before everyone else tried to do the same. In England, these events were to be witnessed many times, in particular during the early nineteenth century. In some developing countries, they are still happening today.

Confidence in the value of receipts would continue so long as the public believed that the goldsmith would exchange them for gold whenever the bearer requested him to do so. Aware that confidence was the key to their success, many goldsmiths devoted their efforts to persuading the public that the new banking institutions were 'prudent' and 'safe'. These soon became catchwords among the banking profession.

In time, the subject of how large or small a reserve was required for safe operation became one of fierce debate. Some argued in favour of a 100% reserve on the basis that if bankers had issued £100 of receipts promising redemption on demand, then they should keep £100 of gold in the vault to honour this promise should they be required to. Others foresaw the hugely lucrative possibilities of holding a lower reserve ratio, perhaps as little as 20% or 30% as a proportion of receipts issued. They cited the tendency of most depositors to leave most of their gold on deposit most of the time as a justification of the safety of their approach.

The debate mattered vitally. If it was safe to keep, say, a 20% reserve ratio, then the remaining 80% of gold could be lent out at interest. £100 of gold could be divided into £20 for reserves and £80 for loans. The lower the reserve ratio, the greater the risk of a bank collapse but also the more that could be lent out. And the more that could be lent out, the greater the interest revenue.

As the process of lending was contemplated, it became apparent to the bankers that there was in fact no need to lend the physical gold in their vaults. Since their own receipts were equally well regarded as money by the general public, it would suffice for these receipts to be lent out as a substitute for gold coins. Such a policy had a great advantage since paper receipts could be manufactured at very little cost, whereas gold itself could not be. For a truly imprudent banker it would be possible to use the entirety of the bank's gold reserves as a ratio for receipts issued. With £100 of gold coins in his vault and a 20% reserve ratio, such a banker could take the risk if he so dared of issuing £500 of receipts in total. Here, the depositors of the coins would receive receipts to the value of £100, and a further £400 of receipts could then be manufactured to lend at interest. In the meantime the banker would attempt to make agreements, primarily with other bankers, to borrow extra reserves of gold should there be heavy withdrawals from his own bank.

The 'fractional reserve' banking system described above relied crucially upon the use of interest in its operation. Why, it might be asked, did the banker not print receipts and spend them on his own consumption if it is in fact true that he had the power to manufacture money? The answer is that the act of spending his own receipts would eventually lead to bankruptcy. If such a course were followed, it would be almost certain that at some future time the spent receipts would return for redemption in gold - gold which never existed in the first instance. By lending the receipts instead, the banker could charge interest on the amount lent. Upon repayment of the loan, the receipts could be destroyed as easily as they had been manufactured. But the interest charge would remain as revenue. And if a loan was repaid using gold coins, then these could be kept in reserve to redeem the still outstanding paper notes at a later date.

Gradually, word spread among the wealthier classes that the provision of banking 'services' was nothing other than the most profitable business idea of all time. An increasing number of entrepreneurs therefore established their own banks in order to cash in on the new game. Thus the banking sector would grow to be one of the largest sectors of the economy. Though competition today ensures that the *rate* of profit made by any one banking company is more modest than it once was, the *amount* of profit made by the banking sector as a whole is huge by virtue of its size within the overall economy. In 1999, the banking sector was the most valuable on the London Stock Exchange measured by market capitalisation.

The bankers faced many practical hurdles in attempting to grow their business as we shall see. Not least was the fact that the banks charged interest on money that only they could create. How then could borrowers hope to repay loans of this manufactured money *plus* the interest charges? Imagine that, initially, the total amount of state money in existence is £100. If the banks now create £400 of bank money there will be a total money supply of £500. Let us further imagine that the £400 of bank money is loaned for three years at 10% interest per year, and that an amount of £532.40 will therefore be due for repayment. Now, if the total money supply at the beginning of the loan period is only £500, where will the extra £32.40 come from? Since the £32.40 does not exist initially, it is impossible to repay this part of the loan unless new money is created from somewhere.

The required new amount of money could only come from two sources. Either the bankers would have to expand the supply of bank money, in other words lend yet more, or the state would have to increase the supply of state money. This simple fact would have enormous repercussions for the economy as the practice of fractional reserve banking spread.

Without the creation of new money, many borrowers would eventually default on their loans. With the creation of new money, default could be avoided. The economic survival of both businessmen and private individuals therefore came to depend in large part on the bankers' willingness to extend loans of newly manufactured money.

The unrepayability of old loans places society in a game of economic 'musical chairs'. For those unfamiliar with musical chairs, it is a game often played in England in which, say, eleven children run around a group of ten chairs whilst music is playing. When the music stops, all the children must find a chair to sit down on but because there is one more child than there are chairs, one child will always remain standing when the music stops. This is the child who has 'lost', and he is removed from the game. So it is with the unrepayable loans. When new loans are not forthcoming, old loans become unrepayable. Under these circumstances, everyone is trying to repay their debts, but a sufficient quantity of money with which to do so simply does not exist. At least one person must go bankrupt and be 'removed from the game'. Life becomes an aggressive competitive struggle to avoid being the one who is left standing when the music stops. The policies of government, the actions of businessmen and the daily life of ordinary people are all affected by this ongoing struggle in a deep and disturbing way.

In an effort to rescue the worst of the financial problems comes the State. In those periods of recession that occur when the quantity of new loans is insufficient to allow repayment of old debts, the state finds itself obliged to pay welfare benefits to the unemployed, to cut tax rates and so on. The money that the State requires to undertake this expenditure can be manufactured by the State itself or it can be borrowed from the banks in the form of bank money. Quite why the State would want to borrow money manufactured by the banks at interest when it could manufacture state money interest-free is one of the unanswered mysteries of our time. Yet this is what happens most of the time in most of the countries of the world.

Since the greatest proportion of new money is nowadays created through loans made by the banking system, money supply expansion is accompanied by a more or less continuous increase in the amount of debt in the economy as a whole. Combined private and public debt as a proportion of gross domestic product has therefore grown substantially in the each of the seven largest economies of the world over the last thirty years. Every developed country runs a national debt. And every one of these countries has a private sector that is heavily in debt. As Michael Rowbotham comments in *The Grip of Death* (1998), despite decades of hard work using ever more productive technology, society in the developed world finds itself more in debt than it ever has been.

Year	UK	USA	Japan	Malaysia
1970	81	136	113	60
1983	85	151	198	144
1993	149	187	250	169

source: IMF International Financial Statistics Yearbook 2000

TOTAL DOMESTIC DEBT (PRIVATE PLUS PUBLIC)
as a % of Gross Domestic Product

We are faced with a choice, in effect, between continued expansion of debt on the one hand and widespread business and personal bankruptcy on the other. The increase in money supply that results from the creation of new debt can and often does encourage general price inflation, but, since almost every developed economy nowadays suffers from such inflation, this is regarded as an acceptable part of modern life.

In the 17th Century when modern banking was just beginning, the long term consequences of the industry's standard practices were perhaps unforeseeable. Yet some individuals saw beneath the veneer presented by the bankers and their lobbyists in public life. They petitioned the state to legislate against the bankers, arguing that whilst most people had to work to earn money, the bankers could simply print it. But the state had other ideas.

The Bank of England

Naturally, the bankers would not wish to suffer loan losses. This kind of event would have the same ultimate effect as an expenditure of bank money by the banker himself, in other words a loss of control of the manufactured money. It therefore became common for bankers to avoid profit-sharing investments and to focus instead on interest-based loans supported by collateral. The collateral would act as a cushion to protect the loan in the event of failure of the borrower's business. In this case, the banker would be able to seize and sell the collateral in order to reclaim full or part repayment of the loan amount.

These criteria for extending loans naturally biased the lending of manufactured money towards the rich. After all, the rich were the ones with the most wealth to offer as collateral. Those without collateral, the poor, though possessing potentially profitable business ideas, might not so easily attract the required funding. Thus it was that the government itself, having the right to raise tax and therefore being the most secure of all borrowers, would become the prime focus for the lending activities of the bankers.

In 1694, King William III of England was persuaded to invite loan offers from private individuals as a means of raising funds with which to wage war against France. Interest at 8% would be paid on the borrowings, financed through a variety of taxes, predominantly upon beer and ale. Repayment of the principal amount would also be made from the revenues thereby generated. On condition of £1,200,000 being advanced within a certain period of time, a charter was to be given under the Tonnage Act of May 1694 to establish *The Governor and the Company of the Bank of England*.

The new Bank would be allowed to take deposits of coinage and issue paper money. Several kinds of paper were issued, in an effort to remain within the rather unclear requirements of the Act regarding the Bank's issuing activities. The various papers included 'sealed bank bills', 'cash notes', and in due course 'bearer banknotes'. The bank's shareholders included many entrepreneurs who were keen to obtain a foothold in the new and seemingly highly profitable business of banking, but it was the bank itself that lent the King the required amount of money. £720,000 was paid in cash and the remaining £480,000 in sealed bank bills created by the Bank for the very purpose (for a fuller description see: Feaveryear, A. E., *The Pound Sterling*, Clarendon Press Oxford, 1931).

In evidence of amounts lent to the State by the Bank, the former would issue the latter with government debt obligations, these known at first as 'tallies', and later as 'stocks' or 'funds'. (In this context, a stock is synonymous with a bond, that is a tradable document displaying the terms of a loan between the borrower of money, the *issuer* of the bond, and the one who has purchased that bond, the *bondholder*). Often the Bank would sell these bonds on to smaller investors, more or less immediately, at a profit margin. By avoiding ownership of the bonds for anything but a short period of time, the Bank would minimise the risk of incurring a loss should their market price unexpectedly fall.

The government increasingly came to fund part of its expenditure by borrowing money from the Bank of England. Fortunately, the Bank was in a position to aid the government in its times of need. It was privileged by an Act of Parliament with the right to manufacture promissory notes which were increasingly being used as money. The Bank was therefore able to meet the government's borrowing requirement by printing more promissory notes. Thus money supply and government debt grew together. According to William Cobbett in *Paper Against Gold, 1812* the aggregate of the outstanding bonds and other borrowings, the 'National Debt' as it became known, grew from £16,394,702 in 1701, to £52,092,235 in 1727 and £257,213,043 in 1784. By 1810, it had reached £811,898,082. The state's outstanding debts were beginning to spiral out of control.

Of course, the Bank could not simply print paper notes without maintaining a sufficient level of gold coin reserves. Over time, it therefore sought to attract greater amounts of gold coin as deposits for its vaults. Though no notes under £20 were issued until 1755, the outbreak of the Seven Years War in 1756 gave rise to a substantial borrowing requirement on the part of state. The Bank of England now issued notes in the denomination of £10. By the time France had declared war upon England in 1793, notes in denominations as small as £5 were being issued in ever more strained attempts to obtain gold from depositors. In this manner the Bank maintained what it saw as a prudent reserve ratio whilst the lending of paper money to both the state and private borrowers expanded.

The insufficiency of reserves to meet large scale simultaneous demands for redemption of its promissory notes was one consequence of the Bank of England's money manufacturing activities. Thus it was in February 1797, that the Bank was permitted by an Act of Parliament to cease the redemption of promissory notes in gold. Following this 'Suspension of Payments', paper money issue increased with the production of £2 and £1 notes. In a letter to the King in 1805, the Earl of Liverpool commented:

When the situation of the Bank of England was under the consideration of the two Houses of Parliament in the year 1797, it was my opinion, and that of many others, that the extent to which the paper currency [system] had been carried was the first and principal, though not the sole cause, of the many difficulties to which that corporate body was then, and had of late years, from time to time been exposed in supplying the cash necessary for the commerce of the Kingdom.

The Bullion Committee of 1810 reported to Parliament that the Bank of England had taken the opportunity of the Suspension to print large amounts of paper money that had no gold backing, and had thereby profited itself substantially. The Committee was concerned that the scale of profits available to the creators of money was so great that the State should share these profits on behalf of the people. More specifically it encouraged Parliament to insist that the Bank of England maintained a full reserve of gold against its paper note issues.

The Bank meanwhile feigned ignorance of the problem. It promoted the 'real bills' doctrine which held that the manufacture of money out of nothing was not harmful to the economy so long as that money was used to finance real trade. Industrialists would issue bills of exchange in the normal course of their trade, and the Bank would purchase those bills with newly created money.

The Bullion Committee rejected the Bank's argument for it knew very well that the creation of money was the issue, not the use to which newly created money was put. Industrialists' need for cash was limitless. To use their need as a limiting factor in money creation was therefore a wholly erroneous policy. In due course, Parliament made the decision to require the Bank to resume redemption of its note issue in gold and this occurred gradually in the years following 1816. Cobbett argued that this remedy did not address the dangers of a 'paper money' system at all. In *Paper Against Gold* he rages against the moneyed interests in the City. He talks of national debt and inflation as children of the paper money system, and introduces us to the monetary conditions of his time :
We see the country abounding with paper money; we see every man's hand full of it; we frequently talk of it as a strange thing, and a great evil; but never do we inquire into the cause of it. There are few of you who cannot remember the time when there was scarcely ever seen a bank note among Tradesmen and Farmers ... If you look back, and take a little time to think, you will trace the gradual increase of paper money and the like decrease of gold and silver money...
Cobbett, W., *Paper Against Gold* (1828) p. 5

Though Britain's dominant position in international trade and increases in global gold production may have supported the gold coin circulation, the banking system continued to encounter crises even after the period of the Suspension had ended.
There was a great diversity of practice and many banks crashed - eighty-nine between 1814 and 1817 alone, though many such were small indeed, with under fifteen shareholders.
Thomas, H., *An Unfinished History of the World* (1981) p. 467

Due to its perceived soundness, the Bank of England's notes were often used by the so-called country banks (those operating outside London) as part of their reserves. A double pyramid of money supply expansion thus came to operate. For example, imagine that for every one pound of gold held at the Bank of England three pounds of Bank of England paper money were created. If now, for every one pound of Bank of England paper money held in a country bank, three pounds of country bank notes were issued, then for every one pound of gold at the Bank of England nine pounds of bank money would come into circulation.

The 1825 crisis exemplifies the type of problem that can be encountered when there is a shortage of reserves in the banking system. Many customers of country banks were demanding redemption of their country bank promissory notes, and would accept only gold coins or Bank of England notes. Representatives of the country banks were in turn approaching the Bank of England in order to acquire (by withdrawal of deposited money or by outright borrowing) gold coins or Bank of England notes. With these amounts, the country banks hoped to satisfy their own depositors' demands for withdrawal. The double pyramid was now working in reverse.

The Bank of England duly obliged, lending freely so as to provide the necessary cash to the country banks and others. However, the demand was so great that the mint had to work flat out in order to turn gold bullion into coinage. Meanwhile, the printers printed Bank of England notes as fast as they could. In December 1825, six London banks and sixty-one country banks ceased payment in gold. Chown quotes Clapham's account of the period:

The public was clamouring ... for money, Bank [of England] notes or gold. Neither notes nor sovereigns could be made fast enough ... By the evening of Saturday the seventeenth, the Bank [of England] had run out of £5 and £10 notes. However a supply came from the printers on the Sunday morning.

Chown, J. F., *A History of Money* (1994) p. 153

So the system wavered between banking crisis and reserve shortages on the one hand, and the profitable operation of fractional reserve banking on the other.

From Receipts to Cheques

The authorities eventually acted to counter the dangers posed to the health of an economy in which numerous private issuers of paper money were active. Under Peel's 1844 Bank Charter Act, the right to issue most kinds of note was restricted to the Bank of England (which was of course obliged to redeem its notes in gold). It was envisaged that this reform would cure the banking system of its previous ills but new banking technology, in the form of the cheque and account statement system, would soon render the legislation ineffective.

At the time of Peel's Act, the country banks had not adopted cheques as a means of clearing payments to any great extent. However, they moved quickly to do so as their right to print notes was removed. Once more, public confidence was essential to the successful operation of the new system. Where once the public felt sure of its ability to convert receipts into gold, it had now to be persuaded that the figures printed on account statements could be similarly converted.

Let us examine the cheque and account system as if there were but a single bank operating in the economy. This bank has several customers of which A and B are two. Both A and B start with a zero balance on their current accounts. Customer A now gives customer B a cheque for £100 in payment for goods, and customer B deposits this cheque with the bank. The banker credits account B with £100 and debits account A with the same amount. B is now in credit and A in overdraft to the amount of £100 and the goods have been paid for. The amount of new bank money in existence is the £100 that forms the total of customer B's account.

Two simple conclusions can now be drawn. Firstly, that one group of bank customers must always be in debt to an amount that equals the existing supply of bank money. Secondly, that if A now repays his overdraft by depositing a cheque of £100 drawn on Customer B, then the bank money transferred from B to A simply vanishes. Bank money stands in complete contrast to state money. Gold coins are never destroyed in the act of repaying a loan.

Confusion on the above matters can arise because the banking system is seen merely as an intermediary between depositors of money and borrowers of money, profiting only from the margin (or 'interest spread') between interest rates paid to savers and interest rates charged to borrowers. But if the entire banking system is viewed as one very large bank, then it has the potential to act not only as an intermediary between saver and borrower, but also as a creator of money. It is however unjustified to single out commercial banks in this analysis since deposit-taking institutions in general, building societies for instance, play their own part in the money creation process. Though the issues raised in the following discussions relate to deposit-taking institutions in general, we will continue to focus on the commercial banking system only.

The following analysis is similar to that given by most standard economic texts on the subject of the 'deposit multiplier'. Imagine an economy in which there are three Banks, A, B and C. Each operates a 20% reserve ratio. Initially there are £100 of modern state money (notes and coins) in circulation and none of this state money is deposited with the commercial banks. Now, if the holder(s) of the state money deposit all of the notes and coins with Bank A, that bank's balance sheet will read :

```
ASSETS
cash                    £100

LIABILITIES
deposits                £100
```

To meet its reserve requirement, Bank A decides to keep £20 of the deposited sum and lend the remaining £80. Having done so, Bank A's balance sheet appears thus :

```
ASSETS
cash                    £20
loan                    £80

LIABILITIES
deposits                £100
```

The borrower of the £80 now spends this sum and the individual receiving it deposits it with his bank, Bank B. Bank B maintains a 20% reserve ratio, and therefore lends £64 of the £80 deposited with it. Its balance sheet is then :

```
ASSETS
cash                    £16
loans                   £64
```

LIABILITIES
deposits   £80

The borrower of the £64 spends it in turn and the individual receiving the £64 deposits it with his bank, Bank C. Bank C's balance sheet now reads:

ASSETS
cash   £64

LIABILITIES
deposits   £64

In this example, the amount of deposits outstanding in banks A, B and C is now £244. This is the total money supply in this simple economy since it represents the amount of money that can be used by customers wishing to pay by cheque. The process of depositing and re-depositing funds that is seen above, referred to as 'multiple deposit expansion', finds its limit under certain assumptions when the total amount of deposits in the banking system reaches £500. This amount is given by the quantity of state money initially deposited, multiplied by the inverse of the reserve ratio (£100 × 1 / 0.2 = £500). The deposit multiplier has a value of 5 here. Before the process of multiple deposit expansion began, in other words before the intermediation of the banks in the financial system, the money supply stood at £100, which was entirely comprised of state money.

The banks have reasoned that all of the deposits made by depositors will not be withdrawn on one day. If this reasoning is proved incorrect then each of the banks may collapse. If the maximum amount of deposits withdrawn in the form of state money on any one day does not exceed reserves, then there will be no collapse on that day. This type of banking system is especially unstable in times of crisis if large numbers of depositors wish to withdraw state money. Realising this, modern banks, like the goldsmiths of old, also make arrangements to source new reserves of state money in the event of high withdrawals.

However, in the modern financial system it is the central bank that guarantees to lend an unlimited amount of state money to the commercial banks should it ever be required. This 'lender of last resort' function, essential to the stability of the modern economy, prevents the recurrence of bank runs as long as sufficient amounts of state money are quickly made available when required. It is worthy of note that this guarantee can only be given because the state too has now adopted paper (and more recently computer entries) as the basis of state money. Were state money to be made of precious metal, no such guarantee could be completely trusted. Even the state does not have access to unlimited supplies of gold and silver.

'Liquidity' and the Banking System

The lender of last resort function carried out by the central bank is only one line of defence, the last line by definition, against a collapse in the banking system. We shall briefly review the other avenues that are available to modern banks for sourcing those reserves of state money which are required from time to time.

In the event that reserves at any one bank branch are severely depleted, the bank in question may of course transfer surplus reserves from other branches. Often, commercial banks make the withdrawal of large amounts of state money by customers subject to at least one day's notice. This requirement provides the bank with sufficient time to acquire the necessary reserves, if not from their own branches then from other sources as described below.

Instead of withdrawing state money from a bank in order to buy goods or services, customers may prefer to pay by cheque or debit card, for example. Where payment is effected in this manner, and where it takes place between two customers of the same bank, that bank merely alters the balances on the two customers' accounts as described in our earlier example. Otherwise, where payment is made to a customer banking with a different bank, then the 'paying bank' must transfer reserves of state money to the 'payee bank'.

For the purpose of making transfers of state money reserves to other banks, each commercial bank holds an account with the central bank. The balances in these accounts are termed 'operational deposits' (and are distinct from 'non-operational deposits' which cannot be withdrawn and which are called for by the central bank from time to time in order to effect monetary policy of one description or other). State money held in operational accounts can be transferred to the central bank accounts of other commercial banks. This is the normal method for settling the net amount of cheque payments between banks due on any one business day, a process for which a central 'clearing house' is responsible. The balance on an operational account can also be withdrawn by a bank in the form of state money, for which purpose the central bank operates regional storage centres where state money is held and disbursed as required.

Since payments made between commercial banks tend to cancel one another, in the same manner that gold coin withdrawals and deposits cancelled one another in our example of the early goldsmith, commercial banks only need to maintain a small balance on their operational account at the central bank. However, in the event that a bank has insufficient reserves of state money in its operational account to meet payments due, it will be necessary to source extra reserves or arrange to go into overdraft. The sourcing of reserves may be carried out in several ways.

Reserves may be obtained by borrowing from other banks on the wholesale interbank money market (sometimes known as the 'parallel market' in the UK since it operates alongside the 'discount market' to be described shortly). A bank with surplus reserves may in this way lend its surplus to obtain interest on otherwise idle funds and the borrowing bank may simultaneously alleviate its reserve shortage. The interbank money market is now a feature of every developed economy.

As a second option, commercial banks in the UK may obtain new amounts of state money by approaching the discount market. In order to understand this process, a brief digression is in order.

The UK discount market is separate to the wholesale interbank money market and the institutions at its centre are termed 'discount houses'. The term 'discount' arises from the principal activity of institutions which lend money by buying short term bills at a discount to face value. For example, a three month government bill is a document in which the government promises to pay, to the holder of the document, three months after the issue date, the face value written on the bill. A buyer may pay 95% of that face value to own this three month bill on the day of issue and will therefore have discounted the bill by 5% (or, more precisely, discounted it at an annualised rate of 20%).

Financial market operators closely monitor the level of the discount, the so-called 'discount rate' (which should not be confused with the type of discount rate that was discussed in Chapter One), because it may act as a signal of trends in the level of short term interest rates throughout the economy. It should be noted that a discount rate is not the same as an interest rate. If one pays £95 for a bill that repays £100 in three months time, the rate of the discount is 5% (£5 divided by £100) but the rate of interest is 5.26% (£5 divided by £95).

The central bank influences the discount rate by withdrawing state money from, or injecting it into, the discount market at appropriate times. Injection of state money may be carried out by buying 'eligible bills' from the discount houses, or by lending money to them directly. On the other hand, when the central bank sells eligible bills to the discount market, state money is received in return and is thereby withdrawn from the market. (Eligible bills are simply government bills, or the bills of major companies, so-called 'commercial bills', that the Bank of England is prepared to purchase at a discount).

The discount houses may lend to, or borrow from, both the commercial banks and the central bank. With state money borrowed from the commercial banks, the discount houses are able to buy government bills, in other words lend to the government. With state money borrowed from the central bank, the discount houses are able to lend to the commercial banks by buying bills from them. The understanding in the discount market is that the central bank will always lend what is required of it to the discount houses, and that the discount houses will always lend to the government or commercial banks the amounts requested. These arrangements can be seen to countenance the possibility that the central bank lends to the discount houses amounts which it subsequently borrows back.

Most of the loans advanced to the discount market by the commercial banks are available for immediate or very short notice withdrawal should the commercial banks wish, being 'money at call' or 'overnight money'. In satisfying their requirements for state money, commercial banks will often withdraw these deposits as a first resort. If such amounts, and others, prove insufficient, then the commercial banks may become outright borrowers from the discount market. Borrowing by the commercial banks may then force the discount houses themselves to borrow from the central bank. As far as a commercial bank is concerned, money withdrawn or borrowed from the discount market will be placed in its central bank account and hence alleviate any shortage of reserves.

Because the central bank agrees to lend the discount market whatever amount of state money is required of it, the central bank cannot necessarily control the amount of state money supply in existence. State money supply is therefore said to be determined 'endogenously'. Given that the central bank guarantees to provide extra reserves in this manner should the commercial banks require them, a safety net is effectively provided that enables fractional reserve banking to be practised with impunity. This is one major reason that bankers in every nation have at one time or other lobbied for (and succeeded in obtaining) a central bank to oversee the banking system. With a central bank, even if bank runs do occur, the bankers need not worry. They can simply ask the central bank to provide as much state money as is required to meet demands for withdrawal.

Commercial banks may also bolster their reserves by selling their investment holdings, or by issuing new bonds and shares of their own for sale to investors. However, the clearest sign of a liquidity shortage, as far as the public are concerned, arises when commercial banks attempt to improve their reserve ratios by 'calling in' overdrafts and other loan facilities.

The Manipulation of Money

'Fiat money', another term for modern state money, is money whose value in exchange for goods and services exists by fiat, in other words by order, of the state. The excess of value in exchange over and above the cost of production of such money is termed 'seignorage'. Thus by producing £100 of notes, perhaps at a cost of £0.01, the state has created fiat money with a purchasing power of £100 and seignorage of £99.99. The greater the cost of production of fiat money, the lower the seignorage. Thus 'commodity money', gold for example, has a lower seignorage than paper money (assuming that the cost of acquiring gold bullion and minting it into gold coins exceeds the cost of acquiring and printing paper). Common to both these forms of money is a face value that is exchanged for goods and services, whether that face value be by fiat or otherwise.

In many ways, modern fiat money bears a similarity to an 'IOU'. An IOU could stand in evidence of a debt owed by a buyer to a seller, amounting to the value of the goods or services acquired by that buyer. Where the seller has faith that the IOU will be honoured by the buyer when the time comes for repayment, the seller will accept the IOU and complete the transaction. The issuer of this IOU acquires goods and services of a value that exceeds the cost of production of the IOU. In a primitive economy where IOU's were the only medium of exchange, the total value of IOU's outstanding would represent the aggregate amount of credit extended by the sellers to the buyers. This is the amount of wealth that Soddy refers to as society's 'virtual wealth' and it equals the wealth that some members of the community have given up in favour of promises by other members to repay at a later date.

In a modern day goods-for-cash transaction, the seller receives a similar piece of paper of little or no intrinsic value. The distinction that must be made is that the state's paper money is accepted in final payment for goods and services, whilst a paper IOU drawn up by a private individual is simply a promise to make final payment at a later date. That piece of state paper that we call 'money' is only money because the state says so, and because we agree to be bound by the rules of the state. But once upon a time, paper notes were regarded by the public only as a promise to pay 'money' (meaning gold or silver coins) at a later date. How things have changed.

Nowhere in the issue of either an IOU or state money need an interest charge arise. Certainly, gold does not bear interest in order to exist. It does not have to be borrowed in order to exist. It simply exists. The state's paper money need not bear interest in order to exist. Its existence need not be dependent on a loan transaction. It simply exists. However, bank money cannot be created other than by a loan transaction and will therefore inevitably bear interest as a condition for its existence.

The first proposal in this work is for a monetary system that is not based on an interest-yielding money supply. This does not mean that money cannot be invested in the hope of some kind of return. It simply means that there should not be a cost, a rent or any other charge extracted by the *issuer* of money for the subsequent usage of that money.

Frederick Soddy writes:
By allowing private mints to spring up, Parliament has fundamentally and perhaps irretrievably betrayed democracy. Before the [First World] War it was customary even in the works of apparently respectable economists to find absolutely dishonest hair-splitting distinctions between the invisible money so created and paper notes. The latter were really money and the former was not! In fact the reader can always tell in such standard works on the subject when he is approaching the fishy part of the business. The essential fact, the creation of new money, becomes obscured in a cloud of anticipatory justification and special pleading.
Soddy, F., *The Role of Money* (1934) p. 30

The banking lobby has tried hard to label this kind of criticism as that of an extreme or somehow unbalanced mind. But the more one looks, the more one sees how widespread the criticism has been:
The unlimited emission of bank paper has banished all her specie [in England], and is now, by a depreciation acknowledged by her own statesmen, carrying her rapidly to bankruptcy, as it did France, as it did us .... Private fortunes, in the present state of our circulation, are at the mercy of those self-created money lenders, and are prostrated by the floods of nominal money with which their avarice deluges us.'
Thomas Jefferson in a letter to John Wayles Eppes on 24 June 1813, Jefferson, *Writings* (1984) New York: Literary Classics of the United States

And I sincerely believe with you, that banking establishments are more dangerous than standing armies; and that the principle of spending money to be paid by posterity, under the name of funding, is but swindling futurity on a large scale
Thomas Jefferson in a letter to John Taylor 28 May 1816, *Writings* (1984) New York: Literary Classics of the United States

The distress and alarm which pervaded and agitated the whole country when the Bank of the United States waged war upon the people in order to compel them to submit to its demands cannot yet be forgotten. The ruthless and unsparing temper with which whole cities and communities were oppressed, individuals impoverished and ruined, and a scene of cheerful prosperity suddenly changed into one of gloom and despondency ought to be indelibly impressed on the memory of the people of the United States. If such was its power in time of peace, what would it have been in a season of war, with an enemy at your doors? No nation but the free men of the United States could have come out victorious from such a contest; yet, if you had not conquered, the government would have passed from the hands of the many to the few, and this organised money power, from its secret conclave, would have dictated the choice of your highest officials and compelled you to make peace or war, as best suited their own wishes.

President Andrew Jackson, Address to the American people, 4 March 1837, recorded in *Richardson's Messages*, volume 4, p. 1532

The government should create, issue and circulate all the currency and credit needed to satisfy the spending power of the government and the buying power of the consumers. The privilege of creating and issuing money is not only the supreme prerogative of government, but it is the government's greatest creative opportunity. By the adoption of these principles, the long-felt want for a uniform medium will be satisfied. The taxpayers will be saved immense sums of interest, discounts and exchanges ... money will cease to be the master and become the servant of humanity. Democracy will rise superior to the money power.

President Abraham Lincoln, *Senate Document 23* 1865

Reginald McKenna, one time British Chancellor of the Exchequer and later the Chairman of Midland Bank writes:
I am afraid that the ordinary citizen will not like to be told that the banks or the Bank of England can create and destroy money.

McKenna, R., *Postwar Banking Policy* (1928), p. 93

Almost two centuries after Jefferson's comments, one might have thought that society would no longer allow itself to be 'at the mercy' of greedy money manufacturers. But, as we shall see, the scale of money manufacture has increased dramatically with the spread of fractional reserve banking. The result is that, in many countries today, banking is by far the most profitable of all business activities.

Country	Bank profits	Non-bank profits
United Kingdom	20.62	- 0.97
France	7.99	- 2.41
Spain	4.79	4.13

TOTAL PROFITS OF BANKS VERSUS NON-BANKS IN THE FORTUNE GLOBAL 500, BY COUNTRY, FOR 2001 (US$ bns.)
Source: Fortune Magazine, Vol. 146, No.2, Europe, August 2002

Central banks from time to time buy or sell financial instruments on the open market. These so-called 'open market operations' are often undertaken not because the state wishes to repay debt or borrow money, but instead because there appears to be too much or too little money in circulation in the economy. When the state pays off old debt by issuing new amounts of state money, that debt is said to have been 'monetised'. In due course, the new amount of state money may be used by the banking system as a reserve upon which to create further amounts of interest-bearing bank money. (Alternatively, the state may encourage an increase in bank money supply by first selling bonds to the banks and then spending the money that it has raised thereby. The money that the state has borrowed from the banking system will thus return to the banking system and the state is therefore acting as a credit-worthy borrower upon which fractional reserve banking can be practised.)

When the central bank employs open market operations in an attempt to reduce the amount of state money in circulation, it does so by selling bonds or bills to the banking sector *without* then proceeding to spend the funds so raised. Thus, the amount of state money in circulation contracts and the growth of bank money supply is in due course restricted. (If this really is the intended result, it is one that is short-lived. Because government debt pays interest, the state must ultimately repay more state money to the commercial banks than was borrowed in the first place.)

In many countries this [money creation by the state] is a straightforward operation because the treasury has the legal right to issue currency with which it can pay for government spending. In the United States, this process is somewhat more complicated, because the Treasury does not have the legal right to issue currency to pay for goods and services, but can only issue securities. Financing government spending with money creation then takes on a more circuitous route in which the Treasury sells bonds to the public which are then purchased by the Federal Reserve ... This last method of financing government spending is frequently called printing money because high powered money (the monetary base) is created in the process. It is also referred to as monetizing the debt, because as the two step process described indicates, government debt issued to finance government spending has been removed from the hands of the public and has been replaced by high-powered money.

Mishkin, F. S., *The Economics of Money Banking and Financial Markets* (1992) p. 421

Customers of commercial banks, both those in debit and those in credit, will find their account balances increasing over time due to the application of an interest rate. One of the greatest economic fallacies of our time is that raising the interest rate reduces money supply growth and hence restrains inflation. In fact, raising the interest rate only encourages those credit and debit balances to increase faster. Hence, in the long run, both money supply and the level of debt in an economy expand. This is not a background against which inflation can easily be restrained.

Whatever the course of monetary policy, a serious conflict eventually arises. Bank money supply cannot grow for ever if reserve ratios have a lower limit and the supply of state money remains fixed. But as we have seen, in the application of interest, bank money supply is forced into a continual expansion. The manner in which this conflict is resolved determines the subsequent performance of the economy.

The commercial banks ultimately have two options. They must eventually act to prevent their reserve ratios from falling to too low a level. They do this either by calling in existing loans or by sourcing new reserves from the state. As we have seen, the former approach destroys money as fast as loans are repaid and thus results in a vicious recessionary cycle. The latter approach allows a continued expansion of money supply.

Given the economic and political consequences of monetary contraction, most governments tend to choose an increase in money supply when given the choice. Achieving this goal may involve an increase in the amount of state money or bank money, or both. As Mishkin shows, new state money is often created through the issuance of government debt, hence government debt tends to increase substantially when this policy is relied upon. And where an increase in bank money supply is encouraged through other means (for example by lowering the statutory reserve ratio for the banks), this will tend to result in an increase in the amount of debt owed by private persons and corporations.

Since the state's tax revenue largely depends upon the value of sales and earnings within the economy, as bank money supply increases so too does the state's tax revenue. Hence, where an economic boom results from increased private borrowing of bank money, the state's own borrowing requirement often falls. This gives the politically beneficial appearance of good housekeeping. But in the long run, debt must grow. It is only a question of the proportion in which that debt is shared between the private sector and the state. When recession bites, the state's welfare payments (unemployment benefit, for example) rise strongly, and the budget deficit reappears.

Many people refuse to see inflation as a particular evil. "What's so bad about inflation?", they ask. The debt situation, however, is another matter entirely:

Relieved of their annual debt repayments, the severely indebted countries could use the funds for investments that in Africa alone would save the lives of about 21 million children by 2000 and provide 90 million girls and women with access to basic education
United Nations Development Programme, *Human Development Report* (1997) p. 93

Because the interest gets paid before the food and medicine is purchased, one might justifiably argue that the banking system is killing people. Of course Hollywood doesn't make films about the Debt Holocaust, and few journalists remind us of what is happening.

We do however hear occasionally of the 'Corrupt Dictators' argument, which blames the borrowers for having wasted their borrowings on such extravagances as palaces and armies. Perhaps we should ask who lent them money in the first place. There are dozens of countries that are labouring under unrepayable debt, not just one or two. Are they all corrupt? If so, did not the Western lenders learn their lesson after the first few bad experiences? Or did they wake up one morning to find that all of their borrowers had suddenly turned rotten? Like so much else, the corruption is at least as much in the West as it is in the developing world, but it is harder to detect, buried in the workings of a complex monetary system and camouflaged by professional smiles.

If we enquire into the motivations of the Western financial establishment, then there can be no doubting the desire to exert political influence upon borrowing clients. The 1997 Asian financial crisis offered another such opportunity, one of loan assistance in return for policy change. We have seen this many times over the last fifty years. It can be dressed up in many forms, perhaps as 'conditionality' or 'structural adjustment', but never is fractional reserve banking mentioned as a cause of the problem. Ultimately, more loans are granted, loans which as we have seen are unrepayable in aggregate. Not one developing country that I am aware of has taken IMF or World Bank assistance and subsequently managed to escape from its debt. Western colonialism nowadays relies more heavily upon the global monetary system than it does upon an army.

More on Money Supply

Some statistics on money supply expansion would be instructive at this stage, but first we must recognise that just as different types of money exist, state money and bank money for example, so too do different measures of money supply. Since each different measure includes different kinds of bank account or financial instrument, economists often disagree upon the correct choice of measure to follow in monitoring the course of monetary policy.

Taking the UK as an example, M_0 describes the amount of notes and coins in circulation outside the central bank plus the operational deposits of the commercial banks at the central bank. It is a 'narrow' measure of money supply. M_1 is a 'wider' measure of money supply and equals M_0 plus the net amount of current account deposits in the banking system. M_2 adds to M_1 the amount of various time deposits whilst M_4 includes deposits at building societies, certain money market instruments and other items, giving a wider measure still.

Year	UK (£ billion)	Japan (Yen trillion)	Malaysia (Ringgit million)
1968	16	39	3,263
1978	56	168	17,521
1988	393	408	60,135
1998	835	578	291,801

source: IMF International Financial Statistics Yearbook 2000

M2 MONEY SUPPLY FOR VARIOUS COUNTRIES

Above we see one of the measures of combined state and bank money supply (M_2). Notice the consistent growth of money supply in every case, as predicted by the theory of interest bearing money. The following table shows how much of this money supply has been created by the banking system.

Year	USA	Japan	UK	Turkey	Indonesia
1968	87.7	88.7	79.5	41.7	13.1
1978	89.9	88.8	84.1	36.3	52.0
1988	91.5	90.4	95.0	69.2	78.2
1998	89.3	89.3	96.2	72.0	87.6

source: IMF *International Financial Statistics Yearbook 2000*

% OF M2 MONEY SUPPLY CREATED BY THE BANKING SYSTEM
(1 - M0/M2) for various countries

The above should serve to remind us that while the state is in control of the paper-money printing presses, the more important fact is that the commercial banks nowadays manufacture by far the greater proportion of the money that is used by firms and individuals in their daily transactions. They indeed have a license to manufacture money.

Some economists have argued that the above state of affairs is quite unjust and many of them are quoted in this work. Others have questioned why the level of money supply, and variation in it, matters in the first instance. They say for example that the banking system's activities are actually good for the economy because the benefits outweigh the disadvantages. So although economists generally agree that changes in the amount of money supply do have *some* kind of an effect upon an economy, the relationship that exists between money, output and prices, is one of fierce debate.

In essence, the argument sways back and forth among those economists who feel that changes in money supply will lead to changes in the level of prices in the long run with no effect upon real variables such as output, in other words that money is 'neutral', and those who feel that changes in money supply *can* influence real variables in the long run. The question is simply whether the manufacture and spending of an extra amount of money brings into existence an extra unit of production or simply an increase in price of existing units. It is probably the case that the truth lies somewhere between these two viewpoints, though where exactly is dependent upon the initial condition of the economic system. In an economy starved of money, more money will probably produce more trade and get people back to work. In an economy with too much money, yet more money will probably create only more inflation.

The 'neo-classical' contention holds that money supply is a major determinant of the general price level in an economy. Few would doubt that it was an increase in money supply that contributed to the massive inflations in inter-War Germany, and more recently in post-Communist Russia. (Of course, the standard Western economic propaganda has us believe that Moscow is responsible for this reckless printing of money, while the money manufacturing activities of the dozens of newly licensed Russian commercial banks goes unmentioned.) Falling prices have, conversely, been related by Professor Fisher to a contraction of United States money supply during the Great Depression of the 1930's.

The simplest mathematical description of the proposed relationship between money supply and price appears in Fisher's Quantity Theory of Money (1911).

$$MV = PT$$

M = money supply
V = volocity of circulation
P = average general price level over period
T = number of transactions during period

The formula is regarded as a truism since the amount of money in circulation multiplied by the number of times it is used must equal the average price level multiplied the number of transactions made at that price level. What makes the theory useful, according to its proponents, is that V and T are assumed to be stable over short time periods. Under one further assumption, namely that causation runs from M to P, changes in P can then be managed by controlling M.

If it is fair to say that changes in money supply can affect the general price level, then an examination of both state and private issuance of money becomes of vital importance to any economic analysis. Many writers have agreed in this. Frank Knight commenting on Soddy's *'Wealth, Virtual Wealth and Debt'* (1926), wrote:

In the abstract it is absurd and monstrous for society to pay the commercial banking system interest for multiplying severalfold the quantity of the medium of exchange when a) a public agency could do it all at negligible cost, b) there is no sense in having it done at all, since the effect is merely to raise the price level, and c) important evils result, notably the frightful instability of the whole economic system.

Frank Knight: *Saturday Review of Literature*, (1927) *p. 732*

John Plender writing in the *Financial Times*, 23 July 1994, comments :
The human and financial resources that central banks pour into supervising commercial banks appear to deliver precious little. Despite all the effort, the English speaking economies have experienced one banking crisis per economic cycle since the mid-1970's, running from the property crash in 1974, to the Third World debt disaster in 1982, to the property and junk bond fiasco of the late 1980's, and the simultaneous Savings and Loans debacle. Taxpayers have ended up footing a multi-billion Dollar bill.

Friedman, in contrast, attempts to show that current arrangements need undergo no basic restructuring, since under his proposals the commercial bank creation of credit could be controlled with resort to various tools of monetary policy. We have already seen that such procedures can be highly unreliable and, if successful at all, only at great cost to economic activity. In *'Free to Choose'*, Friedman argues that the state should rigidly adhere to a policy that allowed growth of between 3% and 5% per annum in the monetary base. This growth would accommodate the requirements of increased economic activity as population and trade expanded. Friedman goes still further in *'Monetary Policy : Tactics versus Strategy'*, arguing that the state should freeze the monetary base once and for all and simultaneously abolish bank reserve requirements.

Friedman's last suggestion would prevent the state from creating money but allow the banking system to do so. Thus the state would have to borrow money created by the banks at interest, to the cost of us all, when it could instead have manufactured its own money interest-free. The policy would also strengthen the ability of the private sector to change money supply arbitrarily as dictated by the profit motive, and with predictable results.

The UK Experience

It has been argued on many occasions that, with proper management by the state, the private issuance of money can be regulated so as to have few ill effects upon economic conditions. The reality is sadly different. Over the years, many of the devices employed to achieve regulation have been abandoned by the authorities in charge of monetary policy. The 'corset' (applied to limit the growth of bank deposits), 'directives' (issued by the central bank to influence commercial bank lending policy) and special deposit schemes are just some of the devices that have at one time or other been in vogue and subsequently slipped out of vogue when found wanting.

In the UK during 1981, the previously existing reserve ratio of 10% for banks was phased out in favour of a much less stringent regime. The new monetary arrangements came into effect on 20 August of that year with little public fanfare for such a far-reaching development. As a result of the change in policy, commercial banks were to hold an amount equal to only 0.5% of their 'eligible liabilities' in reserve in the form of non-operational deposits at the central bank. A bank's eligible liabilities are, broadly speaking, the total amount of Sterling deposits that it has outstanding under categories specified by the Bank of England. In addition, an average of 6% of eligible liabilities were required to be held in the form of liquid deposits, mainly with the discount market. By 1998, the non-operational reserve requirement had been reduced to 0.15% and other reserve requirements were abolished entirely. As always, a lower reserve ratio allows the banking system to create more bank money for every unit of state money that they hold. Those expecting another UK property boom were not to be disappointed.

A key statement with regard to the role of the banking system in expanding money supply appears in the *Bank of England Quarterly Bulletin* for September 1981 :

The abolition of the reserve asset ratio will provide the banking system with somewhat more flexibility to draw on liquidity (subject to the needs of prudent banking) to meet temporary drains. But in the longer term an improvement in the liquidity of the banking system would be consistent with the achievement of the monetary target only if the growth of the banking system's lending to the private and overseas sectors is restrained.

'Restrained' how? Not by self discipline it would seem. Wynne Godley, in his 1993 economic forecast, *Financial Times* (4 January 1993), comments on the aftermath of the Bank of England's relaxation of controls:

> ... previous recoveries were initiated by the removal of credit controls which caused a spurt in lending for expenditure on durables and housing. This cannot happen now because there are no credit controls to remove, and because the balance sheets of banks and other lending institutions have been severely weakened by bad debts incurred during the Lawson boom.

Without formal controls, many authorities in the developed economies are now content to rely upon a single weapon to combat bank creation of money. That weapon is interest rate policy. Higher interest rates, reason some economists, reduce the amount that consumers are willing to borrow, thereby lowering demand for goods and services and ultimately reducing the upward pressure on prices. In this manner, the man in the street has been educated to believe that in order to control inflation, interest rates must rise. But the man in the street has been misled.

Deposit-taking institutions are often said to make a profit by paying lower interest rates on the money that they borrow than is charged on the money that they lend, in other words by charging an interest spread on the money that passes through their hands. As we have seen, this argument camouflages the raison d'être of commercial banking, which is to manufacture money and lend it at interest. There are then two methods of increasing profit in this business: one is to lend more money in total; the other is to increase the size of the spread. *The actual level of interest rates may at times be immaterial in influencing either of these two methods.* Expansion of bank money supply may continue even when interest rates are high.

If people want to borrow money in order to buy a consumer item, they are often quite unconcerned whether the interest rate charged on the money that they borrow is a few percent higher or lower. For many individuals there is an overwhelming desire to enjoy the item and worry about loan repayments later. It is not obvious that higher interest rates stop individuals borrowing money, except where those rates become truly penal. But attempts to halt a monetary expansion by imposing penal rates of interest on the economy can severely handicap or even destroy the businesses of existing borrowers.

When unemployment and business bankruptcy rates increase it is hardly surprising that the level of demand for consumer and investment goods collapses. The natural reaction of any business to such circumstances is then to reduce profit margins and thus to subdue upward pressure on prices. 'So the remedy works!' cry the monetarists. 'Yes', reply the critics, '... but at what cost?'

One result of a long term addiction to the interest rate medicine is an unnecessarily volatile business environment in which long term planning is difficult and confidence becomes weak. In this climate, investment programmes suffer and hence product quality declines. When the recovery comes, domestic products may not so easily compete with the quality or price of foreign counterparts. In the *Financial Times* on 30 January 1993, Christian Tyler describes the views of Robert Bischof, one of 100 managers chosen by Chancellor Kohl to revitalise east German state industry:

... (Bischof) knows only too well how easy it easy for a foreign company entering the boom-and-bust British market to cut the native opposition to shreds. He has done it himself. Bischof agrees with Germany's President, Richard von Weizsacker, that it is not people but the system that determines the success or failure of an economy. "Under communism you could work yourself to death and get nowhere. That is very true in Britain, too... These ups and downs are destroying the social fabric - resources, capital, everything" ... For example, he says Anthony Barber and Nigel Lawson, the Tory Chancellors responsible for the two big artificial booms of the post-war period, should be awarded the Iron Cross for services to German exports.

Brian Reading criticises one-dimensional assumptions about the relationship between interest rates and the growth of money supply:

Any such national government which endeavours to make money tight by making it expensive, secures precisely the opposite result. Higher interest rates cause capital to flow in from abroad and instead of dear money becoming scarce it becomes plentiful. ... High interest rates cause money supply growth to accelerate and are inflationary. Low rates make money scarce and are deflationary. ... British money supply growth has not been slowed by keeping interest rates high. On the contrary as Tim Congdon of Shearson Lehman points out "To conclude that monetary policy has been tightened since December is fantastic. Is it really necessary to point out that the first quarter of 1988 saw the fastest credit growth ever?" Bank and building society lending rose nearly 70% over the last twelve months. Mortgages have never been more readily available, and, as a result, the property market - particularly outside London - continues to boom. ... Courage is required to bring down rates at a stroke to a level at which they can hardly go lower. ... But making money so cheap would work wonders in making it scarce, so ending the excess growth in credit which is now fuelling inflation. ... Sharply lower interest rates would curb the growth of credit for speculative purposes, while enhancing the supply for productive investment. Industry could buy more of the best machines with which to beat its competitors.

Sunday Times, London (22 May 1988)

Reading contends that the growth in the wider UK monetary aggregates during the 1980's reflected the financing of a spectacular property boom that peaked in the latter part of the decade. (We would argue that the property boom reflected the growth in the monetary aggregates.) One might argue that since the price of a home is the largest item of expenditure incurred by most households in the UK, it should be included when calculating the headline inflation statistics. Not so. The conventional argument against the inclusion of house prices is that the cost of financing a home, in other words the interest charge on a mortgage, more accurately reflects the cost of housing for a private household. If this is the case, then we have a perfect example of the manner in which higher interest rates increase inflation.

Anticipating the impact of higher interest rates upon the cost of living for those households with a mortgage, UK Chancellor of the Exchequer Nigel Lawson argued in 1988 that even mortgage interest payments should be excluded from the inflation figures. This statistical change would have produced inflation figures that totally ignored both the cost of purchase, and the cost of financing the purchase, of private residential property. The pressure to massage downwards the inflation figures on the part of this Chancellor was undeniable since he himself regarded inflation as the 'judge and jury' of his economic policy. Lawson's proposals were adopted in the United Kingdom in the form of an additional set of monthly inflation statistics, and the old set of measures were retained. Nevertheless, the various headline inflation statistics presented to the UK consumer still ignore changes in residential property prices, and indeed other asset prices.

The collateralised approach to bank lending found rich pickings in the UK property boom during the 1980's. Homeowners in particular were encouraged to 'unlock the equity' in their homes by taking out personal loans secured on their property. One could not ask for a clearer example of the vicious circle with which creation of money stimulates asset prices and thereby encourages further creation of money. The essential problem for the government of the time was that the new money thereby 'unlocked' was often used by borrowers to finance consumption of consumer goods. Of course the prices of consumer goods *are* accounted for in headline inflation and cannot be excused away as easily as mortgage interest costs. As a result of the new consumer demand, not only consumer prices but imports too began to rise substantially.

By the Summer of 1988, a dose of the interest rate medicine was viewed by the authorities as unavoidable. Pleading against this course of action, George Hodgson, Chief Economist at Citicorp Scrimgeour Vickers, wrote:

Indeed one of the long term solutions to the trade account problem must be to improve the supply side of the economy. Such an improvement could well be on the way with signs of a major surge in companies' capital expenditure. If there is one sure way of jeopardising this, it is to raise interest rates aggressively this Summer.

The Times, London (11 July 1988)

Hodgson's view went unheeded amidst the clamour to restrain money supply growth by raising interest rates. By the end of 1988 base lending rates were 4.5% higher than a year earlier. The monetarists argued that more 'expensive' money would restrain money supply growth, and hence inflation, but M_4 expanded by almost 19% in the twelve months to January 1990. The monetarists argued that higher interest rates would strengthen Sterling, making import prices lower and hence restraining inflation still further, but the currency dropped in value on the foreign exchanges by almost 10% on a trade weighted basis in the eighteen months to April 1990. Meanwhile, headline inflation increased from 4.6% in June 1988 to 10.9% in September 1990.

Monetarists argue that their policy prescriptions take time to have any effect. This is undoubtedly so and, undoubtedly too, severe recessions do restrain inflation temporarily. However, I shall argue shortly that the interest rate medicine would be quite unnecessary were the defects in our monetary structure to be rectified. Even where the structure remains as it is, the chain of causation specified by the monetarists in reducing inflation is wide open to debate. For example, the Bank of England's own analysis confirms at least one earlier proposition. Brian Reading writes:

Indeed, the Bank's calculations show that, unless Sterling meanwhile rises, a one point rise in interest rates leaves the retail price index 0.2% higher two years later and unchanged after three years. ... Higher interest rates increase inflation in the long run through the damage they do to the supply side of the economy, without unambiguously reducing inflation in the short term.

Sunday Times, London (27 May 1990)

Reading then argues that higher interest rates increase the attraction of a currency for foreign investors, causing inflows of 'hot money'. If the lender is willing, it is the borrower who must restrain himself:
> It is only when interest rates rise so high that we can't afford to borrow any more that credit growth slows down.

Will Hutton comments:
> ... as the evidence mounted that success in lowering inflation had little to do with monetary targets, the government persisted in believing that the cause of low inflation was monetary stability. In fact, the chain of causation runs from economic strength ... to price stability - but the government, fixated on financial variables and free market economics, believed that the chain ran the opposite way.

The State We're In (1994) p. 74

Barry Riley in the *Financial Times*, 21 August 1993, reasons thus:
> Here is the puzzle, that while the Germans struggle to control monetary growth through high interest rates, low US rates have coincided with exceptional monetary weakness. The answer lies in time lags. The short term consequence of high interest rates is a rise in deposits, until the economy slumps and loan demand collapses. The short term consequence of low interest rates is a flight of savings from the banks, and thus a monetary contraction, until eventually the economy expands vigorously under the influence of cheap money and the borrowers return in numbers.

So, some basic ideas are being challenged. Overall, one might be forgiven for thinking that confusion abounds. Does increasing the interest rate reduce inflation or increase it? Why does money supply sometimes expand and at other times contract despite similar monetary policies? Is economic strength or economic weakness a cure for inflation?

Only those who understand that modern money is created for the sake of profit can know the correct answer to these questions. The authorities avoid the necessary lobotomy of the existing monetary structure and adopt instead interest rate manipulation as the medicine of first recourse. In 1990 John Major as UK Chancellor of the Exchequer justified a high interest rate policy by saying that 'if it isn't hurting it isn't working'. These are words that one might expect of a quack. If such a blunt instrument works at all, it does so primarily through the mechanism of recession and bankruptcy.

The 100% Solution

Despite a repetitive cycle of monetary inspired inflation and deflation, the authorities in the interest-based economies have yet to tackle the problem of fractional reserve banking. In fact, as we have seen, they have rather encouraged it. This situation, prevailing as it has for some three centuries in the UK, inevitably lends credence to those theories that suggest government to be a puppet of the bankers. Once in every generation or so, a new group of individuals stand up to challenge the bankers. And so far, every time, the bankers have won.

The amateur pamphleteer who discovers the trick of debt enslavement and stands up to criticise the slave masters, he can safely be ignored. Even an academic of standing can be treated this way since the public does not generally spend its time reading the ideas of professors in monetary economics. It seems that this is what happened to the proposals of Irving Fisher in *100% Money* (1935), wherein he advocates the implementation of a 100% reserve ratio system.

In an introduction to his book, Fisher describes how the total money supply of the USA in 1929 was $27 billion, of which $23 billion comprised bank money. By 1933, total money supply had contracted to $20 billion, of which $15 billion was bank money. The commercial banks had destroyed $8 billion of their money in the process of calling in their loans, whilst the state had issued a further $1 billion of its own currency. Resources were abundant, workers were available to work and society required work to be carried out. But without sufficient money to facilitate business transactions, millions of workers remained idle.

The crucial argument in Fisher's book is that private firms should have their right to manufacture money removed and that the state, under constitutional regulation, should take over this function in its entirety. From this moment on, only the state would have the power to create money. The assumption in all of the above is, of course, that the state is a better guardian of money supply than private enterprise.

Fisher proposed not only to confine the production of money to the state, but also to define the circumstances under which the state might alter money supply. Alterations would only arise if demanded by economic activity. Fisher's measure of changes in economic activity was based on the change in an index of general price levels in the economy over any one period. Depending upon such changes, a currency commission would be empowered to issue or retire necessary amounts of state money. Where economic activity increased, due perhaps to population growth or technological innovation, Fisher believed that existing amounts of money supply would be insufficient to enable the required number of transactions to be completed and that the general price index would therefore tend to fall. The currency commission might then sanction an issue of new money. A contraction of money supply would be indicated under opposite circumstances but, in both cases, the general price level would be used as the yardstick by which the need for money supply alteration was measured.

In the banking structure that emerges from Fisher's discussion, there would be two basic forms of bank account. One account would take the form of a non-interest-bearing current account against which a commercial bank would hold 100% reserves. These funds would be available for immediate withdrawal. This type of account would exist on the premise that if funds are available for immediate withdrawal, they cannot simultaneously be invested in a business, government or personal loan. If current account funds cannot be used for such purposes, they most certainly cannot be earning interest. A bank would naturally charge the depositor a fee for the various services provided in relation to the account. The second type of account would take the form of an investment account. Money deposited in an investment account would be unavailable for withdrawal by the depositor until the end of an agreed term. This term would be the period for which the money was loaned by the bank as an intermediary. Since the money was loaned, a return of some kind would be due to the depositor. Again, the bank might itself take a commission or fee, based on its costs in intermediating the savings and loan transaction, and could compete with other banks on price and service.

Having established these two basic types of account we may now examine what precisely would constitute money in this banking system. Since the investment accounts would not be subject to immediate withdrawal by the depositors, their money would not be available to support their own purchasing activities. As far as the holders of such accounts would be concerned, their money would be loaned to borrowers and it would be those borrowers for whom that money provided purchasing power. Therefore investment accounts could not be included in the measure of money supply. The total of all investment accounts in existence would merely signify the total of loans of *existing* money made in the economy and could not be counted as *new* money. The current accounts on the other hand would provide immediate purchasing power to their holders, and would therefore have to be included as a measure of money supply. Since 100% reserves would be held against the current accounts, there would be no possibility for the banking system to create new amounts of bank money.

Under present arrangements, it is clear that the above distinction between currently available deposits and locked in 'term' deposits is highly blurred. This is one reason for the conventional debate as to what actually constitutes money supply. Under the prevailing monetary system it becomes possible to include a single customer's term deposit of state money, as well as subsequent deposits generated from that first deposit, whether they be current or term, in the wider measures of money supply. In contrast, where state money on its own forms the money supply, multiple counting would be impossible.

... in the end, the only marked difference between the deposits under the new and old system would be that the bank loans (and investments) would tend to correspond with time deposits instead of with checking deposits, as now. This might seem, from a bookkeeper's point of view, a very slight difference. But the difference would be fundamental, because the time deposits, not being subject to check, would not be a part of our medium of exchange actually used for circulating goods.

Fisher, I., *100% Money* (1936) p. 81

Commenting further, he notes that :

Under the 100% system the time deposits would absorb savings and expand loans correspondingly just as now. But the demand deposits would operate differently. That is, any money deposited in a checking account would stay there and not be lent out. The circulating medium would not be expanded by such deposits but would merely be redistributed. Loans would go up with savings but the circulating medium would not go up with either ... banks would make loans just like anybody else, either out of their own savings or out of somebody else's, precisely as the earliest lending banks did before they were perverted by somebody's "bright idea" to lend other people's money while still letting these other people think they had that money to use as money.

Fisher, I., *100% Money* (1936) p. 81

Fisher is of the opinion that where constitutional guarantees exist, the state will manage changes in money supply with greater responsibility than profit motivated private firms. Traditional instruments of monetary policy would become unnecessary and defunct. Where today the state hardly knows what money supply is, let alone how to control it, the Fisher approach clearly identifies money, and places it under the control of the state. In order to eliminate the practice of fractional reserve banking, he proposes that the state would first enact legislation requiring the clear separation of currently available deposits from term investment accounts as detailed above. 100% reserves would then be applied, again by legislation, to current accounts. Given that bank money supply will exceed state money supply before the change-over, sufficient amounts of state money would be created well in advance of the restructuring so as to enable the commercial banks to achieve the required cash ratios.

As to the manner in which the newly manufactured state money would actually find its way to the commercial banks, Fisher suggests a neat solution. The state would simply buy back outstanding government debt using the newly created money (in other words the debt would be monetised). In the same way that the national debt was first created through the manufacture of bank money, it would now be repaid through the manufacture of state money. The national debt would disappear at almost no cost. The newly created state money would be paid into either the current accounts or the locked-in investment accounts of those who had sold their government bonds, and the newly established 100% reserve system would begin to operate.

Bank assets :	cash	10
	private debt	70
	government debt	20
Bank liabilities :	current deposits	30
	term deposits	70

BEFORE THE FISHER RESTRUCTURING

Bank assets :	cash	30
	private debt	70
Bank liabilities :	current deposits	30
	term deposits	70

AFTER THE FISHER RESTRUCTURING

The 100% reserve system advocated by Fisher contrasts with the current fashion for reserve ratios in modern banking systems that are far closer to 0% than 100%. Be it ignored or criticised, Fisher's solution is a sound one. No bank depositor would lose any part of any deposit that he held before the restructuring process began. Holders of government debt would receive the fair market price for their holdings. Most importantly, there would be no inflationary implications to this endeavour, since the newly created state money would simply replace amounts of bank money that already existed before the restructuring. There would be no expansion in money supply as a result, only a change in its composition.

In Fisher's monetisation we find a solution that unwinds the errors of the past, with beneficial consequences for the future performance of the economy. Jefferson, Franklin, Cobbett, Knight, Soddy, Tobin, Simons and Hayek are among the many notable Western writers who have all argued in this same direction.

Chapter three

THE CURRENCY GAME

> *A review of the modern foreign currency market is given, focusing upon the means whereby central banks seek to control it. The impact upon economic activity of these various attempts at control is described, with reference to the international gold standard era and the Bretton Woods agreement. Precious metals are proposed as being a better foundation than state and bank money for a monetary system. Conventional bankers and economists often blame the gold standard for economic failures of the past. In fact, these failures resulted from the practice of fractional reserve banking.*

A True Gold Standard

The arguments thus far have suggested that the sole authority to manufacture money should be that of the state. From hereon we must ask whether there is any way of ensuring that the state does not abuse this authority. A monetary system in which the state has full control of money supply may not be sufficient to guarantee monetary stability. We must identify a way in which the state can be prevented from manipulating money supply for its own political or economic gain.

In the aftermath of Sterling's exit from the European Exchange Rate Mechanism in September 1992 it was often said that these problems occur because of poor government, not because of greedy speculators. It was argued that if only the government would engage the correct economic policy, none of this would happen at all. The simplest antidote, as former prime minister Heath pointed out at the time, would seem to involve not having such a thing as foreign exchange at all. Whilst this particular proposal might meet resistance from some in the foreign exchange market, a single currency would at least fulfil the supposed objective of increasing efficiency. With a single currency there would be no exchange rate to gyrate in the first instance, no transaction costs to pay and a release of valuable human resources into the wider economy. But what form should this new single currency take?

Any textbook worthy of the name will inform its reader that a reliable form of money must bear certain distinguishing features. Money should be durable; potatoes would be bad in the role of money because they rot. Money should be portable; bricks would be unsuitable because they are heavy and do not fit in your wallet. Money should be homogeneous; cows would not act as good money because some cows are of better quality than others and because to pay a price of half a cow would entail killing ones cow. Finally, money should be scarce if it is to be used as a countervalue in everyday transactions; if ten Dollar notes grew on trees they could not be used as money. As a store of value, it is interesting to note that gold out-competes every national currency over the long term.

	1900	1990	Average annual change
Purchasing Power Index ~ Gold[a]	130	150	+0.16%
Purchasing Power Index ~ Sterling[b]	100	2.4	-4.06%

Sources: [a] *Gold As A Store of Value*, World Gold Council, Research Study No. 22, November 1998;
[b] *Economist* 1995

PURCHASING POWER OF GOLD AND TOKEN MONEY IN THE UK

Some writers argue in favour of a *full* (or *pure*) gold standard under which the amount of state paper money in issue would be fully backed by stocks of gold held in government vaults. Each unit of issued paper money would then be convertible on demand into gold at a specified rate and, conversely, gold bullion would be convertible into paper money at this same rate. A government currency office of some description would therefore be established in order to exchange gold for paper money and vice versa. Constitutional guarantees would ensure that the state could not cheat on its obligation to keep a full stock of gold against its paper money issuance. Money supply could then expand only when the state received new amounts of gold from external counterparties and issued paper notes in return. Money supply could contract where counterparties exercised their right to demand redemption of their paper money in gold.

Critics ask why society should direct its resources towards digging for gold and silver when it could instead be building homes and hospitals, for example. Why not just have the state manufacture paper or electronic data as money, and forget about keeping gold or silver stocks? On this point, we should note that society is already devoting immense resources to the maintenance of the interest-based monetary system. The developed economies are typically spending up to 10% of their GDP on the banking sector and, according to Huber & Robertson (see: *Creating New Money,* New Economics Foundation, London, 2000), some £21 billion is paid annually to the commercial banking system in the UK alone for its 'service' of creating money. This cost dwarfs anything that would be spent on mining and minting gold and silver coins in the long run. And of course the mining of gold and silver only needs to be paid for once, whereas interest on bank money has to be paid annually in order to keep it in existence.

Other critics point out that under a pure gold standard the amount of paper money supply would be determined only by the amount of gold that was available to the government in first establishing the standard, plus any amounts that private entities were subsequently prepared to exchange at the currency office. Would not the state then be giving up its control of money supply in favour of a metal whose availability could alter in an unpredictable way? What, for example, of a situation in which large new discoveries of gold were presented to the state for conversion into state money? What guarantees would there be that the supply of gold would in any way correspond with those amounts necessary to maintain price and, or, economic stability?

The hollowness of the above argument is revealed in the following two tables of comparison data which show that the growth of gold supply has been both lower and more stable than the growth of M_2 money supply over the long run.

In the first table, US dollar data is shown, but most other currencies have shown higher growth rates than the dollar, thus reinforcing the argument. The greater risk, clearly, is that too much paper and electronic money will be produced, not too much gold.

	1915	1950	1997	Average annual change
Total World Gold Stock (estimated) [a]	24,000	50,000	134,800	2.12%
US Money Supply M2 USD billions [b]	17.59	150.81	5392.9[c]	7.23%

Sources:
[a] *H. C. Wainwright & Co. Economics Inc., USA;*
[b] *Report of US Commerce Department 1970;*
[c] *IMF Financial Statistics Yearbook 1997*

**GROWTH OF THE GLOBAL GOLD STOCK
VERSUS GROWTH OF M2 IN THE USA**

Secondly, the volatility of returns to gold investors (buy and hold strategies over all possible yearly periods) was lower during the period of the gold standard than since its abandonment. This implies that the value of paper and electronic money remained more stable under the gold standard. In other words, despite the practice of fractional reserve banking, gold acted as a moderating influence on the money creating activities of the state and the banking system during this time. The following table illustrates.

	Gold standard (years as shown)	Post Gold standard (1968-1996)
Britain	1.1% (1596-1968)	10.8%
France	2.3% (1820-1968)	10.5%
USA	2.0% (1796-1968)	10.5%

Source: *Gold As A Store of Value, World Gold Council, Research Study No. 22, November 1998*

**VOLATILITY OF GOLD PRICE RETURNS
(ALL POSSIBLE BUY-HOLD-SELL STRATEGIES)**

Gold is not usually found in massive quantities in an easily obtainable form. Exceptions to this general rule do occur, if one happens to be a ruthless Conquistador in South America for example. Nevertheless, on a global scale and in the long run, the rule holds that gold requires effort to extract. This is the key. Precious metals have a cost attached to their production. Paper money and bank money have practically no cost attached to their production.

Clearly, it would not be worthwhile mining gold if the costs of production exceeded the value of the gold produced. Where gold *is* money, then in times of falling prices gold mining companies will find that the cost of labour and equipment is less than the value of gold that can be produced by employing that labour and equipment. The mining companies will therefore produce more gold. This would be the simple market mechanism whereby money supply would expand under the model proposed here, and is the model proposed in the Classical theory of money that was widely accepted in seventeenth century England. It is a mechanism that has nothing to do with interest on receipts, bank credit creation or the printing press, one that tends towards economic justice and it is backed by the force of the free market.

Some or all of the amounts of newly produced gold will eventually be offered for conversion to paper currency at the government office of the country whose prices are the most competitive. Thus the producer of gold will access the maximum purchasing power for the gold that he produces. The tendency will be that the country with the lowest prices, most desirable produce, or most exciting investment opportunities, will attract the most gold for conversion into paper money at its government's currency office. The resulting expansion of money supply will tend to counter any international imbalances in purchasing power and thereby act as a form of automatic stabiliser with regard to employment and trade flows.

Where new supplies of gold are not forthcoming, economic activity *might* continue to expand, this time accompanied by a general trend toward lower prices. Robert Barro is one of those who argues this point (see Chapter Seven). Other economists smirk at the possibility of falling prices and economic growth appearing together, proposing a 'lack of downward flexibility in wages' as the obstacle. However, there is some strong empirical evidence of just such an event in English economic history during the period 1821 to 1914. In this, the gold standard era, growth and falling prices were indeed juxtaposed. The Bank of England's index of retail prices falls from approximately 300 to approximately 200 in this time frame (1694 = 100).

Opponents of a gold standard often propose that it may lead to a prolonged recession in one country or groups of countries. Suppose, for example, that Country A experiences a trade deficit and therefore that increasing numbers of foreign companies become holders of Currency A. Of course, these foreign holders of Currency A might later decide to undertake investment into, or purchase goods and services from, Country A. Currency A would thus be returned into circulation in Country A and no monetary contraction would occur there. Otherwise, foreign holders may decide either to maintain their reserves of Currency A outside Country A or to present them to Country A for redemption in gold, in which case a monetary contraction would ensue.

It is upon the premise that monetary contraction causes a fall in output that critics of a gold standard often base their views. A fall in the output of an economy implies unemployment and recession, they argue. But other economists propose that if prices in Country A fall then foreign customers and producers of gold will find the prices of goods and services in Country A relatively more attractive. With the subsequent increase in demand for its produce, arrives the stimulus for a recovery of output in Country A.

Whichever of the two above views is nearest to the truth, it is clear that a country must produce goods and services of sufficiently high quality in order to attract foreign customers and hence to encourage inflows of gold. Low prices on their own are of little attraction if the product is of poor quality. Foreign currency or gold will only be offered in exchange for Currency A if Country A offers something worth buying or investing into. In the event of a long recession, what guarantee is there that Country A will be able to offer such opportunities to foreign purchasers and investors?

A frank response is warranted here. If one nation cannot win the competitive struggle with others, how then can it expect to enjoy continuing prosperity? Tampering with the monetary system will not fend off the results of economic failure. It may even make them worse by temporarily avoiding the collective hardships that spur a harder national effort. In any event, monetary acrobatics will not necessarily result in the production of goods that foreigners wish to buy. In many ways, a country is like a firm. Its living standard will depend partly upon the quality of its produce. A gold standard would simply make the fact clear. Ultimately, the only stabiliser upon which Country A can hope to depend is the hard work and productivity of its inhabitants.

Where the state guarantees to exchange gold for paper money at a defined rate, and vice versa, the mere existence of a guarantee might dissuade individuals from seeking that redemption in the first place. If the state's promise to redeem is never tested on any meaningful scale, what is there to stop the state cheating on that promise without telling anyone? And what guarantee would exist that, at a future date, the state would not simply change the rules and abandon the gold standard altogether?

Ultimately there is probably only one guarantee that a full gold standard could not be revoked to the detriment of the public. It is the guarantee that exists where gold itself forms the state money supply. State money would no longer be issued as paper or accounting entries in evidence of gold stored in a government vault. It would, at least for large denominations, be the physical gold itself. Revocation of this kind of gold standard could not rob the holders of money of the intrinsic value residing in their wallets.

If such a system were enacted globally, there would be a sea change in international currency markets. One ounce of gold coin in the USA would be no different to one ounce of gold coin in Japan, Germany or France. Maybe the ounce of gold would be given a different name in each of those countries, be it 20,000 Yen, 200 Deutschmarks or 1,000 Francs, but there would be little point in trading foreign currency (and therefore paying transaction costs) because of this difference. Foreign exchange speculation would become defunct. International investment and trade would be relieved of much uncertainty.

Judy Shelton writes :

When the value of money can be altered through government policies against which money holders have no recourse, the economic decisions of private individuals are hostage to the ambitions of politicians. Flexibility in the control of money provides the means for government officials to adjust the purchasing power in the hands of the citizens to accommodate budgetary excesses and federal borrowing.
Shelton, J., *Money Meltdown* (1994) p. 347

Shelton quotes Phillip Cagan in *The Search for Stable Money* (1987):
I see no escape from the conclusion, inherent in the position of the advocates of gold, that only a convertible monetary system is sufficiently free of discretion to guarantee that it will achieve price stability. The operation of any inconvertible monetary system introduces a discretion in management that cannot guarantee price stability despite the efficacy of its monetary controls.
Shelton, J., *Money Meltdown* (1994) p. 301

... and Ludwig von Mises from *Economic Policy: Thoughts for Today and Tomorrow* (1979):
Under an inflationary system, nothing is simpler for the politicians to do than to order the government printing office to provide as much money as they need for their projects. Under a gold standard, sound government has a much better chance; its leaders can say to the people and the politicians: "We can't do it unless we increase taxes."
Shelton, J., *Money Meltdown* (1994) p. 343

With gold, no government would be able to devalue for competitive advantage against its trading partners. No businessman would be at risk from exchange rate volatility. No foreign investment gain would translate into a home currency loss. Every individual, company and state entity would know the meaning of value both at home and abroad, and would be able to budget, invest or borrow accordingly. Interest rate brutalisation of a home economy for the sake of currency strength would become a quirk of history, as would all phoney schemes to manipulate currency values. And government would no longer be empowered to rob the citizen by spending money of its own creation. The idea sounds so persuasive that one wonders what historical events must have occurred to so besmirch the reputation of gold as currency.

History of the UK Gold Standard

At the beginning of the Middle Ages, the silver penny was the one denomination of coin in general circulation throughout most of Europe. 12 pennies made one shilling and 20 shillings made one pound, hence there were 240 pennies in one pound. At the time of William the Conqueror in 1066, a pound was just that - one pound in weight of silver

- so one pound of silver was minted into 240 pennies. But through successive debasements, by 1666, the silver penny had lost almost two-thirds of its silver content. Thus, a pound of silver was now being minted into over 700 pennies.

However, the name 'pound' was retained as the unit of currency and so what once was a quantity of metal used in exchange by traders in their daily business, became increasingly a conceptual unit of value. The use of a more or less valueless piece of paper called 'one pound' developed upon this foundation in several stages. Where once a buyer and seller might have exchanged a horse for a pound of silver, they in due course exchanged a horse for an amount of precious metal that bore the name "one pound". Soon they would exchange a horse for a piece of paper that promised to pay this thing called "one pound". Hence money had become a debt, whereas before it had been an asset. Finally came the transition to full token money. The Bank of England eventually abandoned its promise to pay out precious metal coins in return for paper, and the paper pound itself would then be seen by the public as the true representation of value. Thus, modern paper money comprises token value only, and is denominated purely in conceptual units of value.

The above paragraph summarises in very general terms one thousand years of British monetary history. It is a history that is paralleled in other developed countries to one extent or other. Now we should look a little more closely at the role of gold and silver, and how these metals were gradually excluded from our monetary life by the twin forces of interest and bank money creation.

Bimetallism is the name given to a monetary standard in which usually both gold and silver act as the currency of state in a legally defined ratio. Silver coinage of a given weight will be decreed to have the same value as gold coinage of a different weight. Such a standard is said to operate so as to enable sufficient amounts of coinage to circulate in convenient form throughout an economy. Small value (i.e. *low denomination*) coins made of gold might be impractical due to their small size and the effect of erosion, whilst silver coins of the same denomination would be far larger and therefore superior in fulfilling their function as legal tender. The system also alleviates any problems that may initially arise from an insufficient supply of gold reserves at the mint.

A problem arises however when economic agents regard the implied bimetallic ratio between silver and gold coins to be above or below the ratio of the fair market prices for those metals in bullion form. For instance, if the state decrees that a one ounce gold coin has the same value as fifteen one ounce silver coins, there then exists a bimetallic gold and silver standard at a ratio of one to fifteen. Gold coins would be fifteen times more valuable than silver, weight for weight. If now, due say to large discoveries of silver, the market value of silver bullion declines so that an ounce of gold bullion is now worth sixteen ounces of silver bullion, entrepreneurs will engage in the following procedure. Fifteen silver coins will be exchanged for one gold coin, and that gold coin will then be melted into gold bullion. The one unit of gold bullion will then be exchanged for sixteen units of silver bullion. Sixteen units of silver bullion can then be presented at the mint for conversion into sixteen silver coins, where the entrepreneur previously held only fifteen. The process will be repeated until gold coinage disappears from circulation to be melted in its entirety into bullion form. Where bimetallic ratios vary sufficiently from one state to another, such 'arbitrage' opportunities will inevitably result in the export of precious metal from one country to another, as dictated by the arbitrage equation.

In 1257, Henry III attempted to introduce a gold coin into circulation in England but failed because the bimetallic ratio with silver was set at approximately 10, a ratio that was too low in comparison to the existing bullion market relationship. In the 1279 recoinage of Edward I, round halfpennies and fourthings (later to become known as farthings) were introduced. These small denominations of currency had previously been produced by cutting whole round pennies into halves or quarters.

In Italy meanwhile, gold coinage was coming into fashion. Genoa issued a gold coin in 1252 to be followed by Florence and Lucca. Venice relied on Byzantine coins for a time, but subsequently issued gold ducats that were to become widely accepted throughout the eastern Mediterranean. Here is an example of a common currency that does not necessitate political union. The rise in the demand for gold that resulted from the increasing issue of gold coins subsequently raised gold bullion prices throughout Italy. The bimetallic ratio between gold and silver in Venice rose from approximately 1 : 10 to above 1 : 14 in the late thirteenth century, contributing to the failure of Henry III's gold coinage in

England. Meanwhile, the existence of widely recognised and reliable monetary units, and an accumulation of gold stocks, helped to establish the pre-eminence of the Italian banking community.

Attempts at employing a precious metal standard as a basis for monetary stability have often failed due to quite primitive fraud on the part of the state in debasing its coinage. The process of debasement was evidenced by a reduction of the precious metal content of the existing unit of currency, either by means of a reduction in the purity of the coin or by a reduction in the weight of the coin, or perhaps by a combination of both. To enact the debasement, a recoinage would be ordered by the state in which existing coins would be decreed invalid as legal tender and recalled to the state mint. There they would be melted down and minted into a larger number of new, debased, coins. The new coins would be returned into circulation on a one for one basis, the excess being retained by the state for its own expenditure. Here is a clear early example in which the state effectively confiscates wealth from the citizens in order to raise revenue. (The modern counterpart is the expansion of the state's paper money issue, which devalues the existing money supply through the mechanism of inflation. This modern approach has the advantage that it can be achieved in a far less conspicuous manner. No recoinages required here.)

The 'Great Debasement' of 1542 to 1551 in England saw the weight of the silver penny fall by a third, but more importantly, the silver content of the new lighter coins was itself reduced. At worst, only one-quarter of the new coins' weight comprised silver, the remaining three-quarters being made up in copper. When the surface coating of silver was eroded from a coin, the underlying copper would show through. The first part of the coin to erode in this manner was typically the nose on the impression of King Henry, hence the King's nickname 'Old Copper Nose'. Gold coins were also debased in metal content by a factor of one-third. Bimetallic ratios altered, due to these debasements, from one unit of gold to approximately eleven of silver, down to a ratio of one to five.

So it was that Henry VIII, who had inherited from Henry VII a reputable solid currency, bequeathed through six recoinages each of increasing seignorage, a vastly debased currency to his son Edward VI. Under Protector Somerset, the debasement continued through five further recoinages. The period of Tudor inflation that coincided with these events has been written about extensively elsewhere. Wherever debasement occurred, Gresham's Law would operate. 'Bad' money would drive out 'good' money. Coins that had not been debased would vanish from circulation, often for export and subsequent conversion into bullion, and to the profit of the money changers through whose hands many coins would pass.

Sir Isaac Newton's reformulation of the currency in 1696 left the country formally on a silver standard, but because of the overvaluation of gold under the statutory bimetallic ratio, gold guineas became the more common form of payment in England. The export of silver continued, due to its overvaluation, contributing to a general scarcity of silver.

In order to avoid the by then familiar problems of bimetalism, under the formulation of the gold standard that became fully operational in Britain in 1821, silver coinage was decreed to be legal tender only in amounts of up to £2. A subsidiary silver standard was therefore said to operate, since transactions of substantial size could only be undertaken in gold sovereigns or gold backed paper money. Silver was, in other words, subsidiary to the main monetary standard based on gold. Arbitrage between silver and gold on any scale could not now occur.

The 1797 Suspension of Payments, under which the Bank of England was no longer obliged to redeem its paper note issue with gold, had given the country an inconvertible paper currency until the gold standard officially returned in 1821. The standard was achieved gradually under the terms of Lord Liverpool's 1816 Act, in which one sovereign was defined as one hundred and thirteen grains of fine gold. The sovereign was issued from 1817 and came into circulation gradually. Bank notes remained inconvertible until April 1817 when the Bank of England offered to cash notes of under £5 for gold, as long as they were notes that had been issued before 1816. As there were only £1 million of such notes in circulation, the demand for cashing was low. In October 1817 the Bank offered the encashment of all pre-1817 notes. In 1821, all notes were made redeemable into gold and a full gold standard came into being. The circulation thereafter comprised convertible paper money, gold sovereigns and subsidiary silver coinage.

The British approach formed a model that was copied elsewhere, in the colonies and by competing powers. Portugal adopted a gold standard in 1854, Canada in 1867, Germany in 1873, the USA in 1879, Austria-Hungary in 1892 and Russia and Japan in 1897. However, until the adoption of the new gold standards, a variety of standards existed internationally. For instance, Germany had been operating a silver standard, the United States a bimetallic gold and silver standard, and Russia an inconvertible paper currency system.

If a gold standard is to operate without a circulating currency exclusively comprising gold, then it is essential that the amount of paper currency in circulation must be fully backed by stocks of gold. But if excess issuance of state money is prohibited by the law of the gold standard, it seems reasonable that commercial banks should incur a similar prohibition where their own form of money supply is concerned. To enact a gold standard without prohibiting fractional reserve banking would therefore seem pointless, but this is in fact the very history that Chown describes when he writes:

Issues of country bank notes rose from an average £4 million in 1821-3 to £6 million in 1824 and £8 million in 1825, a major factor fuelling the boom. This enlarged circulation was in principle payable in gold ... the public had become accustomed to accept Bank of England notes in redemption of country bank notes ... country banks actively discouraged the redemption of their notes for gold but a successful petition against a Bristol bank in June 1825 brought home to the public their right to demand redemption in gold.

J. F. Chown: *A History of Money* (1994) p. 152

The Bank Charter Act of 1844 began the process of withdrawing the right of private firms to issue their own paper money. Peel's Act aimed to remedy the activity of those "self created money-lenders" so criticised by Jefferson. However, we have also seen how it was that the banking community moved to exploit the loophole left by Peel's Act after 1844, namely the possibility of using the account and cheque system in place of the gold and receipts system that had previously dominated. Chown summarises the mechanism whereby fractional reserve banking long ago compromised the gold standard:

The United Kingdom gold standard did not ensure short run stability nor did it prevent trade cycles and financial crises. These arose from fluctuations in size of the credit superstructure built on the gold base...

J. F. Chown: *A History of Money* (1994) p. 72

It was the financing of the 1914-18 war that first exposed the Achilles' heel of the British gold standard. The exchange rate between Dollars and Sterling (hereafter denoted as \$/£) had been fixed at \$/£ 4.86 (4.86 Dollars to one Pound Sterling) prior to the war. This exchange rate was determined by the gold standards of the two countries. Since one Pound was defined as 113 fine grains of gold and one Dollar as 23.22 grains, one pound had to be exchangeable into 4.86 Dollars (approximately 113 ÷ 23.22). Any other exchange rate would have allowed arbitrage to occur.

For several decades before the war, government expenditure in Britain had fluctuated between 10% and 20% of GDP. But during the war government expenditure rose to approximately 70% of GDP. The pressure to finance this spending through an expansion of government debt (and hence the creation of new amounts of Bank of England paper money) proved irresistible to the authorities. Hence, whilst there was only £34 million of paper money in 1914, by 1918 paper money supply totalled £299 million. At the same time, gold sovereigns progressively disappeared from circulation over the period 1914 to 1918. Gold sovereigns in circulation totalled £166 million at the outbreak of war, but by the end of the war the amount was less than £84 million.

But the Bank of England did not have things all its own way. The government decided during the war to create its own form of money, interest-free, issuing what came to be known as Bradbury's (named after their signatory at the Treasury department). The issuance of these notes was no doubt of much annoyance to the Bank's directors who had proposed to create more of their own paper money for lending to the government at interest, a proposal that was rejected for the obvious commercial reason.

The decision of the Bank of England in 1919 to abandon convertibility into gold sovereigns for all but the £5 note highlighted the facts of the monetary situation. Issuance of paper money had indeed substantially exceeded those amounts that could be backed by gold reserves. The Bank of England was of course aware that few £5 notes were now left in circulation and that the possibility of a drain on its remaining gold reserves would therefore be reduced by this measure.

In the aftermath of the 1919 decision, the exchange rate moved to $/£ 3.50 and Britain no longer intervened in support of Sterling on the New York currency market. Nevertheless domestic pressure in favour of a strong pound soon resulted in Bank of England action to increase interest rates. The pressure arose largely in the City of London whose status as an international financial centre was seen to depend on Sterling's strength. Foreign investors, attracted by the higher interest rates, were thereby deterred from converting Sterling into foreign currency on the foreign exchange markets. Instead, their funds were now to be deposited in Sterling accounts so as to access the higher rates on offer.

The above is an example of the type of policy that sacrifices domestic business activity to international currency concerns. Currency motivated interest rate increases often ignore the reality of the domestic economic climate. Whilst investors may benefit from an increase in the flow of interest payments on their Sterling loans, it is every borrower who must bear the burden. For business entities, profitability may simply be insufficient to meet higher interest charges. An attractive Sterling interest rate may tempt an individual to maintain a Sterling deposit and thus alleviate pressure on the Sterling exchange rate. However, payment of this interest simply presents that depositor with a still larger amount of Sterling at a later date. The holder of Sterling is then confronted with the same ultimate choices - to convert to foreign currency, to convert to gold (if possible), to purchase British goods, or to once more acquire Sterling investments.

As it was, British manufacturers were finding it increasingly difficult to sell their produce abroad. The war had destroyed many business relationships and allowed foreign competition to gain a foothold in some of Britain's most lucrative markets. Furthermore, the lack of investment in non-war related products during the war years had left British manufacturers with product lines that were often old-fashioned or simply irrelevant to the new markets of the twenties. Exports of manufactured goods fell from £1,664 million in 1920 to £943 million in 1925 and £670 million in 1930. The current account balance of trade fell from a surplus of 5.8% of GDP in 1920 to a surplus of only 0.8% by 1930. What hope here then, to provide foreigners with sufficient goods in exchange for their Sterling?

An increase in the interest rate is often no more than a delaying tactic, a Mr. Micawber response, an attempt to stave off the moment when the currency rate falls or the gold is withdrawn. It may work temporarily, even over a period of years, but if the domestic economy cannot produce sufficient output in the meantime, the moment of truth must eventually come.

Now, the British had abandoned the gold standard in 1919 and the economic instability of the time was amply evidenced in wholesale prices. These rose by approximately 50% between 1919 and 1920 and subsequently collapsed by over 40% between 1920 and 1921. Churchill was persuaded to restore a semblance of the old order in 1925. His budget speech proclaimed the return to gold, at the pre-war standard, implying an exchange rate of \$/£ 4.86. However, the return to gold was not quite what it seemed. Convertibility was allowed for international purposes only, being disallowed domestically except where the public could muster sufficient notes (approximately £1,700) to exchange for 400 ounce bars at the Bank of England. Existing reserves were quite insufficient for the purpose of restoring a full gold standard, and Churchill's refusal to allow domestic convertibility into gold was an admission of such.

Despite Churchill's efforts, confidence in Sterling began to wane in the light of economic reality. The moment of truth was near. Between 1929 and 1931, the wane became a collapse. Foreign events did not help the situation. The Creditanstalt bank of Austria collapsed in May 1931 and there followed a rush for liquidity among international investors. London, having established itself as a centre for 'hot' money, was the first target for withdrawals by foreign depositors, but the London banks themselves were in a liquidity crisis. Over the previous years they had lent heavily, especially to borrowers in Germany and Central Europe, but now found that their loans could not be repaid at the speed demanded by foreigners requesting withdrawal of their deposits. Here is a clear example of the problem that can arise where deposited funds are available for short notice withdrawal, yet are simultaneously loaned 'long'. It was the Bank of England that now rushed to the rescue of the bankers, making its own gold and foreign currency reserves available for them to borrow. The requests of foreign depositors to withdraw their funds were thus honoured and the City of London's integrity remained intact.

The national government formed that year under MacDonald had attempted to restore confidence in British economic policy by balancing the budget, but the move was of temporary benefit only. In July 1931, the German currency collapsed on the foreign exchanges and the speculators turned their attention to Sterling. A flood of Sterling deposits now began to arrive at the Bank of England for encashment in gold. The interest rate increase required to persuade foreigners to maintain their holdings in the form of Sterling would have destroyed the fragile domestic economy and was thus deemed to be an unacceptable policy alternative. On 19 September, the Bank of England ran out of gold and foreign currency reserves as the flight from Sterling continued. On 21 September, the gold standard was suspended. Sterling was now free to find a new exchange rate. It dropped quickly from $/£ 4.86 to £/$ 3.80.

Bretton Woods and After

Since bank money supply is synonymous with money created through loans at interest, there must always exist an amount of debt that equals the amount of bank money supply. There is therefore a tendency for both debt and bank money supply to grow in relation to existing rates of interest. But what happens if society does not wish to see a continual expansion in its debt? What if default becomes widespread?

We have seen that if private debt contracts, bank money supply also tends to contract. Under these circumstances, governments almost always decide to counter the monetary contraction by expanding their own borrowings. This chain of causation is rarely recognised by the commentators. The conventional argument is that government borrowing rises in times of recession because the demands upon the government's purse exceed the receipts that are due to it. Obvious, and true. Social security payments rise as unemployment rises, tax receipts from individuals fall as fewer individuals go to work. But the more relevant truth is that a frequent cause, under a fractional reserve banking system, is the failure of loans made at interest (bank assets) to rise in line with the demands of the interest rate offered upon bank deposits (bank liabilities).

History has shown that a government can sacrifice the gold standard for the sake of its spending programmes. Afraid to inflict upon the population the kind of tax levels that are necessary to fund, for example, a war, the state effects an expansion of money supply through any one of the techniques described earlier. Whatever the chosen method of money supply expansion, citizens still pay tax but this time through the mechanism of inflation. New amounts of state money in circulation will then preclude a return to a gold standard at the previous rate unless the authorities are first prepared to contract the money supply by an amount equalling the previous expansion. In the absence of such a contraction, the panorama of all too predictable economic woes comes into view. Soon, concerned investors begin to exchange domestic for foreign currency. The government now feels obliged to raise the interest rate to defend the currency, with temporary effect, but to the cost of the domestic economy.

The Bretton Woods agreement of 1944 aimed to re-establish stability in the international monetary order without addressing the fundamental problem of fractional reserve banking. The objective was to achieve stability in exchange rates between the major currencies of the world. In pursuit of this goal, the United States was to adhere to the pre-war gold price of $35 per ounce that had been established under the Gold Reserve Act of 1934. Note here the devaluation of the Dollar from the previously existing $20.67 per ounce. With the implementation of agreed fixed exchange rates between participating currencies and the Dollar, gold was to act, indirectly, to anchor the international money supply. In theory, as long as the United States maintained a full reserve of gold to Dollars issued, and as long as participating nations intervened to maintain the required exchange rates with the Dollar, the system would operate as intended. Yet, no State operating a fractional reserve banking system could maintain a full reserve of gold to Dollars issued.

As part of the Bretton Woods agreement, both the International Bank for Reconstruction and Development (the World Bank) and the International Monetary Fund (IMF) were established. The main purpose of the World Bank was, apparently, to provide funds for developing nations at subsidised rates of interest. Meanwhile the IMF was to maintain a reserve of gold and foreign currencies comprising the contributions of IMF member states. The reserves might then be loaned, on request of the borrowing country and at the IMF's discretion, and used to maintain the required exchange rates between participating countries.

Due largely to the input of Keynes at the Bretton Woods conference, the IMF charter envisaged that countries would be free to alter monetary and fiscal policy in the light of domestic economic conditions, whilst at the same time demanding that exchange rate stability be a fundamental object of international monetary co-operation. The two goals were, and still are, mutually incompatible.

Governments cannot be given the freedom to allow an expansion or contraction of money supply and simultaneously expect to maintain the purchasing power of their currency abroad. It was precisely in order to overcome this contradiction that domestic convertibility between paper money and gold was not established under Bretton Woods. A further fundamental flaw in design was thereby incorporated at the very outset and in much the same manner as for Churchill's 1925 'gold standard'. Only central banks could ask for redemption of Dollar reserves at the United States Federal Reserve. Had domestic convertibility been allowed, then the expansion of domestic money supply soon to be described would quickly become unsustainable. But with conversion privileges confined to the central banks themselves, individuals and private entities would be prevented from demanding fair value for their currency holdings.

The door to money supply manipulation was thus left open under the Bretton Woods arrangements and, by way of extra precaution, access to foreign exchange for domestic residents was severely rationed throughout the period. Indeed, in the United Kingdom, restrictions remained from the time of their imposition in 1931 until their removal under the Thatcher government in 1979.

The state deficit financing that was encouraged under President Kennedy and later expanded under President Johnson, and that paid for both the Vietnam war and a variety of new social programmes, would ultimately expose the fundamental weakness of the Bretton Woods arrangements. By the middle of the 1960's, the United States was expanding its money supply vigorously. Still, confidence in the Dollar remained. It was the international currency, indeed the prime reserve currency, but the elements of its downfall were in place.

The first real cracks in the system appeared in March 1968, when a two tier gold market was established with an official gold Dollar price available to central banks and a free market price available to private operators. Such was the reaction to the perceived and all but official devaluation of the Dollar in terms of gold, that the private market price of gold bullion now rose substantially above $35 per ounce.

In an attempt to remove the emphasis that had been placed under the Bretton Woods arrangements on the Dollar as the reserve currency, Special Drawing Rights (SDRs) had been created at the 1967 IMF annual meeting. Originally defined in terms of gold, but by 1974 as a basket of major currencies, they were used from 1970 onwards to settle transactions between central banks. The move was of course sponsored by the inflation of the US money supply that had by now been occurring for some years. SDR's however never challenged the Dollar as a reserve currency, being an invention for use primarily by the central banking community.

The election of Richard Nixon in 1968 set the stage for the final chapter in the Bretton Woods saga. Nixon, in his desire to stimulate the domestic economy, pressured the Federal Reserve into an expansion of US money supply during 1970 that further detracted from the Dollar's appeal to foreign investors. Dollars were increasingly exchanged on the markets for various European currencies that were now offering substantially higher interest rates. Since US imports had been rising in line with the expansion of money supply there, increasing amounts of Dollars were finding their way into foreign hands. Foreign central banks were committed under the Bretton Woods agreement to buy up these excess Dollars on the foreign exchange market in order to maintain the predetermined fixed exchange rates. Often, the foreign central banks would pay for the Dollars that they were forced to purchase by issuing new amounts of their own currencies, one mechanism by which inflation is said to be 'imported'. The Bretton Woods agreement allowed for these Dollars to be exchanged at the Federal Reserve for gold, but the problem was that the gold reserves of the United States were far below the amount of Dollars in the hands of foreign central banks. Aware that they would cause the collapse of the

Bretton Woods arrangements by asking for redemption of their Dollars in gold, the foreign central banks chose instead to hold their Dollars as reserves.

The 'Eurodollar market' that subsequently developed, partly in response to increased commercial holdings of Dollars outside the United States, was beyond the reach of the Federal Reserve's monetary tools. A *eurodollar* was the term used to describe a Dollar held outside the United States, and *eurocurrency* the general term for a currency held outside its home country. Though simple in concept, the implications of a eurocurrency market for monetary policy are complex. The authorities in one country cannot extend their banking or tax regulations to another country. United States reserve requirements for example cannot apply to banks taking Dollar deposits in, say, London. On the other hand, UK reserve requirements could not apply to those Dollars since Dollars are not the currency of the UK. In this regulatory vacuum existed, therefore, the scope for a large expansion of Eurodollar deposits.

From the depositors' point of view, the market offered tax-free returns out of sight of domestic authorities. Corporations soon understood the appeal of the euromarkets, and began to raise funds through long term bonds issued as *eurobonds*. Eurobonds were simply bonds denominated in a currency that differed from that of the country in which the bonds were issued. Investors could claim their interest payments anonymously and tax-free, the attraction being obvious, and as a result would usually accept a lower interest rate on their investment than was available in the domestic currency market. If the watered down gold standard of Bretton Woods was intended to engender stability in monetary conditions internationally, the euromarket was just another kick in its teeth.

In January 1971, foreign central banks held twenty billion in Dollar reserves. Question marks began to arise in public as to the ability of the US to redeem this amount in gold. In May 1971, foreign central bank holdings had risen to $32 billion as Dollars were now dumped in massive quantities onto the foreign exchange markets. US gold reserves meanwhile amounted to only $10 billion. Where private citizens might long before have demanded redemption in gold of their abundant Dollars, central banks instead valued international monetary order above the value of their own Dollar reserves. The purpose of the original design of the Bretton Woods system, in preventing domestic convertibility for currencies, was thereby clear to see. Various institutions had been free to expand Dollar money supply, to their various advantages, whilst private holders of those Dollars had no recourse whatever to fair value in terms of gold. Private holders therefore sought refuge in the only possible way, by exchanging their Dollars for other currencies. In seeking to delay the final hour, the foreign central banks merely magnified their own torment.

On 15 August 1971 Nixon announced that the United States would no longer allow convertibility of Dollars into gold for foreign central banks. He further attempted to camouflage the inflationary results of years of monetary expansion through a series of measures that included wage and price controls.

The Smithsonian Agreement of December 1971 followed in the wake of the Bretton Woods collapse. It allowed for a 2.25% fluctuation band around new central exchange rates between the major currencies, and an official gold price set at $38 per ounce. The United States let it be known that it would not defend this price and the gold link was therefore a useless gesture. The Smithsonian Agreement soon faltered. Though Sterling devalued against the Dollar in June 1972 and the Italian Lira in January 1973, the Swiss Franc and the Deutschmark showed increasing strength. As one currency revalued against the Dollar, investors raced to sell their Dollar holdings at the fixed rates offered on the remaining currencies still within the system. An official gold price of $42 per ounce was set in February 1973, but by March the private market price for gold was already more than double this. The pressure on the Dollar was too great to be accommodated by the Smithsonian Agreement and on 12 March 1973, under the Brussels Agreement, all Dollar links to gold were formally abandoned.

The era of global floating exchange rates was thereby ushered in. Major currencies were no longer to be pegged to a reserve of intrinsic value, nor to one another. The Keynesian and Friedmanite schools had argued that such a system would allow governments to 'tune' their domestic fiscal and monetary policy to their own economic benefit. What these economists were effectively advocating was the sacrifice of currency as a store of value, in favour of currency as a tool of economic policy. Other theorists developed their various ideas to describe where exchange rates would stabilise. However, seemingly logical theories of 'purchasing power parity' seemed not to describe the reality. Instead, speculation and hot money would flow in search of the highest real rates of return available and would increasingly dwarf currency transactions based on trade in goods and services.

US money supply continued to expand through the 1970's. In 1979, the gold price stood at $450 per ounce and US consumer prices were rising at an annual rate of 13%, a post 1940's peak. A major policy change was now implemented by Paul Volker, the new Chairman of the Federal Reserve. On 6 October 1979, Volker announced the Federal Reserve's new focus on control of US money supply as a policy target in controlling inflation. It would now allow interest rates to go wherever markets drove them.

The Plaza Accord in September 1985, the Louvre Accord in February 1987, and a variety of not so public agreements between central bankers since then, have aimed at providing the international currency markets with some form of stability. But we are left today with a monetary order that is in no way conducive to exchange rate stability. If stability is the goal, then a floating exchange rate system unattached to any absolute store of value is not the tool for the job.

In the modern financial world, it is the activity of the speculator that makes the system particularly unstable. Such an agent aims to ride the crest of a wave from one currency to the next, hoping to jump to another wave before the current one devalues, and in the meantime take the interest yield on offer. Currency transactions that are determined in this fashion have little to do with activity in the real economy. Meanwhile, the politicians' efforts are directed at talking their currencies up or down, tinkering with the monetary apparatus, pulling this lever or that, never truly knowing what each lever does. Some businessman watch these antics in helplessness. Others quietly wait for the pre-election boom.

A fully backed gold standard, preferably a gold coinage, would put an end to the arbitrary state creation of money. A 100% reserve ratio for commercial banks and deposit-taking institutions would do the same for the private creation of money. Both policies in combination would eradicate the problems that I have identified here, for as long as they remained in place. One policy without the other would eventually result in failure. Here lies a real danger. When a sound monetary arrangement takes the blame for failures borne of another cause entirely, then a generation may pass before that arrangement is restored it to its rightful place at the heart of economic policy. I believe that the gold standard has taken the blame for fractional reserve banking. In fact the latter was the guilty party.

The European single currency debate of the 1990's passed by without so much as a semblance of regard to the ideas contained herein. If debated at all, there would certainly be objections to these proposals from the banking community itself. Even at the professional level there is often little awareness of the monetary phenomena that arise as a result of our current monetary and banking structure. Simple misconceptions can form the backdrop to discussions on the subject, and sometimes the most basic conclusion is dismissed in a flurry of apologia for the established system.

If money is not allowed to function as it should, if it is used to make both political and monetary profit at the cost of the people, it cannot simultaneously fulfil its intended role as the lubricant of economic life. Where a nation is prepared to pay for today's standard of living today, to borrow today only what can be repaid tomorrow, and to leave the monetary box of tricks alone, the future will be the best it can be. Instruments of monetary policy that have on occasions camouflaged the illness by almost killing the patient must become a thing of the past. It *is* possible to eradicate monetary factors as a cause of economic instability. Where economic problems remain, they will result from real factors, cartels perhaps, maybe trade disputes, even famine or war. We will always face those problems. Why add to them?

Chapter four

WEALTH CREATION AND WEALTH TRANSFER

> *Gambling on a roulette wheel employs resources and people, and so does farming. But whilst farmers produce the food that allows man to live, casinos simply transfer wealth from losers to winners. It is because wealth rots that new wealth must constantly be produced in order to replace portions of the old stock of wealth that have suffered from decay. If mankind were to engage solely in wealth transfer processes, the stock of wealth could not be maintained let alone increased. Wealth creation is therefore fundamental to the survival of mankind. Mechanisms of wealth transfer are examined, in particular the parts played by collateral and leverage. It is proposed that these various mechanisms conspire to promote speculative booms, which in turn can have a dangerous impact upon the allocation of resources.*

Gambling or Investment?

We have seen that a monetary value cannot be put upon all forms of wealth. One cannot, for example, put a price on the air that we breathe. Many statistics that purport to describe the wealth of a nation can therefore be extremely misleading. Gross domestic product (GDP), for example, is a measure published by government agencies that aims to show the value of new wealth produced in the domestic economy over a given period. Statistics on Net Domestic Product (NDP) account for depreciation in the stock of wealth (the 'capital stock') from which GDP is derived. However, changes in wealth that arise due to the deterioration or improvement of such things as beautiful views, social stability or the quality of education are largely excluded.

The point is made by Christopher Ormerod in *The Death of Economics* (1994), p. 28:

> But there is no reason in principle why other factors, such as environmental ones, should not now be thought to be especially important and hence included in the national accounts, despite the fact that many of them, such as pollution, exist but are not bought and sold. Similarly, work done in the household is not given any value in the current conventions used to construct national accounts. So the various daily tasks of cooking, cleaning, washing, ironing and child care are assumed to add no value to the economy.

The concept of 'adding value' referred to here, is of great importance in the following discussion. Using Georgescu-Roegen's approach of relating value to the enjoyment of life, added value can be equated to the net added enjoyment of life that arises at some point in time, present or future, from a given activity. An economic process that resulted in no increment in enjoyment would then be referred to as a 'zero value-added' process, whilst one that actually reduced the amount of enjoyment would be termed 'value-subtractive'.

A growth in wealth cannot always be inferred from the making of an accounting profit, and an accounting profit does not always arise from a growth in wealth. The existence of one does not necessarily signify the existence of the other. As Ormerod highlights, family members do not produce accounts for their domestic duties. They do not calculate a money profit in respect of their duties and the authorities, whose job it is to collate statistics measuring economic activity, do not therefore register such added value in measurements of GDP. It might be possible to remedy any underestimation of added value by imputing a value to household work even though it is rarely charged for. Imputed values could then be incorporated into the relevant national statistics, though of course the problem of subjectivity arises in any such endeavour.

There is however another dimension to the struggle of relating accounting profit to growth in wealth. For an example of this we need look no further than a casino. Here, the winner of a game of chance wins what the loser loses, less the casino's cut. As a result of this cut the gambling process is usually highly profitable for the operator, as it is for the winner, obviously. In order to create wealth in net terms an economic process must however do more than simply transfer existing wealth between participants. Some proponents of gambling argue that it produces pleasure to those who win and is thereby creating a form of wealth. Pleasure is indeed a form of wealth, but one need only consider the fact that losing is highly unpleasurable in order to see that even in this sense the amount of net wealth created in the gambling process is close, if not equal, to zero.

Now the gambling fan may counter with the assertion that the revenues made by the casino are in part used to pay salaries and thereby allow the employees to 'enjoy life'. Surely then, the gambling process cannot be zero value-added or value-subtractive? This latter argument is again dubious because it ignores the fact that the money used to pay the croupiers' salaries is simply transferred from other individuals who might be equally capable of 'enjoying' wealth purchased with that money. Furthermore, it pays no attention to the opportunity cost of gambling, in other words the wealth that could otherwise have been created by the efforts and resources of those involved in the gambling process.

Many individuals argue in favour of gambling on the basis that all human activity involves a kind of gamble. The argument proposed is that to criticise gambling is to criticise any form of activity whose outcome is uncertain. If the investment of money on a roulette wheel is to be mocked, why not then the investment of money in a new business? Here is one possible reply. When crops are planted the farmer risks an early frost or a disease. When a new oil refinery opens, the operator risks malfunctions and destructive accidents. These are all risks, that is for sure, but they are risks which must be taken if we are to have food to eat or petrol to run our cars. For an individual to say that 'planting crops is a risk and gambling at the roulette wheel is a risk, therefore I might just as well direct my efforts towards roulette', is to ignore the fact that farming is essential for the maintenance of life whilst roulette is not.

From this perspective, the operation of a national lottery has often been criticised. The infrastructure that is devoted towards this process of wealth transfer could instead have been directed to other sectors of the economy and created new wealth. Furthermore, if the state genuinely wishes to raise extra revenue for charitable causes and the arts, then the existing taxation system could in fact be used to raise the required revenues at far lower cost. If the Inland Revenue already exists, why bother setting up what is in effect a whole new taxation infrastructure to duplicate it?

Soon after the opening of the UK national lottery, on 17 December 1994, Joe Rogaly wrote in the *Financial Times*:

> The national lottery is fantasy finance. ... It is a tax on the poor derided by the rich, a machine for the creation of a spurious sense of self satisfaction for the pathetic boobies who toss their coins into the maw. There is nothing of worth in this crap game, no net gain for charities, no work of art saved or building erected that could not have been financed by less preposterous means, no true promise of glory for the millennium, no benefit to anyone save perhaps the shareholders of Camelotta Suckers, plc. ... Games of chance, according to the Koran, are abominations of Satan. "They ask you about drinking and gambling," says the holy book. "Say; 'There is great harm in both, although they have some benefit for men; but their harm is far greater than their benefit'." Drinkers may demur, but, as to the lottery, the Islamic view is sheer common sense.

The above ideas are of relevance to any debate on the economic worth of financial market speculation. Some regard speculation simply as a form of gambling whose impact upon resource allocation is similar to that of a casino. However, there is at least one important difference. Financial market speculation can affect a variety of economic variables such as exchange rates, interest rates or commodity prices, whereas the placing of bets in a casino cannot. Through its impact upon the price mechanism, speculation can then have an effect upon resource allocation that is far wider than its own domain.

Many proponents of speculation adhere to the view that there is indeed a value-added process going on here. Three common arguments are as follows. Firstly, because of the volume of speculative transactions in the major markets, let us use the market for foreign exchange as an example, end-users requiring foreign currency will find a liquid market in which to transact. Were no speculative operators to exist, an end-user might come to the market looking to exchange one currency for another but find no counterparty willing to trade at a reasonable price or in a reasonable size. Speculation provides this willing pool of buyers and sellers, and hence a market in good volumes. It is in this sense that speculation is held to create value. Secondly, the difference between the price at which the end-user may buy or sell a foreign currency (the 'bid-offer spread') becomes very narrow due to the competition between speculative participants in the market. The more the speculation, the narrower the spread between the bid and offer prices, and the lower the effective costs of transacting for end-users. Thirdly, as speculators trade out profitable opportunities, the market price tends towards 'efficiency'.

Whilst it is possible that benefits are derived from liquidity and low transaction costs, the chief beneficiary often seems to be the speculator himself. For this agent, the need for speedy execution of trades in large size and at short notice is paramount. Agents in the real economy place less emphasis upon such features. One buys a banana in order to eat it, not to sell it a higher price later. Is it quite so vital to the functioning of the real economy that a foreign exchange deal should take less than one minute to complete? Would a business transaction that has taken several months to plan, be cancelled because the necessary foreign currency can only be obtained at one week's notice?

The supposed improvement in price efficiency that is ascribed to speculation is even more debatable. The level of efficiency in a marketplace is commonly held to hinge upon the degree to which available information is accounted for in current prices. This approach seems to relegate the purpose of a marketplace to one of secondary importance only. Can a market be efficient if it does not allocate resources towards projects that maximise wealth creation? Paul Volker, in an interview with the *New York Times* in the Autumn of 1990, cites the destructive effects upon confidence and business planning that foreign exchange volatility can cause. In pinpointing speculation as the primary cause of such volatility, he asks what possible argument of efficiency could justify an increase of 30% followed by a decrease of 30% in the Dollar/Yen exchange rate over the first few months of 1987. Are we to assume that efficiency has nothing to do with stability in the market price?

If the acquiring of foreign exchange is necessary to fund a foreign business project, then the act of trading one currency for another may indeed enable a value-additive project to take place, but in 1992 central bank statistics compiled by the Bank for International Settlements estimated that speculative trading accounted for over 95% of the $880 billion of global daily turnover. A lot can therefore be seen to ride on the efficiency argument. It must at least overcome the criticisms voiced by Volker on the volatility issue.

In order to maximise turnover, financial intermediaries usually find that volatility of some amount is quite desirable. It is less easy to persuade a client to buy a Dollar for one hundred Yen if in all likelihood the Dollar will still be worth one hundred Yen tomorrow. Yes, it takes two to gamble, but should a financial institution actually encourage the client to place his bets? Gestetner, Gibsons Greetings, Metallgesellschaft and Orange County have all lost at the gambling game to the value of several hundred million Dollars. A skewed incentive system exists within many financial institutions that rewards those who encourage clients to gamble the most. Little wealth creation here, but often a commission for the salesman.

Red faces turned puce at Banker's Trust, an American investment bank in a legal battle with Procter & Gamble, a consumer goods company. Leaked documents and tapes reveal that bank staff talked about a "rip-off factor" attached to complex deals involving derivative sales.

The Economist, 7 October 1995

When international bankers act in this manner, they do not promote the function that a financial system originally purports to fulfil. Wealth transfer is the name of this game, uncertainty and resource misallocation its consequence. In order for its reputation to survive the tarnish of such cases as the Procter & Gamble "rip-off", the financial market must be structured in a manner that meets the genuine needs of its clients on a less predatory basis. Clients that borrow or invest should be viewed by financial institutions as potential candidates for a long term and mutually profitable relationship. As it is, for institutions whose income derives from the charging of commissions on traded volumes, the object of business strategy becomes the maximisation of turnover. Once more, purpose is of secondary importance only and, for some members of this club, the efficiency argument becomes the last refuge of the scoundrel.

In order to continue our discussion of financial market speculation, we must briefly turn our attention to the futures markets. As their name implies, these are markets in which a buyer and seller agree the terms of a transaction to be settled at a future date. For example, a buyer may agree to purchase one hundred ounces of gold from a seller at $400 per ounce, delivery and payment to be made the following December. This is a December gold future contract traded "at $400 in one hundred ounces".

Both counterparties to a futures trade must deposit an amount of money on the trade date, the 'initial margin', that acts as a cushion to guarantee performance of settlement at the future date. This margin is usually a small percentage of the value of the underlying asset traded, and it is held by a central clearing house for safe-keeping. All futures markets work on this principle of 'margined trading'. The central clearing house becomes the counterparty for both the buyer and seller, standing in between them to guarantee against default, and it uses the margins received from buyers and sellers in order to honour this guarantee.

Notice that full payment for the item traded, and the item itself, is not exchanged up-front. In this manner, the futures market allows a seller to sell what he does not own, the process of 'short selling', and the buyer to buy without paying the full price immediately. Both counterparties simply wait until the future delivery date to complete the exchange of countervalues. (Alternatively either party may decide to 'close out' the trade prior to delivery by entering into a new trade, opposite to the one first traded. In this case, a profit or loss is realised, one that is determined by the difference between the two futures prices).

Even in markets where more or less immediate delivery and payment is required, so-called 'cash' or 'spot' markets, similar trading strategies may be undertaken. In order, for example, to sell in the cash market a bond that a trader does not own, he simply borrows that bond from a bond lender for a given period of time. Having borrowed the bond, the trader then immediately sells it. Before the end of the borrowing period, the short seller hopes to make the expected profit by buying back the bond at a lower price in the market. The borrowed bond can then be returned to the lender as originally agreed.

The above methods of trading are in my view a major sponsor of speculative activity. If agents wish to place bets on the future value of an asset, it is much less costly to do so where full countervalue need not be parted with at the outset. Little capital is required to enter a futures trade and the return, on this small amount of capital employed, becomes far greater than the percentage change in the price of the asset itself. Here we have a simple example of 'leverage', a subject to be addressed in more detail shortly.

Where a seller can sell goods that he does not own, and do so in large volumes, the equilibrium of a marketplace can be severely distorted. Of course, the same destabilisation can be encouraged in the opposite direction if buyers do not have to pay the full price of their purchases up-front. Such activity may also generate a trend for others to follow and thereby become self-fulfilling with regard to profitability. Whilst the real sector sees producers and consumers aiming to balance production and consumption in a marketplace, the speculative sector aims to profit by anticipating the price movements that allow this balance to occur. In due course I hope to show that in this way the speculator can distort the very mechanism that determines production and consumption in the real sector. These distortions, whilst profitable for some, can on occasion threaten society at large. Hence, the speculative purchase of foodstuffs in time of famine has been derided throughout history.

In an earlier discussion, I regarded wealth as a stock of varying longevity from which flows of enjoyment arise over time. Now, in order for such stocks to increase net over a period, the value of new wealth produced must exceed the value of that part of the old stock that has depreciated during the period. Since, for example, food stocks diminish as human beings eat and roads deteriorate as cars travel upon them, economic effort is in part a necessary process of running in order to stand still. It is an effort to maintain or replace old stocks of wealth and thereby maintain the flow of enjoyment of life at previous levels. Once again, the entropy process is of relevance. The degree of order in a closed physical system decreases over time unless that system is maintained by an input of energy. Likewise the physical system that is wealth. As any flow of life enjoyment proceeds, the source of that flow deteriorates in its capacity to provide enjoyment.

The crucial point is that if all economic processes within a society were to be value-subtractive or zero value-added, then that society would ultimately find itself in a position of poverty, whether in the material, social or environmental sense. Because of entropy, because all physical structures decay and become less capable of providing the enjoyment of life over time, the creation of new wealth and the maintenance of the old stock of wealth is vital to the long term survival of any society. Profit does not necessarily signify that such a process is occurring. Neither gambling nor drug dealing, for instance, can unambiguously show that their efforts provide new wealth or maintain old wealth for the community, and both absorb the efforts of individuals who might otherwise do so. They are in fact two businesses which, far from creating wealth, may actually destroy it. Yet they are profitable.

The essential explanation of this paradox is summed up in the title of this chapter. Some economic processes create wealth, others simply transfer it. In the modern world we see the latter featuring on an increasing scale. Which of the two approaches to making profit predominates, wealth transfer or wealth creation, will largely determine the happiness and security of our own and subsequent generations. Whilst sections of some communities may attempt to survive on a mix of value-subtractive activities, of which theft is one further example, infrastructure and social cohesion tend to suffer. Even where value-subtractive processes do not quite so dominate the economic landscape, the principle remains the same. Resources that could be employed to contribute to the production of wealth are instead diverted to processes that merely transfer it.

Some of the conventions of our financial environment tend to encourage wealth transfer processes to operate. They are conventions that determine the kinds of economic process in which the various economic players participate, and thus the allocation of resources within the economy. In order to develop this argument, we must now focus upon wealth transfer in a slightly different context.

Collateral and Interest

As described in Chapter Two, most lenders attempt to insulate themselves from the possibility that entrepreneurs will be unable to meet debt repayment obligations by insisting on a cushion of collateral, this to be provided by the entrepreneur himself. In the event that the entrepreneur is unable to repay the loan and interest, the lender of fixed interest funds can seize the collateral and liquidate it in order to recover the required amount of loan outstanding. The result of this seizure of collateral is that, where it occurs, the lender's return results in whole or in part from a transfer of assets from the entrepreneur, not a profit. The use of fixed interest charges in the financing of business activity implies the possibility that at some stage the money return due to the lender of funds may not be met by the profits earned with those funds. A frequent mechanism then employed to meet debt repayment obligations is wealth transfer through seizure of collateral. Even where this mechanism exists there is still of course the possibility that the value of seized collateral would be insufficient to meet outstanding debt. In the UK housing market this latter feature is nowadays given the term 'negative equity'.

It is clear that with the collateralised financing approach, a lender may be able to establish a positive return on invested funds without necessarily having lent to a profitable borrower. If prospective profitability is supposed to be the determinant of the allocation of investment funds within an economy, then collateral based lending criteria may impede the operation of this mechanism. Furthermore, since we have already established that profit is not necessarily synonymous with wealth creation, we can reason that an investor may make a monetary loss on an investment that is value-additive, or a monetary gain on an investment that is value-subtractive. Therefore, even if prospective profitability does determine the allocation of loanable funds, there is then no guarantee that value-additive processes will be preferred to value-subtractive processes as a result.

Wealth transfer need not operate solely on the small scale of entrepreneurial finance. State financing provides an example of the very same process but on a far larger scale. Where the state finances expenditure with money borrowed at fixed rates of interest, such expenditure must either generate sufficient extra tax revenue with which to meet repayments, or the state must allow a seizure of collateral to take place in much the same way as occurred with the entrepreneur of the previous example. Where the state is concerned, we have already seen that the seizure is effected through some kind of taxation, either explicit in the form of higher tax rates, or implicit in the form of devaluation of the currency. The third option, of issuing more debt with which to repay old debt, merely delays and often magnifies wealth transfers.

There is, however, a more subtle process at work with regard to state funding. The existence of a risk-free rate of interest places the financing of private business activity at a disadvantage to the financing of government activity. Why invest in a private project that has an expected but risky return of 10%, when the state offers a risk-free 10%? At every risk-free rate of interest there will be private projects that are financially unjustifiable since they yield the same or less than the risk-free rate, but at a higher level of risk. If any of these projects include essential services such as the provision of health care or education, it is left to the state to provide financing.

Two undesirable phenomena may then result. Firstly, and in the longer term, a substantial burden upon public sector finances may develop as the state is forced into the funding of projects whose expected profitability does not warrant private investment. This burden will probably increase as real risk-free interest rates move higher. Secondly, the financing of state projects can attract funds that might otherwise be invested in private projects. This is the process most frequently termed 'crowding out'. The supporters of the crowding out theory argue that private enterprise is the most efficient mechanism by which to allocate resources in the economy. Without fear of the consequences of non-profitability, the state may fund projects that are highly questionable from a financial perspective. In basic terms, the argument concludes that private enterprise would make far fewer mistakes of this kind. There may be some truth in this analysis, but the crowding out argument must be balanced against the earlier argument that socially desirable projects, being highly value-added in our approach, are often quite unattractive when looked at in terms of profitability. Private enterprise might not invest in such projects no matter what the interest rate, simply because no profit-based measure of value-added appears.

However, if the state is forced to fund essential projects that yield a lower monetary return than the risk-free rate of interest at which it borrows, the result must eventually be the transfer of monetary wealth from the state to the financier of state activity. The provision of new health care facilities, for example, may enable a return to health for certain individuals who then contribute to the productive effort of the economy and hence the government's tax take. The new revenues might be seen as a form of return to the state's investment in health care. But if the return does not meet the costs of financing borne by the state, then ultimately it is the taxpayer who foots the bill for debt repayment to the financier.

It might therefore be argued that the level of risk-free, and thus other, interest rates within an economy should be influenced through the state's monetary policy to approximate with the returns of economic activity. Yet this task is almost certainly an impossible one. Given the diverse nature of business enterprise, and the differing risks and time horizons on which they invest, no one interest rate can possibly reflect the returns available on all types of activity. And since government monetary policy usually revolves around control of short term interest rates, longer term interest rates are often determined outside the authorities control. As we have seen in Chapter Two, monetary policy is often preoccupied with the effort of controlling bank creation of money supply. Such an effort may run contrary to the demands of the real economy in which the level of business activity may require substantially higher or lower short term interest rates than are viewed appropriate for control of the banking system. The conflicting demands of these situations produce impossible dilemmas for authorities in charge of economic policy.

In any event, interest rates cannot be set at a level that fairly reflects the profitability of business enterprise since the rate of profitability cannot be predicted before the event. It must again follow that there are times when the interest charge does not reflect the profitability of the project in which funds have been invested. Either the interest return will be smaller than the rate of profitability, or in excess of it. It is here that the benefit of full equity financing becomes apparent. Equity holders in projects financed purely on an equity basis are rewarded with dividends and capital growth on their shareholdings that, in the longer term, relate quite closely to the profitability of the investments undertaken. The resultant rate of return then automatically provides the correct cost of capital. As long as interest-bearing debt does not form part of the financing for the venture, any profits on the economic processes involved will be shared without a seizure of collateral. (Of course the profits themselves may have arisen from a wealth transfer process, the operation of a casino for instance, but this is another matter entirely.)

One argument sometimes extended in favour of fixed interest financing is that were it not for such funding techniques, entrepreneurs would tend not to engage in certain projects. For example, where the equity-based financier contributes the entire equity capital of the project, the return in its entirety would be due to that financier. Hence, no monetary incentive would exist for the entrepreneur to be entrepreneurial in the first instance. Two criticisms of this argument might be made. Firstly, the financier would not wish to charge a fixed rate of return in these circumstances either, since he himself is in fact exposed to the full risk of the project with no cushion of entrepreneurial funds in the event of loss.

There is then little reason for the financier to limit the upside on his investment by charging a fixed rate of return at the outset. Secondly, and more importantly, there is nothing to stop the entrepreneur agreeing to share part of the profits of the project with an equity financier in a pre-agreed ratio. In this manner the contribution of the entrepreneur may be fairly recognised as an input to the capital of the business venture.

I have so far argued that since profitability for a lender can be achieved through a seizure of collateral, the existence of collateral may compete with prospective profitability as a criterion for determining where a lender allocates his funds. Lenders may be willing to loan funds to those borrowers who have existing assets, but may be unwilling to do so where no existing assets are available as security. The cynics quip that bankers are people who lend you money if you can prove you don't really need it. Others simply note that collateral based financing criteria tend to encourage the circulation of funds among the rich since these are the ones who are most able to offer collateral in the first place. The rich, or those with existing assets, do not have a monopoly on value-added project proposals however. Poor people, indeed poor nations, may have a variety of value-added processes to engage in, but lack the capital so to do. To the extent that capital can only be raised where collateral already exists, the collateralised approach fails this particular group of potential borrowers.

In Chapter Two, I noted the tendency for banks to lend funds that are simultaneously available to depositors on short notice. In this procedure resides the risk of a liquidity crisis, the inability of the banks to satisfy demands for withdrawal of deposits, especially apparent during times of economic downturn. In compensating for these risks, bankers tend to prefer the funding of short term projects that can satisfy the demand for liquidity in the event of such a downturn. Long term projects, those requiring a long term commitment of funds before producing a return, do not compete on grounds of liquidity with short term projects. But once again, short term projects do not have a monopoly on value-added processes. They sometimes revolve around the financing of speculative activities since, under certain economic conditions, these appear more capable of yielding profit than industrial or business processes. Property booms often demonstrate this possibility. Furthermore, we have seen that the very nature of the discounting analysis undertaken by financiers devalues the distant consequences of current actions. Short term projects come out best from the discounting analysis and financiers will thereby favour them if they rely on such analysis in determining where to place their funds.

Leverage and Speculation

Two common conventions of the modern financial environment have now been introduced, namely collateralised loan finance and the existence of risk-free interest-based returns, that affect the decisions of financiers in allocating their funds. In order to describe more fully the manner in which these conventions conspire to encourage wealth transfer processes in an economy, we must also understand the motivation of the borrower of funds. By looking at both sides of the lending and borrowing process, we may better understand why such inequitable practices have survived so long.

If engaged in widely, the process of borrowing money to finance asset purchase can be self-sustaining. Owners of assets are often able to provide them as security for loans. Sometimes the loans thus secured are themselves used to buy further assets and these in turn can be used to secure further financing. Where one particular asset class becomes the focus of this pyramiding of collateral and borrowing, the price of that asset class may begin to rise, allowing further growth of collateral values and thus engendering greater confidence among lenders to lend. Very quickly a 'speculative bubble' may develop. The asset provides the collateral, and a bull market with a pool of debt-financed buyers provides the liquidity. The greater the extent to which this mechanism is employed, the greater the degree of leverage that results. Thus, a small increase in asset price can provide the debt-financed project owner with a large percentage gain on his own capital base. The next table demonstrates how the operation of nine times leverage, being debt at nine times the value of equity, translates a return of 20% on assets into a return of 110% on the owner's equity.

Owner's equity	100
Amount borrowed (at 10% interest)	900
Total project assets	1,000
Profit on project	200
Total asset value after one year	1,200
Interest and principal repaid to lender	990
Total owner's equity after one year (= 1,200 - 990)	210
Return on assets (= 200 / 1,000)	20%
Return on owner's equity (= 110 / 100)	110%

EFFECT OF LEVERAGE ON RETURN TO PROJECT OWNER

The euphoria that is evident among those who operate on the basis of leverage, often turns to distress. This is most obvious in the aftermath of a speculative property boom. Governments may react to asset price booms by raising the interest rate at which all must borrow. As interest rates rise, some borrowers are unable to meet their interest costs and a few begin to default. In the newly cautious monetary climate, the tap of bank money that has financed the speculation is turned off. New buyers therefore become scarce and the boom in prices abruptly ends.

So far so good, at least as far as the authorities are concerned. Speculators however, aware that further capital gains are unlikely in the short term and aware that interest costs on their borrowings are rising, now attempt to sell some of their assets to repay their borrowings. In an unhealthy market, asset prices begin to fall. The net worth of many speculators shrinks quickly as leverage begins to work in the opposite direction to that which was originally intended. Lenders, increasingly concerned by the declining value of their collateral, begin to foreclose on those borrowers least able to meet their repayment schedules. A vicious circle of further asset sales, further asset price falls and further bank foreclosures ensues.

In *The Debt Deflation Theory of Great Depressions* (1933), Irving Fisher describes the deadly combination of falling nominal asset prices and over-borrowing that is debt deflation. For Fisher, the expansion and contraction of bank money supply, 'check-book money' as he calls it, is the crucial catalyst. Fisher writes :

As explanations of the so-called business cycle, or cycles, when these are really serious, I doubt the adequacy of over-production, under-consumption, over-capacity, price-dislocation, mal-adjustment between agricultural and industrial prices, over-confidence, over-investment, over-saving, over-spending. I venture the opinion, subject to correction on submission of future evidence, that, in the really great booms and depressions of the past, each of the above named factors has played a subordinate role as compared with two dominant factors, namely 1) over-indebtedness (especially in the form of bank loans), to start with, and 2) deflation following soon after

Fisher, I., *100% Money (1934)*, p. 106

Gordon Pepper also focuses on monetary causes of asset price inflation and deflation in financial markets and finds a marked correlation. He summarises :

Industrialists focus on the behaviour of the factors affecting individual companies: that is on profits, dividends, earnings and so on. The fact that these are not dominant short-run influences on the level of the equity market is an important explanation of accusations of the City being out of touch with reality and of 'short-termism'. Many of the remedies proposed for curing short-termism are tinkering with symptoms. Attention should now be focused on the underlying causes, that is on flows of funds and imbalances in the financial system.

Pepper, G., *Money, Credit and Asset Prices* (1994) p. 15

The relationship between changes in bank lending and changes in asset price is most striking where that lending is tightly focussed upon a particular asset class, for example house mortgages and property prices. Here, Pepper conducts an analysis that I have confirmed and reproduced graphically below. Separately, I have also related the net change in bank lending against the change in average house price for the UK and found a strong correlation ($r^2 = 0.57$) for 1971 to 2000. Pepper and Fisher have good reason to highlight private sector expansion of money supply as a prime moving force behind the truly major speculative booms of modern times.

During an economic boom, interest and collateral based financing criteria may encourage the banking sector to expand lending, and hence money supply, in the desire to make profit. During the contractionary phase, the same criteria encourage the opposite phenomena to arise. Pepper comments again :

A market's reaction to news is biased when liquidity transactions tend to persist in one direction; the market reacts to good news but tends to ignore bad, or vice versa. Keen observers detect that the market appears to want to go up or down, as the case may be. This is an explanation for intuitive expectations and 'market noses'. Market participants detect that following a trend tends to be a profitable course of action. The herd instinct then prevails. Crowd psychology becomes more important than the behaviour of investors acting as rational individuals. Technical analysis (chartism), which is based on crowd psychology, becomes more important than fundamental analysis.

Pepper, G., *Money, Credit and Asset Prices* (1994) p. xix

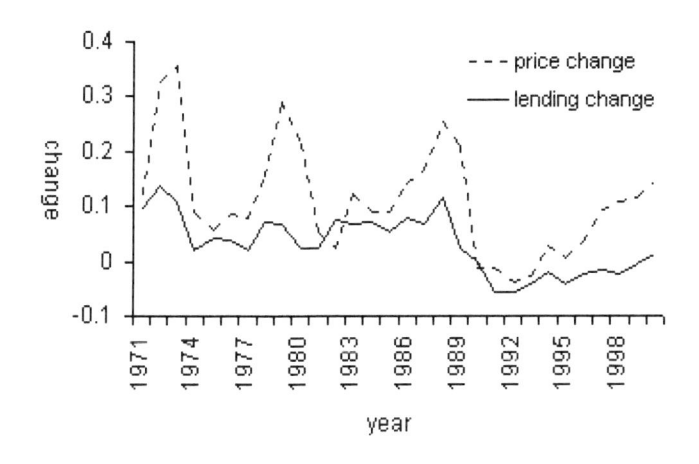

**CHANGES IN AVERAGE UK HOUSE PRICES
AND CHANGES IN UK BANK LENDING**

Many homeowners in the United Kingdom today know how powerful the herd instinct can be. Speculators may buy residential property because the information available to them indicates that house prices are rising. This may be efficiency in the sense of processing available information, but it is often most inefficient in the sense of resource allocation. When enacted by millions of households, the speculative game can become a self-fulfilling money-spinner that strips the price signal of any meaningful relationship to fundamentals. Very quickly, pseudo-technical arguments of the '... buy now while you can still afford it' variety take over. In this environment, it is rarely asked whether the devotion of substantial new resources to the construction of residential property meets a genuine need for accommodation, or simply acts as a tool for the making of speculative profit. In any event, increasing property values encourage the construction of new property. Where genuine non-speculative demand for property exists, the action of this price signal can be highly efficient in allocating resources to the sector.

This may not be the case where the price signal is activated by speculation.

Between 1984 and 1989 in the United Kingdom, loans outstanding for housing purchase rose by over 110%, from £108 billion to £258 billion. During the same period, the ratio of average house price at mortgage approval stage to male average earnings, rose from approximately 3.25 to 1 to almost 4.5 to 1. The official statistics show that average house prices in the south-east, where the debt-financed speculative mechanism was unleashed to the full, rose from £37,334 in 1984 to £81,365 in 1989. The cost per hectare of housing land in this same region averaged £397,800 during 1984 and £895,000 in 1989. By 1992 however, average house prices in the south-east had fallen back to £74,347 whilst the per hectare cost of housing land had collapsed in just twelve months to stand at £636,500 in 1990.

Having leveraged in order to buy, and now unable to meet substantially increased interest charges, many over-indebted individuals began to default. The number of properties repossessed by members of the Council of Mortgage Lenders rose from 15,800 in 1989 to 43,900 in 1990 and 75,500 in 1991. This is but one of the many consequences of debt-deflation.

Pepper's criticism of technical analysis may apply to the short term only, but often the short term is quite long enough for the market correction to prove highly destructive. The charity *Shelter* has in the past estimated that 100,000 low cost permanent homes are needed each year to meet the high levels of low cost housing need in the UK. At the end of 1994, such accommodation would have been welcomed by many among the 127,290 households that were homeless, the 419,890 that were more than three months in arrears on their mortgages, and the several million who were living under 'negative equity'. What did the 1980's boom do for these people?

When the free market mechanism operates in the manner described above, no one can seriously argue that is has resulted in a healthy application of material resources and human effort. Some of the players in this economic game are of course more guilty than others, and some may suffer more than others in the aftershock. But suffer too do some quite innocent bystanders. The value-adding economic agent who did not, or could not, seek any part in the speculative boom, must also endure the full effect of the monetary squeeze that aims to cure it. Once sold at rock bottom prices, the entrepreneur cannot simply re-acquire his business at a later stage. Workers, plant and skills that have taken years to assemble, quickly disassemble, clients find new suppliers and other forms of goodwill evaporate. As any entrepreneur knows, to begin again from scratch is not an easy process. A successful long term business cannot usually be founded in a short period of time since client trust and suitable products all take time to develop. To produce a new model of car or computer chip, a new medicine or aeroplane, or any number of other value-added products, requires long term commitment and long term effort. Businessmen clearly like boom conditions, but they also dislike busts. In fact, stability is probably of far greater value to a businessmen when viewing the long term. It is of little use to experience a boom in which client demand cannot be fully satisfied anyway, if the consequence is a bust in which bankruptcy follows.

The successful quick-buck speculator might like the boom and bust conditions that have afflicted the Anglo-Saxon economies in recent years and short term speculative projects may at times find favour with those collateralised financiers who value liquidity. But this kind of activity does little to encourage the formation of industries that are capable of providing stable employment and added value in the long term. Wealth creation requires economic stability, a commitment to the long term, and a commitment by the financier towards the project he finances. It requires the financier to finance those with ideas and competence, not just those with collateral. We do not hear these phrases often enough in the vocabulary of modern finance and it is not because the talents in this sector are of poor quality. Indeed, the pay rates in the financial sector have attracted many well qualified brains. Rather, it is the structure of our financial system that encourages a harmful set of priorities to dominate.

The nature of discounting, the private creation of money, monetary policy and the criteria for bank lending would not grab the headlines in an election campaign. But they are having a continuing and powerful effect upon the lives of every individual in the modern economy. As Michael Rowbotham writes:

Throughout the economy the scramble to meet costs and repay debts in a debt-based financial system introduces an unrelenting pressure, fostering trends which utterly dominate industry, agriculture and the provision of services. It is a pressure that dominates every corner of our lives, binding us to permanent employment, distorting our economies, forcing them to grow and change at an ever increasing rate and compete with ever greater ferocity. The way this pressure takes effect ... gives far greater substance to the chilling warning of Lord Stamp. 'If you want to be slaves of the bankers and pay the costs of your own slavery, then let the bankers create money'.

Rowbotham, M., *The Grip of Death* (1998)

Chapter five

VALUE JUDGEMENTS

> *In this chapter, the normative and positive approach to economics is reviewed. Positive economics tries to be free of value judgements but is not. Normative economics deliberately highlights its value judgements and makes them central to its discussions. The most essential question that must be asked is "where do our value judgements come from?" Revealed knowledge is contrasted with deductive knowledge. It is proposed that economic activity cannot be based solely upon the foundation of materialism. The value judgements of Islamic economics are introduced and their implications for a variety of economic policies are discussed.*

The Normative and Positive Approach

Conventional economics emphasises its freedom from value judgements. It is an analysis that tends to be of the positive kind, therefore choosing to examine questions of the 'what happens if ... ?' variety. The positive economist might enquire, for example, as to the effects of an increase in tax rates upon tax revenue. This approach stands in contrast to a method which seeks to highlight particular value judgements and use them as a foundation for a variety of economic prescriptions. Here is the normative approach to economic analysis, an approach that concerns itself with questions of the 'what should be ...?' variety. The normative economist may therefore contend with, for example, the degree to which wealth redistribution should be achieved through the tax mechanism.

Despite its pretensions, even supposedly positive economics has its own peculiar set of value judgements. Bentham, for example, proposes that man acts out of a desire to maximise the utility derived from consumption, whilst classical economists such as Smith and Ricardo argue that the profit motive determines economic activity. If discovered in another world-view, such sweeping assumptions would hardly be tolerated by the positive-minded economist. Yet in the pervasive modern concept of 'economic man' resides the ugly sight of one who acts out of a selfish desire to increase his own material wealth. There seems to be little scope for charity, conscience or ethics here.

Value theory, as outlined in the works of neo-classical economists such as Menger and Walras, provides a further example of the type of value judgement that can creep into orthodox economics. Since a man who is lost in the desert will value a glass of water more highly than a bar of gold, the price he will pay for water will be greater than that for gold. Marginal utility theorists proposed that the price of an item is determined by consumers in this 'subjective' manner, not for example by the cost of production of that item as earlier economists had theorised. Thus was born the concept of marginal utility. The pleasure gained from that next glass of water would determine the price of all available units. In a wet country this might not be very much, but in the desert ...

However, the utility theorists made certain assumptions of their own. Amongst these assumptions are that one consumer's utility is independent of the utility of others, and that utilities are 'exogenously' determined (in other words determined by external influences only). But utilities are often inter-dependent, fashion trends being an example of the way in which the preferences of one consumer can affect those of others. Utilities can also be endogenously determined in that today's utility can affect tomorrow's utility. For example, £1,000 of wages today may provide what is regarded by a given individual as a luxurious standard of living, but over time this same individual may become accustomed to his new lifestyle and regard it as rather more of a necessity than a luxury. The satisfaction arising from that same wage thus diminishes and the individual's set of wants changes. Where he once dreamt of owning a motor car, he now dreams of owning two. In this way, today's utility is affected by yesterday's consumption. But since yesterday's consumption is determined by yesterday's utility, an endogenous process is seen to be at work. Utility determines consumption, which in turn determines utility.

Much of 'value-free' positive economics is not, in fact, free of values. The value judgements are there, it is just that they are not immediately apparent. The normative economist reminds us of the rather obvious fact that without first defining 'what should be' in our economic life, we cannot go on to decide how best to achieve it. In defining what should be we are immediately forced to make value judgements. The problems begin to arise when we ask who it is that should be empowered to make these value judgements.

Revealed Knowledge and Deductive Knowledge

It is a common view among many religious denominations that, where the important value judgements are concerned, the Divine Authority has already pronounced quite sufficiently. This is a comforting idea in that it conveniently removes at least one source of argument and confusion that can arise where men are left to make such judgements for themselves. For others, the approach is merely an abdication of intellectual responsibility.

Naturally, the manner in which modern value systems are constructed does not go uncriticised itself. Sessions of Parliament in the United Kingdom often provide a good example of the kind of battles that can occur between groupings that hold opposing value judgements. To favour the rights of the businessman or the rights of the poor? Here, in a simplified form, is one typical confrontation between capitalist and socialist that is debated on most days of the political calendar across the widest spectrum of topics. Opposing value judgements can severely hamper the legislative process, for on some occasions even the objective of policy is in question and not simply the best means of attaining it.

By implanting a secular order where a religious constitution once existed, the politicians have usurped the Higher Authority's right to make value judgements for us. Religion may be a private matter, it may have little to do with the day to day running of the affairs of state, it may have little pedigree where economics is concerned, but why are the value judgements of politicians to be held in any greater esteem?

Whether we allow our own value judgements, or those of a supposed Divine Being, to rule our lives is an essential question for society to address. The battle here is chiefly between two camps. The one believes that science and religion have little common ground, whether in our physical understanding of the universe around us or in the political, social and economic foundations of our daily lives. The other camp proposes religion as the source of guidance for all aspects of life. Hence the argument between 'men of science' and 'men of religion' that takes place in the secular societies. For some, science has disproved religion and all religious guidance can safely be ignored. Therefore values derived from the Bible, for example, are no more worthy than values derived from the man next door.

Where western thought is concerned, Dr. Maurice Bucaille argues that this supposition of 'conflict' between science and religion has arisen largely because of a number of inescapable contradictions between a Biblical text, which for many represents 'religion', and current scientific knowledge.

It was at first held that the corroboration between the scriptures and science was a necessary element to the authenticity of the sacred text. Saint Augustine, in letter No. 82 ... formally established this principle. As science progressed however it became clear that there were discrepancies between Biblical Scripture and science. It was therefore decided that the comparison would no longer be made ... The existence of these contradictions, improbabilities and incompatibilities does not seem to me to detract from the belief in God. They involve only man's responsibility. No one can say what might be original to the texts, or identify imaginative editing, deliberate manipulation of them by men, or unintentional modification of the Scriptures.

Bucaille, M., *The Bible, The Qur'an and Science* (1981) p. ix

Conflict between theologian and scientist is far less evident in the Muslim world. This is in part because Qur'anic guidance in the physical sciences has not so far contradicted the results of mankind's scientific investigation. The Qur'an does not ask us to reject our most basic scientific knowledge by telling us that God created the Earth's plant life before creating the Sun (Genesis 1:1). Rather, in the scientific sphere, the guidance of the Qur'an predates many modern scientific 'discoveries'. Modern astronomy confirms that the Earth and the heavens were once joined together and that the universe is expanding (Qur'an 21 : 30), and that the Sun too follows an orbit of its own (Qur'an 36 : 40). Whilst nineteenth century scientists in Europe were proposing their unlikely theories of human reproduction, followers of Islam already knew that it is the male sperm that determines the sex of the off-spring (Qur'an 53 : 45/46).

The scientific commentary in the Qur'an dates from a time when men could not discover the above facts 'scientifically'. The existence of these mysteries is of course no final proof of God's existence, although it would be interesting to hear them explained away by the secular scientist.

Given the Muslims' faith in the Divine origin of the Qur'an, it is not difficult to understand why the methodology of study under Islam combines both an inductive approach and the deductive approach common to western study.

Under the deductive approach, attempts are made to identify the specific from observations of the general. "A causes B, B causes C, therefore A is the cause of C", argues the deductive thinker. For example, if tar enters the lung when tobacco smoke is inhaled, and if tar is observed to cause cancer of the lung, then one might deduce that smoking causes lung cancer. Here is the basis of a scientific method of investigation that has had many benefits for humanity.

However, deductive thinking, based as it is on observations of the world around us, is not always secure against error. Knowledge obtained by deduction changes according to the evidence at our disposal and is limited by our ability to understand the world around us. As Ormerod points out, Copernicus and the Church came to opposite conclusions by analysing the same data. The Sun rose in the east and set in the west. Surely then the Sun orbits the Earth, argued the Church. Most surely the Earth orbits the Sun, replied Copernicus.

In the inductive approach, the specific comes first and the general follows from it. "A and B are true, therefore C is true" argues the inductive thinker. Scientific investigation confirms that the astronomy of the Qur'an is accurate, similarly its biology, proof that the Qur'an must be from God.

The inductive approach is often criticised for lacking the scientific method that is common to deductive thinking. However, some things cannot be discovered through scientific investigation. In these cases, knowledge revealed to man by God is the only means of finding the answers that we seek. Revelation is perfect and has been revealed as a guidance. And by following it, man does not need to learn his lessons the hard way.

As far as attitudes to interest are concerned, the Muslim will be hostile because Islam is against interest. Interest is harmful to society and this fact is part of revealed knowledge. Even if man cannot fathom the thinking of the Almighty, the validity of Divine guidance must remain unchallenged.

The world view of Islamic economics requires an appreciation of the fundamental difference between value judgements borne of a religious inclination, and those that arise in the non-religious mind. If there is an afterlife, a God, a Day of Judgement and recompense for all Earthly deeds, then our economic analysis should surely attempt to account for this state of affairs. If there are no such afterlife realities, we may carry on as before, searching for our own answers, on our own, in a world where each individual has a right to disagree and where absolute truth cannot often be identified. I do not feel comfortable with this latter and rather lonely proposition. Of course, this discomfort is not a conclusive argument against 'atheistic' economics. I do however argue that modern economics caters little for a belief in God, a belief held in some form by several billion people, and all that this implies for the motivation behind worldly economic behaviour. Value judgements can inform economic activity, so why shouldn't they inform economic analysis too? In the remainder of this work I have simply chosen the Islamic set of value judgements as my starting point.

The Foundations of Islamic Economics

In my introduction I proposed that the economic ideas identifiable in Islam provide what is possibly the last established opposition to the essentially capitalist world-view that is now in the ascendancy. However, Islamic economists do not generally aim to re-invent the economic wheel. Many western principles are themselves a fundamental part of Islamic belief and, in many cases, western principles have themselves been developed through contact with the Muslim world of old.

The Qur'an is regarded by Muslims as the ultimate reference when establishing Islamic law. Under no circumstances can the injunctions of the Qur'an be negated or annulled by reference to any other source.

The practice and traditions of Prophet Muhammad s.a.w., known as *sunnah* (literally 'way' or 'path') and recorded in the *ahadith* (singular *hadith*), are next in order of importance when deriving Islamic principles. During the time of Prophet Muhammad s.a.w., ahadith were passed on orally by those who had committed them to memory. A definitive compilation of ahadith was not attempted until some time after the Prophet Muhammad's s.a.w. death when, in response to growing unease at the hundreds of thousands of varying and contradictory ahadith that had become widespread, the major compilers and biographers began to produce what have now become standard works. The six most authentic ahadith collections, the *Sihah Sitta*, are those of Bukhari, Muslim, Tirmidhi, Abu Daud, Nasa'i and ibn Majah.

The ahadith inform us that the Prophet Muhammad s.a.w. said "... after I am gone differences will arise among you. Compare whatever is reported to be mine with the Book of God. That which agrees therewith you may accept as having come from me. That which disagrees you will reject as a fabrication". Thereafter arose a strict scientific method, under which ahadith were scrutinised for authenticity. For example, the honesty and virtue of the one reporting a hadith, as well as the chain of reporting (the *isnad*), had to be well established in order for the hadith to be authenticated by the early compilers.

Islamic scholars, *ulema*, may encounter an issue upon which there is no specific guidance in the Qur'an or Sunnah. In such a case, they may indulge in *ijtihad*, the forming of independent judgements, so as to guide Muslims in the relevant activity. The resulting jurisprudence is termed *fiqh* (literally 'comprehension') and the passing of a judgement is termed a *fatwa*. Fiqh may be derived in two ways. Firstly, through achieving a consensus among ulema, termed *ijma*, and secondly through deduction by analogy with existing principles, termed *qiyas*.

Importantly, where a legal rule (the *hukm*) is concerned, jurists will attempt to discover the grounds or 'ratio decidendi' (the *illa*) upon which that legal rule is based. They may not agree upon what the illa actually is, of course, which results in differences in ijtihad between the jurists. It may also require some investigation in order to discover what the wisdom (the *hikma*) behind the hukm actually is, though this is a discovery that may be beyond the human mind. As an example, the hukm is that the thief must have the hand cut off. The hikma may be that such a punishment deters theft and makes the world a safer place to live in. The illa is the act of stealing wealth of a value in excess of the specified threshold (*nisab*), this amount being between two and ten dirhams, or quarter of a dinar, according to which jurist one follows. So the theft of a slice of bread would not normally invoke the punishment of amputation since the illa is not met.

Shariah, literally 'fount' but more commonly translated as 'Islamic law', thus comprises rules that are explicit in the Qur'an and Sunnah, as well as rules that are derived therefrom by means of ijma and qiyas. There are four major Sunni schools of thought, these being the Hanafi, Maliki, Shafi'i and Hanbali. These schools were not established in order to found a new variant of Islam, rather they sought to establish new methods of studying existing guidance. (The minority Shia sect has its own schools of thought and these are not referred to in this work).

Islam has a great deal to say about the regulation of human activities, and not just in the economic sphere. It is a religion that highlights its value judgements, prescribing them as a basis for the guidance of mankind. Three foundations underlie this prescription. They are *aqidah*, the articles of faith which embody a Muslim's belief, *akhlaq* which embodies the moral and ethical code of Islam, and Shariah. Shariah is often regarded as having two different aspects, namely *ibadat* (the law pertaining to devotional matters), and *muamalat* (the law pertaining to civil activity).

Aqidah comprises six elements of belief. These are a belief in the oneness of God (*tawhid*), in the coming of a Day of Judgement, in the divine scriptures, in the prophets through whom those scriptures were revealed, in the angels who serve God and, finally, a belief in predestination.

Tawhid is the most fundamental belief in the religion of Islam. Worship is to be directed to the one God. Other forms of worship, whether they take the form of devotion towards humans, material possessions, or one's own reputation, are contrary to the teachings of Islam. If materialism is seen as a religion, then it is a religion that Islam strives to eradicate.

On the Day of Judgement, the record of worldly life will be brought to bear as witness for or against each individual that has lived on Earth. Ultimate justice will on this day be disbursed by God in recompense for past deeds. In Islam, the worldly life is seen merely as a test, for which eternal paradise is the potential prize. Here is a reward for one's worldly efforts that is infinite, non-monetary and hard to incorporate into a conventional economic analysis. But if this recompense really does exist, in fact even it is only imagined to exist, then where does it leave the validity of our materialist models of human motivation, based as they are upon such foundations as worldly self-interest and worldly wealth maximisation?

The scriptures revealed by God are provided for the guidance of mankind. Man is not perfect and hence his own laws cannot be perfect either. Man-made law is subject to alteration and revocation, often to suit the ends of the law-makers themselves.

Muslims regard Islam as the 'final revelation' from God to mankind. They believe that many individuals were called to Prophethood by the very same God prior to the advent of Prophet Muhammad s.a.w. Among these individuals were Noah, Abraham, Moses and Christ, all of whom are deserving of respect. Thus it is that other religions embody some or many of the principles laid down in Islam. Islam certainly does not claim to have a monopoly on truth, rather it claims to be free of those human manipulations which have muddied, over time, the guidance embodied in other faiths. It is not therefore surprising to find followers of other religions sharing many of the prohibitions of Islam, including those on usury.

Under muamalat, the enactment of forbidden (or *haram*) activities is punishable by an Islamic court of law. Major haram activities include murder, adultery, theft, the consumption of intoxicants, gambling, the practice of astrology and usury. Any form of involvement, directly or indirectly, with such activities is prohibited irrespective of the desirability of the perceived outcome that might result therefrom. The principle in Islam is that the ends do not justify the means. In fact, the Prophet Muhammad s.a.w. is related to have said that "only good can come from good", and it would therefore seem that under Islam the means justify the ends. Importantly, the principle of necessity, *al-darura*, provides an exception to the above rules of prohibition. Where survival is threatened for example, a Muslim is allowed to consume prohibited food or drink. Otherwise, any action that is not specified as haram is automatically permissible or *halal.*

In aqidah and muamalat one may begin to recognise the set of value judgements that informs the Islamic economic model. Muhammad Haykal in *The Life of Muhammad* argues that a society which founds itself upon economic activity, but gives little weight in public life to faith, is incapable of achieving happiness for mankind. The material economic outlook pits man against man as competitor rather than co-operator, be it worker against capitalist, or entrepreneur against socialist planner. Haykal comments that :

The victory of materialist thinking (in the West) was largely due to the establishment of western civilisation primarily upon an economic foundation. This situation led to the rise in the West of a number of world views which sought to place everything in the life of man and the world at the mercy of economic forces...

If it is correct that material possessions provide short-lived improvements in an individual's happiness, then it is unsurprising that more material wealth becomes the goal of conventional economic policy. Perhaps it is shopping that is now the opium of the people. Islam, in contrast, aims for a regulation of human activity that at the same time offers an outlet for its expression. As Haykal points out, Islam does not deny the human desire to accumulate private wealth, but this desire is not supposed to dominate as is the wont of purely capitalist society, nor is it totally suppressed as in the communist prescription.

Under Islam, the desire to accumulate wealth is regarded as a God-willed fact of human nature. The struggle against the sometimes conflicting desires to accumulate wealth yet to follow the religion of Islam, is then seen as being one of the forms in which the test of life presents itself. Power and wealth are as much a test of human qualities as poverty and weakness since both have in attendance their own peculiar temptations toward sinful behaviour. The actions of worldly life must therefore be undertaken with consideration for both the present and afterlife consequences, and worldly self-interest is not the sole criterion upon which action should be predicated. Economic man is replaced here, as in other religious world views, by an altogether less materialistic kind of individual. Wealth is not an evil of itself and it is not a principle of Islam that heaven is only open to the poor. It is simply that the accumulation of wealth should not become an end in itself.

Neither can a utopian equality of wealth be implied as a goal of policy in the Islamic model. The Qur'an stresses that inequality in wealth has been established on Earth quite deliberately, resulting as God intended from the differing aptitudes and degrees of good fortune which He has bestowed upon different members of mankind. No fair policy is seen as capable of completely erasing the resulting inequalities and no policy to achieve such a goal is viewed as desirable. Accepting disparity in wealth as 'natural' does not however amount to the same thing as acquiescing to the existence of poverty. In fact, the avoidance of hardship is regarded as a fundamental prerequisite for the maintenance of faith.

In Islam, conditions that enable individuals to achieve success in the afterlife become the focus of public policy, not simply the improvement of material standards of living. The state should encourage resources to be allocated with this objective uppermost in mind. This policy is often described as maximising social welfare, or encouraging what is in the public interest (*maslahah*).

The idea that mankind is God's *khalifa* or vice-regent on Earth has been interpreted by some to suggest that man is a guardian of wealth that ultimately belongs to God. However the correct interpretation of the khalifa concept, according to Ibn Kathir, is that each man is a vice-regent of the previous generation. God needs no vice-regent since He is all powerful and ever-present. For those who are blessed with the enjoyment of God's wealth comes the responsibility of ensuring that those without it are not left in need. This, for the wealthy, is another of the tests of life.

In order to understand the approach to providing social welfare more fully, one should be aware of three categories of resources that have been identified by such scholars as al-Ghazali and al-Shatibi. Their approach is to an extent reflected by western economic thinking, for example in Maslow's 'hierarchy of needs'. Under the Islamic formulation, necessities (*daruriat*) are those items and activities required in order to sustain the 'five foundations of life'. These foundations are usually classified as being religion, life, mind, honour and wealth. Conveniences (*hajiat*) are those items that ease the burden of human life but which can be done without if not available. Refinements (*tasiniat*) then include all other permitted goods and services, being those that do not remove a burden from human life but rather act to brighten or adorn it. Refinements are therefore synonymous with luxuries.

A distinction between need and want now appears. Fahim Khan is one economist who emphasises that human wants are unlimited whilst human need is not. He continues :

Whereas want is determined by the concept of utility, need, in the Islamic perspective, is determined by the concept of maslahah. The objective of Shariah is the welfare of the human being ... Whether a Mercedes car has utility can be decided on the basis of different subjective criteria. For example, because it is good to show off in; or because one likes its design; or because it is manufactured by ones own country or by a country that one likes, etc. There could be innumerable criteria on the basis of which one may decide whether something has a utility. This is not so in the case of maslahah. The criteria are fixed for everyone and the decision has to be made on the basis of this criteria. This property of maslahah vis-à-vis utility is capable of enhancing the predictability and validity of economic policies because the criteria available for decision making are known.

Khan, F., *Essays in Islamic Economics* (1985) p. 36

Islamic scholars proceed to argue that the state's economic policy must be designed so as to encourage the resources of both the state and the private sector towards necessities first, and only thereafter towards conveniences and refinements. Left to its own devices, the market mechanism may be a practical device in providing wealth in return for work, but it is certainly not efficient in distributing wealth according to need. The building of luxury residences by a wealthy elite in the midst of a deprived majority would clearly contradict the principles laid down here. Such an allocation of resources would not maximise social welfare and might in fact decrease it as a result of resentment among the poor. Thus arises one justification for the intervention of the state in resource allocation.

There is no Malthusian paranoia in Islam. Naturally, there is a limit imposed by technology, environment and population upon the wealth-creating capacity of an economy. However, constraints determined by the physical endowment of natural resources are far less evident. Dire predictions of resource depletion have been in vogue for many decades. Meanwhile Christopher Booker in the *Sunday Telegraph*, 29 May 1994 writes:

On April 19th for instance, the House of Commons was informed that in 1992, under the latest figures, we paid for the growing and destruction of 40,503 tonnes of cauliflowers, 49,370 tonnes of tomatoes, 154,943 tonnes of oranges and 336,992 tonnes of peaches. This means the destruction of four billion peaches - nearly 1,000 tonnes for every day of the year - mostly bulldozed into the ground in Greece. A Government minister, Michael Jack, solemnly assured MP's that the British Government strongly disapproved of this practice and was "pressing the (European) Commission for a radical reform of the arrangements". But that is exactly what politicians have been saying every year for a decade, and nothing will be done this time either.

Today one hears poorer countries being advised on how best to avoid overpopulation on the basis that too many people require more resources than are available. Yet the average resident of the industrialised countries consumes some ten times as much energy and seven times as much meat as the average sub-Saharan African and one is therefore tempted to ask who, exactly, should be having fewer children?

	Sub-Saharan	Industrial
Meat consumed (Lbs/person/year)	11.2	77.36
Energy consumed (LbsOE/person/year)	450	4569

Source: UNDP, Human Development Report, 1997/1999
LbsOE: Lbs of oil equivalent as of 1994 (1000 Lbs. = 1 Ton)
figures for Meat and Cereals as of 1995, figures for population as of 1994

COMPARISON OF CONSUMPTION
Selected regions

Introductory texts on economics inform us that the "economic problem" is one of limited resources being chased by unlimited want, but it seems that the economic problem of our time is more one of fulfilable need left unfulfilled. Excess resources can often be seen where the pessimists choose not to look (aren't the unemployed a resource?), and whilst wants are indeed unlimited, need is not. In 1930's America, such a view was close to the heart of Robert Doane. In a country with millions of miles of road and hundreds of millions of acres of farmland and forest, he famously lamented how incredible it was that any individual could be in need.

Muslims believe that God has endowed the Earth with sufficient resources to last mankind until the Day of Judgement. As we have seen, one main focus of attention under Islam is how this wealth can be distributed among mankind so as to avoid need. Private wealth is not spurned in Islam but conditions are imposed upon those to whom it is granted by God. For example, at the time of the early Islamic state, those who left land uncultivated for three years would risk confiscation of their land in favour of those who could manage it productively. In general, owners are required to use their wealth for the common good, without harming the environment or others, without being extravagant in their use of wealth and without directing it towards the production of prohibited goods and services. The private owner is not permitted complete freedom over the manner in which he manages his wealth.

Perhaps most important in the Islamic theory of distribution is the system of *zakat*. Zakat, literally 'purification', is a wealth levy that applies to Muslims only and varies, according to the nature of the asset in question, from between 2.5% (for personal wealth such as gold and silver) to 20% (in the case of treasure trove when discovered, for example). The revenues raised from zakat form a substantial source of the funding for welfare payments in the Islamic economic system.

The various forms of zakat must be paid by each individual whose wealth is in excess of a threshold, the *nisab*. There seems to be some dispute over the setting of the level of the nisab, that is whether it be fixed or variable by the state according to economic conditions. In any event, zakat is not to be imposed where hardship would result from its payment. To this end the inspection of the living conditions of welfare recipients, a form of means testing, was common in the early Islamic state.

Zakat funds are to be directed in their entirety towards eight classes of beneficiary, quoted below, whether they be Muslim or non-Muslim. Other state revenues would also occasionally be distributed to these permitted causes. They might include voluntary charity *(sadaqa)*, the land tax *(kharaj)*, and a yearly poll tax *(jizhya)*. In the early Islamic state, jizhya was levied on non-Muslim able-bodied men only, this group being exempt from military service yet simultaneously protected by the Muslim state army. But it was under the institution of zakat that the greatest means to fund and implement an early welfare mechanism arose.

Alms are for the poor and the needy, and those employed to administer the funds : for those whose hearts have been recently reconciled to Truth: for those in bondage and in debt : in the cause of God : and for the wayfarer ...

Qur'an 9:60

Modern welfare systems exist in recognition of the fact that the happiness of the rich and the happiness of the poor are inseparable in the long run. The conventional wealth lobby tends to stress ideas of punishment for offenders, the free market, survival of the fittest and other predatory theories, but deterrence and competition have little meaning for the poor unless accompanied by hope and opportunity.

Income taxes and sales taxes now predominate as the funding source for many welfare payments, yet despite an increasing burden of tax we find that wealth distribution often remains stubbornly in favour of the few. According to *The Economist*, in the United Kingdom during 1994 some 5% of the population owned more than 50% of the country's wealth. Meanwhile, the poorest 20% laid claim to less than 5% of the wealth. On a global scale, things are far worse. According to the United Nations Development Programme's *Human Development Report* of 1996, the richest 358 individuals in the world owned more financially measurable wealth than the poorest 2.5 billion.

Both nationally and internationally, transfers of wealth from the wealthy to the poor would enable the satisfaction of need for the many at the expense of the wants and luxuries of the few. In seeking to achieve true wealth redistribution, we see one very good reason why it is that value judgements need to come from a Higher Authority and not from a parliament of men. To impose a wealth tax upon a country's rich may in theory provide a solution to the problem of gross inequality in wealth. But in practice will the laws be passed if the law-makers are the rich themselves?

Islam must be viewed as a complete economic and social prescription. It cannot be put in place by the simple passage of laws for, like Prohibition in America, these laws would fail hopelessly without the support of the people. Elements of Islamic law when applied individually may prove as unsuccessful as the policies which they are intended to improve upon. A man cannot be expected to refrain from stealing food if his alternative is death by starvation. For the state to exact a penalty for theft, without having provided an alternative for those who are starving, would be quite wrong.

Chapter six

TRADE OR INTEREST?

> *Here, the Islamic approach to trade and finance is introduced. The prohibition on usury is discussed and the concepts of gharar and maisir outlined. The various forms of Islamic contract that are of particular relevance to economics are summarised and categorised under contracts of exchange, contracts of charity and contracts of investment. The manner in which these contracts are applied in the modern world of Islamic finance is reviewed and criticised. Particular attention is given to a comparison of murabahah and interest. A description follows of the way in which Islamic contract laws might operate so as to prevent some of the economic evils described in the preceding chapters.*

What is Usury?

Islam offers more than general encouragement towards honesty and equity in men's dealings with one another. We have seen, for example, that detailed guidance can be found on the subject of welfare policy with the injunction requiring Muslims to pay zakat at specific rates on specific items. Similarly, when man is instructed to avoid appropriating the wealth of others wrongfully, guidance appears on the means to achieve this goal. The injunctions relating to usury (*riba*), gambling (*maisir*) and deception or uncertainty (*gharar*) are of particular relevance here.

The literal translation of the Arabic word *riba* is increase, addition or growth, though it is usually translated as 'usury'. As the following discussion shows, usury is not to be regarded solely as the practice of taking interest on a loan.

DEFINING ELEMENTS OF RIBA

Riba al-Fadl
(the usury of surplus)

Riba al-Nasia
(the usury of waiting)

TWO FORMS IN WHICH RIBA MAY BE PRACTISED

Riba al-Qarud
(the usury of loans)

Riba al-Buyu
(the usury of trade)

Several methodologies exist for describing riba. Here, two defining elements of riba are identified (*riba al-fadl* and *riba al-nasia*), and two kinds of transaction into which these elements may be incorporated are described (*riba al-qarud* and *riba al-buyu*).

Riba al-fadl involves an exchange of unequal qualities or quantities of the same commodity simultaneously, and could therefore be described as the usury of surplus. *Riba al-nasia*, the usury of waiting, involves the non-simultaneous exchange of equal qualities and quantities of the same commodity and does not therefore involve a surplus but only a difference in the timing of exchange. Some writers employ the term *riba al-nasa* to define such an exchange.

Hence, an exchange in which I part with 100 grammes of gold now in return for 100 grammes of gold to be received from you tomorrow can be described as riba al-nasia. An exchange in which I part with 100 grammes of gold now in return for 110 grammes of gold to be received from you now can be described as riba al-fadl.

It is occasionally argued, quite reasonably in my view, that usurious loans, *riba al-qarud*, combine both riba al-nasia and riba al-fadl since there is both a delay and a surplus involved in such transactions. This is the modern interest bearing loan, wherein a charge is levied by one party on a debtor in respect of an amount owed. It is one of the major forms in which riba may be practised. The original debt may arise from a loan of money or from the purchase of an item on credit. In either case, the debtor enters into a contract to repay the lender a pre-agreed amount of wealth in addition to the original debt in return for a delay in the timing of repayment. Somewhat confusingly, the term riba al-nasia is occasionally used synonymously with riba al-qarud, but in this text the terms are used as defined above.

Some scholars have in the past asserted that the prohibition on riba al-qarud relates only to high interest charges and not to all forms of interest. Others such as Dr. Tantawi, while Sheikh of al-Azhar in Cairo, have argued that bank interest is a sharing of the bank's profit and may therefore be permissible. In recent times it seems that the Sheikh has either changed his opinion on this matter, or corrected an earlier misunderstanding of his opinion by others. In any case, the view in question has now been widely rejected.

Rejected too have been those arguments that proposed fixed interest rates to be haram and variable interest rates halal. It is occasionally argued that if the rate of interest is allowed to vary then this is permissible since the rate of return is not fixed in advance. This of course is a complete misunderstanding of the mechanics of interest. It is simply the manner of calculating interest that varies here, not the fact of its payment. Under variable rates of interest, interest is indeed charged but the rate at which it is charged is determined at the beginning of each sub-period into which the loan is divided.

Riba al-buyu, the usury of trade, is a second major form in which the elements of riba al-fadl and riba al-nasia may appear. In order to avoid riba al-buyu, both the quality and quantity of the exchanged items must match and the exchange must be simultaneous. Hence, if dates are to be exchanged for dates, the quality and quantity of the dates must be the same and the exchange must be made on the spot. (Quite why anyone would enter into such an exchange is another matter, but Mahmoud El-Gamal whilst at Rice University in Houston has pointed out that the requirement may simply exist in order to encourage the sale of goods for cash in order to achieve fair market values for buyers and sellers, "marking-to-market" as he describes it).

A question now arises as to which kinds of item the prohibition on riba relates to, in other words which are the *ribawi* items?

'Gold is to be paid for by gold, silver by silver, wheat by wheat, barley by barley, dates by dates, and salt by salt - like for like, equal for equal, payment being made on the spot. If the species differ, sell as you wish provided that payment is made on the spot'.

Hadith: Muslim

According to Ibn Rushd in *Bidayat al-Mujtahid*, most jurists maintain that the scope of riba extends to more than just the six commodities mentioned in the above hadith. Hence, an exchange of one ounce of copper for two ounces of copper undertaken on the spot would constitute riba even though copper is not mentioned in the hadith. Note also that exchanges of the same commodity within the six (dates for dates, say) as well as different commodities within the six (for example dates for wheat) must not involve delay.

An exchange of £100 of paper money now for £110 of paper money later is also seen as a forbidden transaction. This is so because the paper fulfils the function of money, and in the hadith the reference to gold and silver is interpreted as a reference to all things that possess the characteristic of being used as money (i.e. things that have *thamaniyya*).

However, the illa employed by the jurists in this matter differs. For example, in respect of the prohibition of excess (the riba al-fadl element) Malik asserts that the illa is the characteristic of being food that can be stored, or the characteristic of being the same commodity and one representative of currency. In respect of the prohibition of waiting (the riba al-nasia element) for the four items of edible produce, Malik identifies the illa as being the characteristic of tastefulness and suitability of storage. However Imam Hanifa argues that the illa for all six items is the characteristic is of being something that is customarily measured by weight or volume. Meanwhile, the Zahirite opinion is that only the six commodities are to be viewed as ribawi. Under this view, one ounce of copper can be exchanged for two if the parties wish. In any event, riba al-buyu can always be avoided if a commodity is sold for money on the spot.

Abu Sa'id said that Bilal brought to the Prophet some barni dates and when the Prophet asked him how the dates had been obtained, Bilal replied, 'I had some inferior dates so I sold two sas for a sa'. On this the Prophet said 'Ah the very essence of riba, the very essence of riba. Do not do so, but if you wish to buy, sell your dates in a separate transaction, then buy with the proceeds'.

Hadith: Muslim

It therefore seems that riba al-buyu cannot occur under a money-for-goods transaction. Neither can riba al-qarud occur in a money-for-goods transaction since loans are repayable in kind. If correct, this is an important conclusion since it means that where Person A buys a good from Peron B with money, there can be no riba. This in turn means that even if Person A is asked to pay a higher price for deferred payment than for immediate payment, following the purchase of a good, riba does not occur. We shall return to this subject later.

Some writers have stated that *riba al-jahiliyya*, the usury of the days of ignorance, was the only kind of riba known at the time of the Prophet s.a.w. (This kind of riba appeared where a buyer of a good on credit reached the end of the credit period, whereupon the seller offered to extend the credit period for an extra charge). However, the majority view seems to be that both riba al-qarud and riba al-buyu were well established by the pagan Arabs before the time of the Prophet Muhammad s.a.w. and that he warned his companions that riba could be practised in many different ways.

If forced to generalise about the two major forms of riba, one might say that they occur where both counterparties in a contract do not enter, or cannot be assured of entering at a later date, into a fair exchange of countervalues. For example, in riba al-qarud, the borrower is held to pay an amount of value (interest) to the lender for which there is no valid countervalue. And in riba al-buyu, by exchanging two measures of corn for one measure, one party clearly receives more value than the other.

It has also been brought to my attention that Jesus (peace be upon him) evicted the money changers from the Temple in Jerusalem for practising a kind of usury that seems in all respects equivalent to riba al-fadl. Jewish pilgrims arriving in Jerusalem to pay the Temple tax would wish to do so using the half shekel, this being the only silver coin that did not portray the head of a pagan Roman emperor. The usurers of the Temple made a business of receiving the despised silver coins and giving in return the half shekel. The exchange of coin for coin was simultaneous, but the usurers took more weight of silver from the pilgrims than they gave. Thus, they practised an exchange of unequal weight of silver hand to hand, riba al-fadl. The similarity between this mechanism and the practices of those Kings who debased their currency, is obvious.

It is often suggested that the use of money sooner rather than later is a valid countervalue to the payment of interest, although the benefit of this earliness of use has itself been questioned in Chapter One. However, a little consideration does yield some examples of unfairness in the riba al-nasia transaction and the discussion of entropy in Chapter One is of relevance here. If A gives B corn today under an agreement for B to give A the same amount of corn next year, then B is effectively storing and maintaining corn on behalf of A free of charge throughout the period. The exchange may also result in one party having to provide the other with a commodity that is of more value at one time of year than another. If it is easy for A to provide B with corn at harvest time, it may not be so easy for B to provide A with corn at the outset of the growing season.

Riba is mentioned in a number of Qur'anic verses (2:275-279, 3:130, 4:161 and 30:39) and contrasted with acts of charity. It is seen in juristic writings as one of the means of 'devouring' others wealth. This accords with what we have seen of fixed interest financing mechanisms, relying heavily upon wealth transfer in many cases, for instance where collateral is seized by a lender in a loan default. One might equally argue that the process of money creation also results in the devouring of others' wealth, devaluing their savings through the mechanism of inflation.

Often by reference to less widely known ahadith, some writers regard riba as including a variety of commercial activities such as the artificial bidding up of prices at auction, the payment of commission to a middleman and rent on land. The majority seem to stick with the narrower definitions of riba and classify activities such as money manufacture and auction rigging as fraud or deception.

Whatever the precise scope of riba, in the ahadith the Prophet Muhammad s.a.w. condemns the one who takes it, the one who pays it, the one who writes the agreement for it and the witnesses to the agreement. It is also clear that Allah in due course required the new Muslims of Arabia to give up riba in its entirety.

O you who believe, give up what remains of your demand for usury if you are indeed believers. If you do it not, take notice of a war from God and his Messenger.

Qur'an 2 : 278 to 279

In concluding this short introduction on the subject of riba it is worth reminding ourselves of some common misconceptions. Firstly, the view that 'interest is a guaranteed gain' is not correct. Nothing is guaranteed in life and even modern bank loans do not guarantee that the bank receives its interest. Borrowers do default from time to time. Neither is it true to say that loans at interest are permissible so long as the loan itself is used to purchase a productive asset. Interest-free loans are permissible under Islam for a wider range of purposes than production alone, whilst interest bearing loans are prohibited under practically all circumstances (situations of coercion or necessity being two exceptions that come to mind). Instead, it is the fixing in advance of a gain on money loaned that is the defining feature of modern interest. This is the feature that I shall search for in due course when analysing the practices of Islamic banking.

Gambling, like theft, is regarded in Islam as one form of injustice in the appropriation of others' wealth and therefore has much in common with the concept of riba. The act of gambling, *al-qimar* or *al-maisir*, sometimes referred to as *al-murahanah* or betting on the occurrence of a future event, is prohibited and no reward accrues for the employment or spending of wealth that an individual may gain through means of gambling :

They ask thee concerning intoxicants and gambling. Say, "In them is great sin, and some profit for men : but the sin is greater than the profit."
Qur'an 2 : 219
The Prophet said 'If a man earns by sinful acts and gives it in charity or kind action or spends it in the way of God, God will throw him into Hell after collecting everything'.
al-Ghazali, *The Revivification of the Religious Sciences*, Book 2, Ch.4, p. 77

Can a business investment be so unlikely to bear fruit as to be the equivalent of gambling? Or is the investor in such a business just a bad investor? If today I launch an internet company hoping to be the one, out of many thousands of others, that achieves success in an intensely competitive market, is this gambling or is it investment?

It seems that the best we can do is to look for clues when attempting to answer this question. If there is no wealth creation in the course of the transaction, then we have a strong indication that the nature of the transaction is one of gambling. This feature tends to be present where a process of transformation of inputs into finished goods or services is absent. Secondly, gambling tends to occur where a transfer of wealth is triggered by a future event over which the individual cannot exert influence (watching a ball fall into place on a roulette wheel, for example). The activities of a businessman in developing his product and his market are entirely different to those of a gambler awaiting the result of a bet. Thirdly, gambling typically involves the creation of an avoidable risk. We cannot eliminate the risks of farming since we need to eat, but we can certainly decide not to risk our money on the outcome of tomorrow's football match.

Of the above features, the second on its own may not be strong enough to define the gambling process. For example, a non-voting investor in a business exerts no influence upon the outcome of that business, but such a person can hardly be said to be gambling. Here it helps to draw a distinction between risk and uncertainty. While few Muslim writers differentiate between the two, in the conventional literature risk is sometimes regarded as that which applies when a condition of a system at a future time can be forecast on the basis of past experience. Uncertainty on the other hand is said to exist where the condition of a system at a future time cannot be forecast from an appraisal of past experience. Some people take their holidays in the Summer because the risk of cold weather is minimal, but past experience of the English weather can never inform us if it will be raining during the second week in June. The more specific the time period, the more the uncertainty.

So too with the stock market. Company share prices generally increase over the long term as the economy grows, but we cannot know whether a given company share will increase in price on a particular trading day in the future. Again, the more specific the time period, the greater the uncertainty. I am often tempted to answer the question 'is stock trading the same as gambling' by saying 'it depends on the time period you have in mind'. Day trading is probably gambling (unless one has inside information) and a five year buy-and-hold strategy is probably not.

This brings us back to wealth transfer as a key indicator of the presence of gambling. If the gaining of profit by Person A can only occur at the expense of Person B's loss, then we can be highly confident that gambling is taking place. Of course, the gambling process may be institutionalised (by means of a lottery), or intermediated (by a casino), but the essential characteristic of wealth transfer remains as the defining feature throughout. Here the understanding of gambling merges with that of gharar. As Dr. Sami al-Suwailem points out in *Towards an Objective Measure of Gharar in Exchange (Islamic Economic Studies, Vol. 7, Nos. 1 & 2,*

Oct. 1999, Apr. 2000) using simple game theory, a gharar transaction is shown to exist where one party can only benefit by the other's loss, under conditions of uncertainty. Insurance is given as an example of this, since either the insured pays a premium and receives no countervalue, or the insurer pays out on a claim much more than was received in premium payments.

Whilst Islamic law is clear that gharar should not be a feature of any contractual agreement, it is not easy to know from a reading of the modern literature how far gharar differs from gambling or indeed what its precise scope is. We know for example that it is not permitted to sell what one does not own, the process of short-selling, because this is regarded as a form of deception. But the word gharar is often interpreted as meaning 'uncertainty' rather than deception. Hence, one cannot sell an item of uncertain quality, an unborn calf for example, since the buyer and the seller do not know the precise quality of the thing that they are trading.

If one takes uncertainty to mean a lack of knowledge pertaining to the future outcome, then every act of man bears an uncertain outcome. The outcome of a business venture is unknown at the outset, as is the quality of the unborn calf. Does this mean that a business venture is forbidden under Shariah? Clearly not. Investment contracts are indeed permissible in Islam. So the lack of knowledge as to the profit resulting from entering into an investment contract would not seem to be of the same species as the lack of knowledge that exists where the quality of the unborn calf is concerned. Furthermore, scholars have distinguished between contracts containing minimal gharar (which are valid) and contracts containing substantial gharar (which are prohibited).

In the above exchange transaction, a known amount of money is exchanged for an unknown calf. Hence the prohibition on the grounds of gharar. In the investment contract, each partner gives a known amount of wealth in return for a known share of final profit. There is risk as to the outcome of the investment here of course, but the countervalue to the investment contribution is the percentage share of final profit, not the amount of profit itself. (On the other hand, if one agrees to share the profits of a business venture with one's partner in a fair ratio without contractually defining what is meant by the word 'fair', it can be argued that there is gharar as to the profit sharing ratio and such a contract might therefore be deemed invalid.)

The Islamic literature often focuses upon protecting the buyer from deception and uncertainty in a sale contract since it is assumed that the seller is the one who is better informed of the item that is being sold. However, a contract wherein a given item is sold at a price to be determined in the future according to some specified event involves uncertainty of a type that could be detrimental to the buyer *or* the seller. To limit the scope of uncertainty to cases in which only the buyer is affected seems inappropriate in today's context.

Forms of Contract in Islam

According to al-Ghazali in *Revivification of the Religious Sciences*, and al-Shafi'i in *Kitab al-Umm*, a contract, or *al-aqd*, must be enacted between counterparties who are: capable of understanding the implications of the contract, in other words who are *mumayyiz*; in a sane and mentally competent condition (hence very ill or intoxicated persons cannot make a valid contract); represented by a sighted person if blind, or represented by an agent if unwilling or unable to act in their own name. Here are some terms which, in the opinions of these scholars and in their day, were required to ensure that fairness was maintained in business dealings.

Every contract must satisfy certain basic conditions: it should be expressed in clear and unambiguous terms; it should come into force after an offer, in writing (*bil kitabah*) or verbally (*bil kalam*), is accepted; it must be enforceable in its own right; it must not be agreed under duress; and it is invalid if either countervalue involves a haram item or activity. Many of these conditions are of course regarded as basic to contractual relationships throughout the developed world today.

It seems to be a generally held view among Muslim writers that in matters of the worldly life all practices are acceptable unless expressly prohibited (whilst in matters of formal worship, *ibadat*, all practices are forbidden unless expressly permitted). Hence, any condition may be applied to an exchange transaction so long as it complies with the injunction that:

All the conditions agreed upon by the Muslims are to be upheld, except a condition which allows what is prohibited or prohibits what is lawful.
Hadith: Hanbal

It also seems that contracts with counterparties whose practices do not accord with the tenets of Islam are permissible so long as the above conditions of contract apply:
Hazrut ibn Masud was once asked by a man 'Shall I take a loan from a man whom I know to be a bad man?' Ibn Masud replied 'Yes'. Ibn Masud was asked by another, 'Shall I accept the invitation of a man who takes interest?' Ibn Masud replied 'Yes'.
al-Ghazali, *Revivification of the Religious Sciences, Vol 2* p. 94

The most widely recognised Islamic forms of commercial contract are often grouped into three categories. These are: a) contracts of exchange, where both parties receive a countervalue; b) contracts of charity, where the donor does not arrange to receive a countervalue, and c) contracts of investment where assets (or effort) are invested into a project on a profit-sharing basis. Other forms of commercial contract do of course exist outside of these three categories, for example contracts of surety, and these impact upon a wide range of economic activity.

Although the injunctions on riba, maisir and gharar are general in scope, an investigation of the subject of trade in the ahadith will uncover a flexibility that caters for a variety of specific commercial situations. For example, an individual is permitted to sell commodities for delivery at a future date. In doing this, a farmer who sells produce that he has not yet grown might be accused of selling that which he does not own. However, as an exception, with specific conditions, the Prophet Muhammad s.a.w. allowed this procedure under the contract of *bay al-salam*.

Contracts of Exchange

The Arabic word *bay* refers to any transaction in which ownership of an asset is exchanged between a seller and buyer, in return for money or by barter. Referring to the kinds of absolute sales, ibn Rushd derives the nine possible forms of sale, and highlights the prohibition of the general form of sale that involves the exchange of two liabilities:
Each transaction between two individuals is an exchange, either of corporeal property for corporeal property, or of corporeal property for a corresponding liability, or of a liability for another liability ... Each one of these three again is either immediate for both parties, or delayed for both, or is immediate for one party and delayed for the other. The kinds of sales (that emerge) are thus nine in number. Delay from both sides is not permitted by

consensus either in corporeal property or in liabilities as it amounts to a proscribed exchange of a debt for a debt.

ibn-Rushd, *Bidayat al-Mujtahid*, (1996) p. 154

Commenting further, ibn Rushd examines the three forms of sale that can arise in a market where goods and money are in existence:

... when two commodities are exchanged, one may serve as a currency and the other as a priced commodity, or both may be currencies. When a currency is exchanged for a currency the sale is called 'sarf', and when a currency is exchanged for a priced commodity, the transaction is sale proper ('bay'). Similar is a the sale of a priced commodity for another priced commodity (barter) ...

ibn-Rushd, *Bidayat al-Mujtahid*, (1996) p. 154

Exchange transactions can be for immediate or deferred exchange and it is recommended that future contracts be evidenced in writing.

O you who believe! When you deal with each other in transactions involving future obligations in a fixed period of time, reduce them into writing

Qur'an 2: 282

Spot transactions need not be evidenced in writing but witnesses are recommended.

... but if it be a transaction which you carry out on the spot among yourselves, there is no blame on you if you reduce it not to writing. But take witnesses whenever you make a commercial contract ...

Qur'an 2 : 282

According to most traditional jurists, the item for sale should be under the ownership of the seller and in his physical or constructive possession at the time of contracting the sale.

The messenger of Allah forbade me to sell a thing which is not my property

Hadith: Tirmidhi

The messenger of Allah forbade me to sell a thing which is not my property or something that is not apparent and seen clearly.

Hadith: Bukhari

The subject matter of an exchange contract must have value of some kind. According to the Shafi'i and Hanbali schools, the 'usufruct' of an asset (in other words, the benefit arising from the use of that asset) can be considered as property and thus can be subjected to an exchange transaction, whereas the Hanafi and Maliki schools do not share this view. According to Professor Hashim Kamali at the International Islamic University in Kuala Lumpur, most scholars of later periods side with the Shafi'i and Hanbali schools on this matter.

A sale by public auction, *bay muzayadah*, in which an item is sold to the highest bidder, is disallowed by many jurists apparently on the basis that auctions may be rigged by a small group of well informed 'insiders'. Others see no harm in the practice:

Anas Reported "the Messenger of Allah (Peace Be Upon Him) purchased a piece of hair cloth and a bowl and he said: who will buy this piece of hair cloth and bowl? A man said, I take them for one dirham. The Prophet (Peace Be Upon Him) said: who will give me more than one dirham? A man gave him two dirhams and bought them from him.

Hadith: Tirmidhi, M. A. Mannan in Islamic Research and Training Institute *Developing a System of Financial Instruments* (1990) p. 82

Whatever the truth of this particular matter, such a view does not seem to prohibit the making of a public offer to sell at a given price.

The Shariah permits making [a] public offer with fixed deadlines for acceptance, binding the offeror to abide by the deadline he has fixed.

Hussein Hassan in Islamic Research and Training Institute *Developing a System of Financial Instruments* (1990) p. 40

According to many jurists, a contract of sale must relate to only one transaction. Hence, rather than signing a single contract to cover several separate transactions, individuals should instead enter into each transaction under a separate contract. Here is an important condition. If followed strictly, it helps to prevent usurious agreements being constructed from a set of underlying contracts that may in themselves be quite acceptable (recall the *contractum trinius*). We should however note that the following hadith, often quoted in this regard, has been termed weak by some commentators:

The messenger of God has forbidden making one contract of sale from two sale transactions.

Hadith: Tirmidhi, Nasa'i

The price agreed must be fixed at the time of contracting the exchange transaction, and ownership remains with the seller until delivery is made. In this respect, there should be a formal event that signifies the point at which a contract is concluded, for example a handshake or a signature.

Conditions may be imposed upon a sale, for example the implementation of a service contract on a manufactured item sold to a buyer, or the availability of a warranty against defective goods (see '*daman*').

Both the buyer and seller may be given an option, *khiyar al-majlis*, to cancel a transaction during a given period after conclusion of that transaction. The Hanafi school limits the period of this option to three days, whilst other scholars do not precisely define the period of time allowed. Some have used *khiyar* as the theoretical basis for modern day 'Islamic option' products whilst others have based arguments for the permissibility of options on the existence of the contract of *bay al-urban*. Bay al-urban involves a deposit that may be forfeited in the event that the depositor does not complete the purchase of the specified good by a specified date. However, it would seem that whilst khiyar is widely accepted as a valid contract under Islamic law, only the Hanbali school permits bay al-Urban.

Naturally, individuals will not always be in a position to conduct exchange transactions on the basis of a simultaneous exchange of cash for goods or services (in other words as 'spot transactions'). Where one of the two countervalues in an exchange transaction are not exchanged simultaneously, certain rules, and some exceptions to those rules, apply. The following contracts are widely recognised.

Murabahah is a sale in which the seller agrees to sell his goods or services at a specified rate of profit over cost. Hence, person A (a trader in potatoes) can agree to sell a sack of potatoes to person B for 10% above the cost incurred by A in obtaining those potatoes. If A sells to B at 110, this implies that the potatoes cost A 100. Of course, B must trust that A did indeed incur a cost of 100 in obtaining the potatoes, hence the description of this type of sale as a 'trust sale'.

Murabaha takes place when the seller declares the price for the buyer at which he had bought the goods, and then stipulates some profit in dinars or dirhams. They (the jurists) disagreed, on the whole, over this on two points. First, over that which the seller can count, and which he cannot count, as part of the capital of the goods out of the expenditure he made on the goods, after purchase. Second, when the seller lies to the buyer and informs him of a higher price than that for which he bought the goods; or if he mistakenly informs him of a lesser price than that at which he bought the goods and it later appears to him that he bought them for more.

ibn-Rushd: *Bidayat al-Mujtahid* (1996) p. 256

During the time of the Prophet Muhammad (s.a.w.), murabahah would often be enacted through the appointment of a trader, by another individual, the trader agreeing to buy goods on behalf of that individual and deliver them to a specified location. The trader would perform this service for a fee (the profit over cost) and would bear the various risks of the transaction. These risks included those related to purchase and ownership of the goods until the delivery date, for example the risk of damage to the goods whilst in the trader's ownership, and the risk that the buyer might not be able to make the required payments after taking delivery of the goods from the trader. In the event of a default (for example where the individual who appointed the trader does not fulfil his side of the agreement to buy), the trader in a murabahah only has recourse to the asset in question. He cannot charge further 'fees' where repayment of the due amount is delayed. Here, murabahah can be seen as a contract of exchange in which the buyer pays the trader for the service of delivering a given item.

Murabahah is nowadays often referred to as 'cost-plus financing' and is applied to raw material purchases as a form of short term trade credit. Typically, an Islamic bank will purchase a commodity and then sell it more or less immediately to a client at a higher price. This 'mark-up' is usually quoted as a percentage rate that must be applied to all the costs incurred by the Islamic bank in fulfilment of the murabahah, such as the costs of purchase, storage and transport.

The client can contract to settle the amount outstanding in one lump sum upon delivery of the items, but in modern times of course the purpose of the murabahah is to delay the time at which payment is made or to spread payments over several installments. If the client delays payment, the contract becomes one of *bay mu'ajjal* (often referred to in Malaysia as *bay bithaman ajil* or *BBA*).

Thus, for example, in murabaha, all risks associated to ownership must be borne by the bank even fleetingly before the article is delivered to the client. Otherwise, the mark up will [be] tantamount to riba.

Islamic Research and Training Institute, *Developing a System of Financial Instruments* (1990) p. 6

The *Islamic Research and Training Institute* also quotes the report submitted to the state authorities by the Council of Islamic Ideology in Pakistan:

Safeguards would, therefore, need to be designed so as to restrict its [bay mu'ajjal's] use only to inescapable cases. In addition, the range of mark-up on purchase prices would have to be regulated strictly so as to avoid the ... [appearance] of interest in a different garb.

Islamic Research and Training Institute, *Developing a System of Financial Instruments* (1990) p. 52

Bay al-salam is a contract for deferred delivery of commodities, with a specified delivery date and full advance payment. Originally, the primary use for this form of contract was in the financing of crops and raw material production. Full advance settlement of the agreed trade price is required but the goods that are subject to the transaction need not yet exist. The quantity and quality of the items to be delivered should however be defined, and should not depend upon unforeseeable factors. Thus the quantity of goods purchased under the bay al-salam contract cannot be defined as that resulting from the cultivation of a given plot of land since such a quantity may vary according to climate and other unforeseeable factors. Items must be indistinguishable in nature (in other words 'fungible') in order to avoid delivery difficulties. Hence, rare items, or those that are not precisely specifiable, cannot be the subject of the bay al-salam contract. If, upon delivery, the quality or quantity of the items are found to be other than specified, the buyer has the right of refusal. The buyer does not own the goods until after delivery, but may take a performance bond from the seller.

Whoever wishes to enter into a contract of salam, he must effect the salam according to the specified measure and the specified weight and the specified date of delivery.
Hadith: all Sihah Sitta

About the condition whether the species of the muslam fih [the item that is the subject of the salam] should be in existence at the time of the contract, Malik, al-Shafi'i, Ahmad, Ishaq, and Abu Thawr did not stipulate this and said that salam is permitted for a thing out of its season. Abu Hanifa, his disciples, al-Thawria and al-Awzai said that it is not permitted unless it is the season of the muslam fih. The proof of those who did not stipulate the season is what occurred in the tradition of Ibn Abbas that the people used to contract salam for dates for a period of two or three years, this was approved and not rejected. The reliance of Hanafites is upon the tradition related by Ibn Umar that the Prophet (s.a.w.) said 'Do not contract salam in date-palms until they (the dates) begin to ripen".
ibn-Rushd, *Bidayat al-Mujtahid* (1996) p. 244

Ijara represents the purchase of the usufruct of an asset in return for a payment, where ownership of the asset itself is not transferred. This contract accords with a modern 'operating lease' agreement. Under an operating lease, the one renting-out the asset (the 'lessor') does not recover the full value of the asset through lease payments and is therefore exposed to at least some of the risks and benefits of owning that asset at the end of the rental term. Modern 'finance leases' differ in that the lease payments are structured so as to provide the lessor with a full return of the funds invested in the asset plus a pre-agreed rate of return on those funds. Finance leases therefore tend to look very similar to interest-based loans secured by collateral except that, in the case of a finance lease, the collateral is the leased asset itself. There are however certain legal and accounting differences between interest-based loans and the above forms of leasing agreement that can make leasing a more attractive alternative to the one who is in need of capital equipment.

Under an alternative approach towards Islamic leasing, the one renting-in the asset (the 'lessee') can agree at the outset to buy the asset during, or at the end of, the lease period. In this case the lease takes on the nature of a hire purchase contract known as *ijara wa iqtina'* (literally, lease and purchase). The cash-flows involved in such a lease can again be structured to look very much like an interest-based loan secured by collateral.

Another form of transaction under this category, common today, is *istisna*. This is a contract of exchange that allows deferred delivery at a specified date. The contract relates to the production of made-to-order items and allows a manufacturer to fund the production process by receiving the sale price of his produce up-front. A detailed specification of the item to be produced must be agreed between the buyer and seller prior to commencement of the production process. Some jurists maintain that up-front payment is not a pre-requisite under istisna, in other words that both countervalues may be exchanged at a date in the future. However, we have seen that this kind of transaction is generally prohibited according to Ibn Rushd since two liabilities are exchanged, one a liability to produce the item at a future date, the other a liability to produce payment for that item at a future date.

It is important to note that Muslim scholars have traditionally prohibited the sale of a debt (*bay al-dayn*) at anything other than face value. Thus, if person B lends person A £100, B cannot then sell this debt to person C for anything other than £100. (If B sold the debt to C for, say £90, then C would effectively be earning interest of £10 on a loan of £90).

Where the sale of debt obligations in exchange for immediate payment is concerned, most jurists are of the opinion that such can only occur where the debt is sold at face value. Where the price paid for a debt is not the same as the face value of that debt, the transaction would be tantamount to riba al-nasia and is therefore prohibited. Among the achievements of the Islamic Fiqh Academy (affiliated to the OIC) was the issuing of a detailed decision ... for deeds based on debts, which shall be non-negotiable except where transfer is made with the exchange of the face value of that debt. If they are purchased for less than their face value this would be the same principle as is applied to discounting of bills of exchange which is prohibited.

al-Qardawi, Y., *The Islamic Capital Market Conference, Malaysia* (1996)

A few Malaysian voices dissent here, and they are widely seen as rather liberal for doing so. For instance, Professor Kamali quotes ibn-Taimiyah and al-Darir as being in favour of bay al-dayn, and argues in favour of the transaction on the basis that there is no clear and authentic prohibition to be found in the Qur'an or Sunnah. Then, in their paper *Regulation and Supervision of Islamic Banks*, Jeddah, IRTI Occasional Paper # 3, 2001, Umer Chapra and Tariqullah Khan argue that the discounting of debt is acceptable so long as that debt arises from a productive process. Hence, for example, if a manufacturer sells goods for 100 payable next year, it can then sell this debt for 90 payable today. (Since the purchaser of this debt locks in a fixed rate of return on his money as a result of his purchase, it is hard to see how the transaction can be anything other than riba).

Although the trading of debt is widely prohibited in Islam, there is no such restriction upon the selling of an investment holding. A hotelier might, for example, purchase a property and rent rooms to travellers on a daily basis in order to earn a profit. At a later stage, the hotelier might decide to sell his business to another entrepreneur. This latter transaction is quite acceptable under Islamic law since it involves the sale of an asset, not the sale of a debt.

Shariah permits the disposition of title of ownership, and even goes so far as to permit, according to the Malikites and some jurists, the disposition of debts through pawning and selling under certain conditions ... regardless of whether the pawning of debt is carried out by the debtor himself or anyone else.

Islamic Research and Training Institute, *Developing a System of Financial Instruments* (1990) p. 28

The trading of assets is allowed under Islam in a variety of ways. For example, a hotel could be sold by means of a cash sale to a willing buyer. Alternatively, if the hotel is owned by a company, the shares of that company can be sold instead. The price at which these shares change hands is a matter for the counterparties involved in the transaction to decide. Islam does not prohibit one from buying and selling assets, or certificates representing those assets, at an agreed price according to market conditions. Here is the contract of *bay al-sikak*, sale by document.

Contracts of Charity

Among the contracts of charity that one encounters in the literature on Islamic finance are the following:

Qard hasan, a goodly (interest-free) loan, is extended by a few Islamic banks to investment account customers, by others to needy and underprivileged borrowers such as students and the poor, or occasionally as business development loans for small enterprises. Loans with service charges operate on the same basis as for qard hasan, except that the former incur a service charge applied by a bank for the costs of administration. Service charges were deemed by the Jeddah based Council of the Fiqh Academy in 1986 as not bearing resemblance to interest as long as they are in an amount sufficient to defray administrative costs borne by the lender and no more. This is probably still a rather controversial decision in some quarters, since it may allow the banks to argue that wages are an administrative cost, leading to a situation in which employees of the bank earn a livelihood in the process of making loans of money. Such a payment, benefiting the one who lends money, is something that may well have been repugnant to Abu Hanifa, who refused even to stand in the shade of the canopy of a person to whom he had lent money, for fear that this small benefit might be riba.

It has been suggested by Abdul Gafoor in *Commercial Banking in the Presence of Inflation* (Apptec Publications 1998), that the bank can charge a fee if it is seen simply as a courier that delivers the money of depositors to borrowers. Here the bank is not a lender of its own money, but rather an agent of those who wish to lend their own money, interest free, and pay for so doing. This seems a theoretically coherent proposal, albeit one in which the commercial element of profit is hard to identify. How many lenders would wish to pay for the privilege of lending their money interest free? Many, perhaps. But enough to set up a profitable banking business? And if it is to be the borrowers rather than the lenders who pay the 'fees', aren't we entering into rather dangerous territory?

There is a striking similarity here with the arguments adopted in Christendom to justify the charging of fees on money transfers. John Noonan in *The Scholastic Inquiry into Usury* refers to Durandus of St. Pourcain who suggested in his *Commentariorium* that the state should set up a lending agency to fulfil the need for loans. Wages (not usury) could then be paid to the officials of that agency in respect of their work.

Noonan then discusses the use of 'virtual transportation charges' by the early bankers of Europe. The 'virtual' element of the bankers' fee arose when a client requested a banker to pay money in another city (by drawing a bill of exchange). Under these circumstances, according to Scholastics such as Biel in *Collectorium*, the banker could charge for his service even though physical transport of coin would not actually take place. In due course it would be argued that the transport of money through space was analogous to the transport of money through time, for which a percentage discount on the face value of the bill would be charged. Thus the practice of usury was legitimised.

Under the methodology employed in Islam, loans do not represent investments. A loan is an act of charity for which no material reward can be contracted at the outset. However, according to many scholars, a gift may be given at the end of the loan period as a sign of gratitude to the lender (so long as this gift is not pre-arranged). If an investment is to be made, it must be made on a profit-sharing basis not an interest-bearing basis.

As for *hiba*, gifts, according to *al-Ghazali* they are permissible provided that: a) no goods or services or other benefits are given or arranged to be given in return; b) the recipient has no administrative or state powers, lest a gift should be viewed as a bribe; and c) in the event that a gift constitutes haram property, it must returned, destroyed or given to charity.

A *waqf*, or charitable endowment, is established where a donor gifts an asset in perpetuity to some named cause, specifying that the usufruct of that asset only, not the asset itself, should be used for the charitable purpose. The endowment assets must be held in trust for the beneficiary and may not be sold by the trust. Furthermore, the assets must not be used as security for any other transaction. The trust manager is liable for mismanagement or negligence of trust assets.

Contracts of Investment

Under *musharakah,* all parties to a project contribute finance on a profit-sharing basis and have the right but not the obligation to exercise executive powers in that project. Musharakah can be established as *permanent musharakah* in which invested funds are not subject to repayment in the short term, or as *diminishing musharakah* where invested funds are repaid over time as profitability allows. Divestment terms are to be stated at the outset of the financing agreement. Permission from existing partners is required before raising fresh capital from other parties in which case the old partnership ceases and a new one is created comprising the newly increased number of partners. Where the partnership is not permitted to contract debts, in other words where all subsequent purchases are made for cash, then (negligence excluded) a partner's maximum loss is limited to the amount of his contribution to the total financing and losses are shared according to the financing share of each partner. All partners must contribute capital to the partnership, and profits may be shared in any ratio agreed between them.

According to Imam Hanifa, the contribution of capital to the musharakah is to be made in the form of cash. Imam Malik however argues that a non-cash contribution can be made provided that its cash value can be established prior to employment in the partnership. Thus, material contributions must first be valued or sold for cash before establishing the contributor's share in the partnership. This difference over musharakah arose upon the premise that where separately identifiable assets are employed, no pooling of assets can occur and thus no partnership in business can be established. Imam Shafi'i argues that fungible commodities can be contributed as non-cash capital, but not non-fungible items. Al-Ghazali also argues that pooling of assets must occur and that non-fungible contributions of capital are disallowed.

The above description of musharakah, based as it is upon a contribution of capital from each partner, is but one form of the partnership contract, namely the *sharikat al-inan.* Other varieties of partnership contract exist:

Sharika on the whole, according to the jurists of the provinces, is of four kinds: sharikat al-inan, sharikat al-abdan, sharikat al-mufawada, and sharikat al-wujuh. One of these is agreed upon, which is sharikat al-inan, though some of the jurists did not designate it with this term, and they also differed about some of its conditions ... The other three kinds are disputed and there is disagreement about some of their conditions among those who agreed about them generally.

ibn-Rushd: *Bidayat al-Mujtahid* (1996) p. 301

The *sharika al-abdan* is a partnership in work, in other words one in which the partners contribute their labour efforts but not monetary capital. Imam Hanifa and Imam Malik permitted it generally whilst al-Shafi'i prohibited it. *Sharika al-mufawada* is a partnership that exists where each partner appoints the others to act on his behalf in transacting with his whole wealth, whether present or not. Once again, Imams Hanifa and Malik generally permitted it whilst al-Shafi'i prohibited it. The *sharikat al-wujuh* is a partnership in which the partners contribute their credit-worthiness as support for the trading activities of the partnership. According to Shafi'i and Malik, this form of partnership is void.

Another form of partnership contract, termed *mudarabah* (sometimes referred to as *qirad*), arises in the Arabic language from the word *mudarib*, a user of others' capital. The mudarib contributes management input, itself viewed as a form of capital, to a productive process and can be regarded as an entrepreneur. Under mudarabah, an investor of funds (a *rabb al-mal*) contracts with a mudarib to enter into a business venture on a profit-sharing basis, giving the mudarib full control over the funds provided. Thus, the rabb al-mal is an investor of cash on a 'non-executive' basis. Once again, a ratio of profit-sharing between the mudarib and the investor is agreed at the outset of the project. Meanwhile, losses must be shared according to the financing share of each investor but the investor's maximum loss is limited to his share of the financing. With the permission of the rabb al-mal, the mudarib may contribute some of his capital to the project or raise fresh mudarabah capital from others. Importantly, the mudarib is not allowed to draw remuneration in any other form than profit-share. In the absence of a guaranteed wage, he has no recompense unless the project is profitable.

There is no disagreement among Muslims about the permissibility of Qirad. It was an institution in the pre-Islamic period and Islam confirmed it. They agree that its form is that the Qirad gives to another person capital that can be used in business. The Amil (user of capital) gets, according to conditions, some specified proportion of the profit, in other words any portion that is agreed, one fourth, one third, or even one half.

ibn-Rushd, *Bidayat al-Mujtahid* (1996) p. 284

Islamic partnership law is often seen as compatible with the modern day limited liability shareholding structure. There are indeed conceptual similarities. For example, shareholders in a modern corporation share the profits of that corporation among one another just as partners of a musharakah share the profits of their endeavours. However three important differences appear from a deeper inspection. As Professor Nyazee points out in his treatment of the topic (*Islamic Commercial Law: Partnerships*, 2000) some of the concepts applied in the Western limited liability structure are alien to Islam. These include the application of limited liability, the methods by which new shareholders may enter a corporation, and the absence of any proper application of the Islamic principle that the taking of risk brings with it a commensurate right to a sharing of financial rewards.

Professor Nyazee argues that if a company is seen as a legal entity in its own right, as indeed Western law does see it, then that entity has no share in the profits of the business since all profits belong to the shareholders. However, if there is a bankruptcy, the shareholders bear none of the loss. So the taking of risk and the sharing of reward certainly don't go hand in hand under this view of the limited liability company.

Following Sheikh an-Nabhani, the Hizb ut-Tahrir group promote the idea that unless existing partners to an investment give their permission, then the entry of new partners into the venture is not allowed. In many modern day corporations, there can be hundreds of thousands of shareholders, very few of whom know any other shareholders let alone exercise any management input in the corporation's activities. Any individual can become a shareholder by buying a share, an action that does not require the agreement of existing shareholders. Whilst in mudarabah the investors do appoint an entrepreneur to run the business, the modern corporation sees investors (the shareholders) isolated from the entrepreneur (loosely speaking, the board of directors) to such a degree that they can hardly be said to have appointed him (or them).

The argument proceeds that, in due course, a small but influential group of well connected shareholders (often corporations themselves) come to have influence over the selection of the board of directors, and hence the running of the business. In some bigger corporations, the large numbers of smaller shareholders are typically so fragmented and disorganised that their voting patterns cancel one another when any opportunity to vote presents itself. In this manner, their voices can safely be ignored for extended periods of time. Frequently, these investors are simply not given an accurate picture of what is going on at the management level. With distance and a lack of transparency in the relationship between executives and shareholders, one can understand how scandals such as that involving Enron in 2002 can arise.

The company is considered as a corporate entity, which has the right to sue and be sued in its own name in the courts. It also has its own residence and particular nationality (country of incorporation including where its head office may be registered). Neither a shareholder nor any member of its management, in his capacity as partner or in his personal capacity, fills its place. The only one who has this right is the one who has been authorised to speak on behalf of the company. The one who has the right of disposal is the company, i.e. the corporate personality, rather than the person who disposes directly. This is the stock company and it is a void company in Shar'a. It is one of the transactions that a Muslim is not allowed to participate in.

an-Nabhani, T., *The Economic System in Islam* (1997) p. 152

Other Forms of Contract

Our brief review of Islamic contract types would not be complete without a brief mention of *wakalah*, *rahn*, *wadia* and *daman*, whose application in the field of business is particularly common.

The concept of agency or *wakalah* in Islam is accepted. Hence an agent (the *wakil*) can be appointed, for a fee or not, in order to act in the name of the one who appoints him. The agent is to be seen as doing his employer's bidding and is not to be held liable for the actions that he implements in the normal course of his work. There are of course limitations upon agency. For example, one is not allowed to appoint an agent to performs one's prayer.

Rahn, a pledge of security, may be made provided that the pledge is irrevocable. The pledged item must be saleable in the event of default and maintenance of the pledged item falls to the holder of the pledged item.

A person who enters a contract of safe-keeping (*wadia*) for a deposit, holds that item in trust (*amana*). A trustee does not have to pay compensation in the event of unintended loss or damage to the item held in trust unless payment is received for the performance of the trust, in which case compensation is due. The costs of delivery from safe-keeping fall on the owner. Use of the deposited item by a third party can only occur with the permission of the depositor in which case some jurists insist that all resulting profits or losses accrue to the depositor. (This principle defines the basis upon which an Islamic current bank account is to be established as discussed in Chapter Seven.) The trustee cannot contract another trustee to undertake the safe-keeping of a deposited item without the permission of the owner. In the event of the trustee using the trust item in some manner without the owner's permission, any subsequent loss must be fully compensated by the trustee. Upon the demand of the owner, the deposited item must be returned by the trustee.

The contract of *daman* (which can be translated as surety, guarantee or warranty) exists in various forms. *Daman al-naqs* constitutes a liability to make up a loss and has been applied in Islamic banking as a guarantee against the loss of depositors' funds due to violation of contract on the part of the bank itself. *Daman al-talaf* is a guarantee to make up any loss to property whilst in the custody of the trustee, and *daman al-tarrud* is a warranty given against loss or damage caused to a third party by the sold item.

A Step Forwards or a Step Backwards?

Contracts of exchange such as murabahah, istisna and bay mu'ajjal have been adopted by many Islamic banks over recent years in order to serve a diverse range of commercial requirements. The farmer awaiting ripening of his crops is not the only one who would suffer were forward sales to be totally prohibited under Islam. For example, industrialists too take time to produce their output and an ability to enter into a made-to-order (istisna) contract is therefore of great use to them. However, a heated debate is now occurring within the world of Islamic finance because of the manner in which these various types of contract are being interpreted and employed, and because in practice Islamic financing has come to rely much more heavily upon contracts of exchange than contracts of investment.

The arguments for and against using contracts of exchange as a means of providing finance are not always clearly defined in the literature. Let us therefore clarify the issue at hand before proceeding. As we have seen, it is agreed among Islamic scholars that a businessman is allowed to share the profits of his business with an investor who finances that business. The investor and the businessman agree the proportions of future profit that they will each share prior to the commencement of business.

However, some commentators argue that profit-sharing does not satisfy all of the potential demands for financing in an economy. An individual wishing to buy a house usually buys that house to live in, not in order to make a monetary profit. So how would a Muslim raise the money to buy a house if that house never produces a profit which can be shared with a financier? The answer according to some is for the Islamic banker to use a contract of exchange, such as BBA, instead of a contract of investment.

Imagine, for example, that an individual approaches an Islamic bank having identified a house that he wishes to purchase from a builder. The banker agrees to buy the house from the builder on behalf of the individual at the market price of say £100,000, and then sells it to the individual for a price of £150,000 to be paid in instalments of £7,500 per year over twenty years. The 'mark-up' of £50,000 represents the banker's profit, not an interest charge, argue the Islamic bankers who practise this technique. The bank acts as a trader, they say, buying the house for £100,000 and selling it for £150,000. In this manner, a contract of exchange is used to provide the required finance to the house buyer.

Among the agreements that are normally required by the banker under a BBA contract is a 'promise to buy'. This promise would be given to the bank by the individual *before* the banker buys the house from the builder. Under this promise, the individual confirms that he will buy the house from the bank at an agreed date in the future. With the promise in its possession, the bank purchases the house from the builder and then sells it on to the individual immediately. The banker will usually take some form of security for repayment of the instalments, such as a charge over the house. This is the familiar process of taking collateral that we have reviewed in earlier chapters, and it allows the bank to sell the house in order to repay any outstanding instalments if the individual defaults on the repayments.

So far, there seems to be very little practical difference between the cash-flows paid under BBA (or ordinary murabahah) on the one hand and interest-based forms of finance on the other. An interest-based bank might also advance £100,000 to a borrower for the purchase of our hypothetical house, and require repayments of £7,500 per year for twenty years.

Often there is little noticeable *qualitative* difference between the two forms of finance. Islamic banks tend to take a charge over the house, just as interest-based banks do, and would be empowered to sell it in the event of the borrower's default, just as interest-based banks would be. In this manner, Islamic banks attempt to guarantee receipt of their mark-up to no less a degree than any interest-based bank would attempt to guarantee its interest charges under a conventional loan.

Some say that the difference between Islamic and conventional finance in this case is that, under Islamic finance, the house is transferred into the individual's ownership in the first instance instead of a cash loan of £100,000. Technically, this is indeed the case. There is no loan of money involved, rather a purchase of the house (by the bank from the builder) and a sale of the house (from the bank to the individual). Since no loan is involved, how can interest be involved? A conventional bank may indeed pay the loaned sum of money direct to the builder's account when financing a borrower at interest, but there the contractual documents do not reflect a purchase of the house by the bank. In the interest-based environment, the bank is acting as an agent of the borrower when making the payment of cash to the builder.

A big 'but' remains, for the practical impact of many Islamic banks' activities is that they contract an increase in their holding of money from the outset of a financing transaction, just as the conventional banks do. So does the method by which they fix this gain make the difference? In other words, is riba in the method, or in the result? If Islamic banks enacted murabahah of the traditional kind described in our review of contracts of exchange, there might be less controversy. It is however a different matter when a banker imposes 'promises to buy' or other contractual obligations upon the purchaser. When these techniques are employed, the least one can say is that the Islamic banker enters into the realm of what is doubtful. At worst, a money-for-money transaction has occurred, one which is split for presentational purposes into a money-for-goods transaction followed by a goods-for-money transaction.

If it can be shown that the Islamic bank's rate of return is fixed at the outset of the transaction, at the point at which money is first released by the bank to a counterparty, then the bank is charging riba. And if the bank is charging riba, the bank's counterparty (or set of counterparties as a whole) must be paying it.

Of course, BBA and murabahah contracts allow Islamic banks to compete with conventional banks in the sphere of interest-based lending. This competitive success has been accomplished simply by setting the murabahah mark-up in line with prevailing interest rates. As a result, not only do the cash-flows of modern Islamic financing contracts look like interest, they are also often set at the same level as market rates of interest.

Let us go back to the house, the builder and the individual for one moment, and look at the problem from a slightly different perspective. Now it is of course quite permissible under Islam for the individual to buy the house from a builder for £100,000 in cash and to occupy it more or less immediately. Alternatively, that individual might negotiate with the builder to pay instalments of £5,000 per year for twenty years. The same sale price would then be paid, £100,000, but over a twenty year period instead of in one lump sum up-front. Clearly, there is no interest involved here. In both cases the builder would make his profit, being the difference between the cost of building the house and the £100,000 sale price, and in both cases the individual would buy the house to live in under a valid contract of exchange.

Imagine now that the builder offers the house at £100,000 for up-front payment but at £150,000 for instalment payment over twenty years. If the buyer decides to go for the deferred payment option, does the extra £50,000 represent an amount of interest charged by the builder, or just a further amount of profit that the builder is trying to make? From the house buyer's perspective the deferred payment option produces cash-flows that are the same as those resulting where the house buyer borrows money at interest in order to buy the house without a mark-up. When the builder allows the buyer of the house to pay under deferred payments, the buyer will be in debt to the builder just as he would have been in debt to the bank. And just as the bank requires more in return than it gives, so does the builder. "My price is £100,000", says the builder, "but if you can't pay me now, take the house and pay me £150,000 later".

One of the forms of riba practiced in the 'days of ignorance' is related by Malik in his *Muwatta*. If a debt was due for payment, the lender would say to the borrower 'pay me the amount you borrowed from me, or pay it with an extra amount (i.e. interest) later'. If this procedure is prohibited, what of the builder who says 'pay me the price now, or the price plus an extra amount later'?

... they say 'Trade is like usury', but God hath permitted trade and forbidden usury.

Qur'an 2 : 274 to 275

Perhaps those who oppose BBA and murabahah are the 'they' that the Qur'an is referring to. Could it be that the practice of charging more for deferred payment is in fact permissible in Islam? Unfortunately, even some scholars disagree on this issue. For example, Imam Shafi'i is regarded as being favourably inclined towards the instalment sale of an asset at an increased price, whilst Imam Malik would seem to be against:

(1353)   It reached Malik that the apostle of Allah (may peace be upon him) prohibited two sales within a sale. [Professor Rahimuddin comments: It means that the seller tells the buyer 'I shall sell this cloth to you for Rs. 10 for cash or for Rs. 15 on credit'].

(1354)   It reached Malik that a person told another to buy a camel for him for cash and that he would buy it from him at an appointed time on credit. Abd Allah b. Umar considered it a bad kind of transaction and prohibited it.

(1355)   Qasim b. Muhammad was asked about the case of a man who purchased a thing for ten dinars on cash or for fifteen dinars at an appointed date on credit, and he considered it bad business and prohibited it.

Imam Malik : *Muwatta'*

It may be because there are few scholars with a detailed understanding of financial activities in the modern interest-based economy that a clear consensus is unavailable here. Without a consensus, criticisms of any one 'Islamic' financial product can be met quite easily with the assertion that it is only a matter of opinion as to whether that label is, in fact, warranted.

Some argue that if BBA is indeed a form of interest then a huge number of Muslim shopkeepers should be condemned for charging interest of 50% when selling their stock to customers at a mark-up of 50%. But, in a modern murabahah or BBA contract, the banker agrees to sell goods to his customer *before* purchasing them from a supplier (this of course being the purpose of the promise to buy). In contrast, a corner shop trader agrees to sell goods to a customer *after* buying those goods from a supplier. The corner shop trader takes the risk that no one will buy his stock. Islamic bankers don't take this risk if they can possibly help it.

What is clear and widely agreed in the above matter, is that the builder of our house charges a price which he is free to determine according to market conditions. He may offer this price for payment in any way that he sees fit, either cash up-front or payment by instalment. If his price is too high he may reduce it so that a willing buyer comes forward. The difference between the builder's cost and his selling price is then his profit. But once the selling price is agreed, if the builder then seeks to increase his price in recompense for a delay in receiving payment, he is now attempting to earn extra revenue due to the delay, which is riba.

With regard to the more difficult question of charging a higher price for deferred settlement, the current consensus position seems to be that the builder is offering to conduct a goods-for-money transaction, which as we have seen earlier in this Chapter cannot contain riba, and that Malik is in a minority with his opinion on this matter. An interest-based bank on the other hand is conducting a money-for-money transaction which involves a gain on the money loaned and which is therefore prohibited. So, whilst the builder is free to agree to increase or decrease his price depending upon the timing of payment, the bank is not free to agree to charge riba. The seller of goods on a deferred payment basis can charge however much he likes, more or less than the cash price.

Looking at things another way, if deferred payment at a mark-up is not allowed, then what of deferred payment at a mark-down? Can A not say to B, 'the price is £100,000 but if you buy right now I'll give you a discount of £10,000'? If this marking-down practice is allowed, then it will be valid for our builder to say 'my price is £150,000' and then tempt buyers who are able to make immediate cash payment with the offer of a £50,000 discount.

To the above consensus, I would like to contribute in what I hope is a constructive manner. I agree that deferred payment is clearly permissible in Islam, but in the absence of reliable evidence to the contrary and under current monetary circumstances, I propose that where promises to buy and other contractual devices are employed to close the loop between two money-for-goods transactions, deferred payment at a mark-up simply opens the door for interest-based banks to practise usury on the 'Muslim market'. Money for money with the house in between, as it were.

The brief description of forward market prices in Chapter One helps to explain. As shown there, it is an established principle in the conventional financial world that the forward price of a commodity in a trade is determined largely by the rate of interest over the period. (Recall that with interest rates at 5% per year, with the gold spot price at $400 per ounce and with storage costs at $1 per ounce per year, then the fair one year forward price for gold will be $421 per ounce. And with interest rates at 10%, given the same assumptions, the fair one year forward price of gold will be $441 per ounce.)

Thus we see how the very existence of interest can affect prices where payment is deferred. Most of the Islamic banking industry still depends on the existence of this difference between cash prices and forward prices. It is a difference that arises because of interest and in this sense the most commonly used Islamic banking techniques rely just as much upon the existence of interest as their conventional counterparts.

Hence, if Islamic bankers aren't actually practising usury their talk can sound suspiciously like it: I and my colleague encountered a statement from one Islamic bank in Malaysia during 1997 that the bank would be happy to provide funds through an Islamic debt arrangement at a finance cost of 9% per year. These are the words of the money lender, the language of usury. It is a language that modern banks, leasing companies and finance companies know well.

The debate over deferred payment at a mark-up arises because the bulk of the money that society is forced to use is manufactured by banks at interest. It will be difficult to resolve this debate unless it is first accepted that the problem arises in the monetary system itself. How can Islamic finance be practised with money that bears interest as a condition for its existence? Purge the system of money created at interest, and the forward price premium will largely disappear. The shadow of interest will no longer fall upon the real world of trading in goods and services.

The subject of deferred payment mark-up leads somewhat naturally into a discussion of the acceptability of debt trading in Islam, in particular because the two are linked in many discussions to the proposed existence of the time value of money. Since we have covered the rather weak conceptual basis of the time value of money in Chapter One, here we need only note its expression within modern Islamic financial markets.

As we saw in Chapter Two, the issuance of bonds by borrowers to lenders has been a common practice of large-scale financing for at least the last few centuries. The bond would stand in evidence of an amount of money loaned. The amount to be repaid by the borrower at the end of the loan period would be stated on the face of the bond (which is why it became known as the 'face value'). Part of the bond document would be divided by perforations into separate sections, each section known as a 'coupon'. When an interest payment became due, the holder of the bond was required to tear off the appropriate coupon and return it to the issuer in order to claim his payment. Eventually, the term 'coupon' became widely used to describe the interest rate (calculated as a percentage of the face value) on a bond.

A bond is said to be a 'zero-coupon bond' if no coupons (i.e. interest instalments) are due to the bondholder during the life of that bond. Investors therefore only buy zero-coupon bonds at a price that is below face value so that, when the bond matures, the difference between the purchase price and the face value is realised as a *gain of waiting*. The issuer of the bond guarantees to pay the face value to the bondholder at maturity, and in the event of default the bondholder often has the right to seize collateral.

In the early years of Islamic banking some uninformed commentators argued that zero-coupon bonds are 'Islamic' because no interest is paid during their lifetime. But of course interest is paid, it is just that it is paid all in one go at the maturity date instead of in instalments over the life of the bond.

Now imagine that each instalment due under a BBA is 'securitised', that is, turned into a tradable financial instrument. For example, each instalment to be received by the builder from the house buyer could be securitised into a zero-coupon bond with a face value of £7,500. These bonds can now be bought and sold and, if the builder decided to sell one of them, he would be selling a debt owed to him by the house buyer. And, if an investor purchased that bond at below face value, that investor would be contracting to make a gain of waiting. Thus, the instalment due from the house buyer at the end of year one could be securitised into a *one year* 'zero-coupon bond' with a face value of £7,500. If this bond was bought by an investor at the beginning of year one for £6,818, a gain of waiting of £682 would be achieved by holding the bond for one year. The two year zero-coupon bond might be bought by an investor at the beginning of year one for £6,200, giving a £1,300 gain of waiting over two years.

In Malaysia today, some Islamic finance deals are being concluded on more or less the basis described above. Among the projects so financed was the construction of the new Kuala Lumpur International Airport (KLIA). Here, the financiers purchased assets that the KLIA already owned, such as land and the rights to the future revenues to be generated once the airport is operational. Payment was made in cash for these assets, and the KLIA thereby raised the funds that it needed to continue its construction programme. Having bought the KLIA's assets, the financiers in this deal then immediately sold them back to the KLIA for payment in instalments over twenty years. The final step in this financing process was that the instalments were securitised into zero-coupon bonds and sold at below face value to investors.

... It is the largest such facility to be issued in Malaysia to date. The notes issuance facility is based on a deferred payment basis (Al-Bai-Bithaman Ajil) where the subscribers will buy from the KLIA Bhd assets such as the KLIA concession at an agreed purchase price. The assets will then be resold to KLIA Bhd at an agreed selling price, which comprises the purchase price plus a pre-determined profit-margin. The payment of the selling price by the KLIA Bhd is through the issuance of Islamic primary and secondary notes, also known as Islamic bonds or Syahadah Al-Dayn (Certificate of Debt)... Once again the facility will serve to strengthen the confidence of private debt securities (PDS) players in the Islamic debt instruments and interest free market in Malaysia.

Islamic Banker Magazine, London (March 1996)

Malaysian financial companies are currently rushing to make profits on the bandwagon of Islamic finance. This bandwagon has often been a source of embarrassment to those Islamic bankers who are asked to explain the difference between interest-based finance and the Malaysian Islamic alternative.

Among the inventions coming out of Malaysia in 1996 were Islamic short selling and Islamic debt discounting. Some encourage the development of these 'innovative' Islamic financial products on the basis that Islamic finance should be able to compete with the interest-based sector in order to establish itself. But this argument has little in common with the methodology of Islam. Islam does not teach one to overcome usury by competing with the usurer at his own game, nor does it instruct Muslims

to define an objective and then use what means they see fit in order to attain it. Instead we are obliged to ensure that the means are correct, so that the ends may look after themselves. Usury, like fornication, will never be permissible no matter what name or justification is given to it.
Allah's Messenger s.a.w. said, "A dirham which a man knowingly receives in usury is more serious than thirty-six acts of fornication."
Hadith: Tirmidhi, 2825

The trend towards compromise in Islamic banking is reinforced by the 'pragmatic' attitudes of many Muslim businessmen who work within it. Some are lacking in their understanding of Islamic financing principles, and therefore offer little resistance when instructed by clients to side-step them. Others say they are committed to building a genuine Islamic alternative, but are trapped in the mind-set of a western financial degree course. As for the many non-Muslims who work in the field of Islamic finance it is rather unfair to expect them to carry the flag of Islam on behalf of the Muslims.

Unfortunately, since theory often tends to follow practice in the business world, the danger arises that the definition of usury will come to depend upon what the bankers are practising. This is already happening in academic establishments where positive economists study the 'what is' rather than the 'what ought to be' of Islamic banking and finance. Yet after almost four decades of debate on the subject, no standard theory or statement of practice has emerged because so much of the industry is built upon inescapable contradiction and consistent fudging of the key issues.

In order to build Islamic banking and finance into something more than just conventional banking with the labels changed, Muslim bankers must first study and understand the history of banking in the West. The Islamic law on investment and commercial transactions has a wisdom that goes far beyond the mundane mechanics of sharing profits. Its impact would reach into the very heart of the monetary system. Copying the conventional system in order to 'compete' is one of the least helpful things that Islamic bankers can do. I believe that this approach will lead to compromise on the subject of usury, the fate that eventually befell Christianity.

In the Absence of Leverage

Our brief summary of contract types indicates that a Muslim entrepreneur may obtain the assets that he needs for his business in a variety of ways. For example, he can raise money under mudarabah or musharakah; he can hire the machines that he needs for a production process under a contract of ijara; and he can buy goods under a purchase agreement in which instalments are deferred until a future date when funds are more readily available.

Importantly, by basing his business upon contracts of exchange, the entrepreneur does not need to share the profits of his business in order to develop it. Hence, the Muslim entrepreneur is allowed to make his profits whilst hiring a labourer for a fixed wage under a contract of exchange. In the absence of interest, there is little to discourage commercial activity from continuing apace.

Economists were also taken to task for describing the Islamic economy as equity-based. This would give the wrong impression that all operations in an Islamic economy have to be based on equity-sharing only. It was pointed out that al-Qur'an prohibits riba and permits tijara and that the latter does not have to be equity-based always. Seen in this perspective it would seem that the Islamic economy is profit-based.

Islamic Research and Training Institute, *Developing a System of Financial Instruments* (1990) p. 11

Since Islamic contract law almost certainly prohibits the exchange of two liabilities from forming the basis for an exchange transaction, speculative purchases will only be possible if at least one counterparty to the trade is willing to exchange full countervalue up-front. Since fewer individuals will wish (or be able) to speculate if required to pay full countervalue up-front, speculative trades should decline in both value and number.

It is no longer possible, for example, to buy £100 of gold in the 'Islamic' forward market by paying only a £10 deposit up-front. This would be a typical form of 'margined' transaction employed by a conventional speculator in the hope of selling his gold at a profit before the balance of £90 becomes payable. A 10% increase in the gold price would then translate into a 100% profit on the deposit invested. The prohibition of this type of leverage, along with the prohibition upon short-selling, would anchor the Islamic financial market to the real economy.

The substantial eradication of leverage that is evident in the properly structured Islamic financial system would make conventional corporate finance theory largely redundant. In Chapter Four we saw how a typical modern corporation seeks to improve the rate of profit on the funds it has invested in its own business, through the mechanism of debt financing. The objective was achieved in that earlier example by borrowing money at 10% and subsequently investing it into assets from which a profit of 20% was made. Due to leverage, the owner made a profit of 110% on his own investment into the company. (It may benefit the reader to revisit that example before proceeding with the current argument.)

This last type of leverage, often termed 'gearing', is all-pervasive in the modern world. To my mind, it is also one of the greatest sources of economic injustice after the manufacture of money by the conventional banking system. The mechanism of gearing allows borrowers to own any amounts of profit that remain after the interest charges have been paid. Hence, lenders at interest do not receive a share of company profit proportional to the amount of money that they have loaned to an enterprise. In the example of Chapter Four, the lender provided 90% of the funds for the borrower's business but received only 45% of the profits made, in the form of interest earned. Meanwhile, the borrower provided 10% of the funds and earned 55% of the profit, in the form of growth in net assets.

To the layman it may seem that equity holders are playing a rather unfair trick upon interest-based lenders, but the professional financier will quickly respond that lenders are taking less risk than equity investors. Let us examine this argument a little further.

The risk argument is based upon the fact that, under modern law, interest is paid before dividends. Given that lenders are therefore more likely to receive their interest than equity investors are to receive their dividends, theorists argue that the former should be prepared to receive a lower rate of return on their investment than the latter. The possibility exists of course that a corporate borrower will not generate sufficient returns on assets to pay its interest charges but, for the market as a whole, this has been a short term phenomenon only. (If the phenomenon were to be true in the long run then every corporation would eventually go bankrupt.) In any event, we have already seen how lenders minimise this type of risk by taking as much collateral as possible. A second possibility is that the enterprise will earn just enough to pay its interest bill, but not enough to pay out any dividends to the equity holders. In this case, the lenders will receive their return on investment, but the equity holders will receive nothing. Again, lenders seem to undertake less risk than equity holders.

But the above justifications for lower returns to interest-based lenders ignore a third possibility which is by far the most commonly encountered in the world of large companies. The fact is that, in the long run, larger corporations in the interest-based economy generate returns on assets that exceed their interest costs in most periods. So much so that long term returns on a diversified portfolio of equity shares have *consistently* outperformed long term returns on a diversified portfolio of interest-based loans since the Second World War. This has been true in every major economy and over most time frames that one wishes to examine. Since these are the facts of life in the corporate world, then the risk that academics talk of when justifying lower returns to interest-based lenders seems to exist in the short run only.

If equity holders receive higher returns than interest-based lenders in the long run, then it seems that it is the interest-based lenders who are in fact taking the most risk. Theirs is a risk, proven by long term experience, that interest-based investments will under-perform those of equity-based investors.

In the interest-based system, it is the convention under which money is invested that in part accounts for the level of reward which it receives. Meanwhile, in the Islamic approach, investment is rewarded in line with its contribution to profitability after the fact. Rather than rewarding invested capital according to the level of risk that is perceived at the outset, Islamic principles require that capital is to be rewarded according to the profitability with which it has actually been employed.

Gearing becomes impossible under Islam unless the debt financier is prepared to advance an interest-free loan. However, it is difficult to see why even Muslim investors would advance their funds as interest-free loans to a profit-seeking corporation on any significant scale. Unless some form of charitable project was involved, it would be far more common for them to advance their funds on a profit-sharing basis. Since interest-free loans are unlikely to form a significant part of the capital for a profit-seeking corporation, and since interest-bearing loans are totally prohibited, the opportunity for gearing in the Islamic economy is suppressed.

Under the conventional approach to financing, the choice of debt to equity ratio revolves largely around the level of confidence attached to the business venture under consideration. If the entrepreneur is confident of a return on assets of say 20% per annum, the incentive to fund this opportunity using debt at 10% is far more attractive than a profit-sharing alternative. Why share a 20% profit when one can borrow at 10% interest? But where the businessman is involved in a highly uncertain venture, debt might in fact seem less preferable than equity. Saiful Rosly, in a paper presented at the *Dual Banking Conference, Kuala Lumpur,* (1995) comments :

Thus, the use of debt and financial leverage concentrates the firm's business risk on its stockholders. ... Would mudarabah and musharakah be a viable product worth investing in today? Certainly not in Malaysia. This is because firms will opt for equity when projects are highly risky and push for debt if profit-making is a question of capital alone ... more so in a world where business can make a choice between debt and equity supported by tax laws not in favour of mudarabah and musharakah banking.

Rosly also reminds us that in modern economies there are tax advantages to interest-based funding that do not apply to equity funding. This, combined with the fact that lenders do not under normal circumstances have the right to vote on company policy, makes debt a still more attractive form of corporate financing. Fahim Khan summarises:

... if the profit-sharing system is better than the interest-based system then why does it not prevail over the interest-based system and drive the interest-based system out of practice ... If the interest-based option is permissible, the demand for investable funds will tend to be mainly for projects which are low return or more risky, with entrepreneurs financing high return or low-risk projects from their own funds. Suppliers of funds, aware of this tendency, will find it easier to charge interest rather than make the effort of finding or selecting the more profitable projects ... Only when the option of interest-based financing has been totally abolished will the profit-based system be able to prove all its merits described in the literature.

Fahim Khan : *Essays in Islamic Economics* (1995) p. 177

The practice of gearing tends to produce a bias in commercial activity that Umar Vadillo in *The End of Economics* refers to as 'business gigantism'. Because greater gearing increases the returns on an entrepreneur's own capital, firms are encouraged to borrow money in order to expand the size of their operations. Economies of scale often allow the larger firms to out-compete their small-scale rivals. Furthermore, larger firms often have more borrowing power than smaller firms and can therefore consolidate their domination of an industry sector by smothering new competition. Gradually, the small scale, familiar, community strengthening business is replaced by the massive, anonymous, community destroying alternative. Employer-employee structures dominate under this gigantic system, in contrast to the traditional owner-proprietor-apprentice structure of the small enterprise. The baker who once owned and operated his village shop now works as a disinterested employee of a large supermarket in a gigantic 'out-of-town' shed. The small builder who once built individually designed houses of character now works as a sub-contractor to a massive property development company, erecting characterless swathes of look-alike houses. With all these disinterested employees about, rules and regulations now become commonplace. People whose heart is not in their work have to be monitored, given performance targets, and provided with booklets that tell them how to perform even the smallest aspects of their work.

The supposed benefits that society derives from the operation of this system are highly questionable. The products that are offered to us today are in many cases of an inferior quality to those of the past. As Michael Rowbotham remarks, most of us remember how long our parents' household appliances lasted. In many cases they are still with us. But buy a kettle or a lawnmower or an alarm clock today and see how long it lasts you. Product quality has not always benefited from progress, and if we are told that it is too expensive to produce the quality of yesteryear, then why are we so frequently reminded that society is becoming wealthier?

For most people, the idea of increasing choice also falters upon close inspection. On the surface all appears well. If one takes a short walk down the British high street in search of a mobile phone, there are many shops to choose from. In early 2003, I found Curry's, Dixon's, PC World and The Link offering mobile phones locally. Healthy competition? Not at all. These shops are all owned by the same holding company. Perhaps someone should tell those kind development economists at the World Bank that even in their own backyard the competitive market isn't a reality.

The interest based establishment has today spread its philosophy throughout Western society. It has obtained for itself tax advantages (the tax deductibility of interest does not extend to dividends), extraordinary powers of legal recourse to borrowers' assets, media influence (often by means of very generous advertising budgets), and political influence (many governments cannot survive in the absence of regularly renewed commercial bank lines of credit). But perhaps worst of all is the infection of the academic system by the hand of modern banking. By this means controversy has been manufactured on the topic of money creation where no controversy is due. The practice of leverage, the mechanism that produces so much demand for bank money, has simultaneously been promoted as a key ingredient of any 'good' financing strategy. Today it is taught at colleges and universities everywhere.

Even our children are not spared the barrage of propaganda in favour of existing arrangements. This ranges from the indirect and subtle (the establishment of mini-banks in British schools by National Westminster Bank during the 1990's, for example) to the more direct promotion of pro-banking ideas such as the following:

The HSBC Money Gallery at the British Museum attracted millions of visitors after its formal opening in 1997. A 'Resource Pack for Teachers' was created to help teach the history and value of money to students; and, to facilitate distance learning for those unable to visit the gallery, a CD-ROM, The World of Money, will be released in June 1998. The book, Money: a History, will soon be available in Korean, Japanese, French and German, and the children's book, The Story of Money, is being reissued in paperback and in Danish.
1997 HSBC Group Annual Report

Although no sane person would think of commissioning a known thief to write a manual on home security, we have alas reached the stage where banks are being allowed to write the history of money. If it is true that the victor writes the history, perhaps we can conclude that the bankers have won the world.

Chapter seven

BANKING AND MONEY UNDER ISLAM

An Islamic banking structure is outlined here. The system relies upon profit-sharing and the eradication of fractional reserve banking. It allows investment and other financial activities to continue in line with the demands of both modern life and the principles of Islam. 'Monetary policy' becomes largely redundant under this approach. The chapter concludes with a brief discussion of money in Islam and it is proposed that Islamic banking, in conjunction with a precious metal currency standard, would form the basis of a fair and stable wealth creating economy.

An Islamic Commercial Banking Structure

From the discussions of Chapter Two emerges an Islamic banking system that differs greatly from the present incumbent. The current account would work on the basis of *wadia*, being a deposit of funds that is available for immediate withdrawal. A 100% reserve ratio would apply to this account. A service charge could be applied to these accounts so as to remunerate the deposit-taker for the costs of administration. Normal withdrawal and transfer facilities would apply in order to effect an efficient payments system and deposit-takers could compete on both service charges and the quality of services available. Monzer Kahf in *The Islamic Economy* (1978), and S. M. Yusuf in *Economic Justice in Islam* (1971) both support the adoption of these measures in conjunction with the abolition of interest.

Some writers argue that the deposits under current account could be used by the banks to advance interest-free loans, though under the wadia injunction this could only occur with the permission of the depositor. There would of course be little to prevent a bank offering a form of current account in which funds deposited were explicitly made use of in such a way, but in this case two essential restrictions would remain. Firstly, deposits would be available for immediate withdrawal only if liquidity was available and, secondly, any risk arising from the on-lending of funds would accrue to the depositor.

Investment accounts would operate in a different manner. Here, the bank could act as the depositor's agent and investment advisor and charge a flat fee for providing its advisory and agency services. Alternatively, it could act as a mudarib and invest the investment account funds in return for a share of the profits. For example, the bank could offer potential depositors an 80% share of profits on investments, the remaining 20% accruing to the bank. The *share* of profits due to the depositor and the banker on an investment account would be agreed prior to the depositing of funds.

Nejatullah Siddiqi in *Banking Without Interest* (1988), proposes a two-tier arrangement as the basis of operation for investment accounts, one tier being the depositor-bank relationship and the other the bank-business relationship. Each of these tiers could operate on either of the two profit-sharing principles of mudarabah or musharakah but other forms of investment, into leasing contracts for example, would provide the banks with a variety of opportunities to earn diversified returns on investment account funds.

Over time, different banking institutions would experience various degrees of profitability on their investments. They would thereby establish a track record, on the strength of which customers might be more attracted to one bank than another. The expertise of each bank in investing the investment account funds would thus be vital to that bank's reputation among depositors and banks would also be able to compete with one another by offering more attractive profit shares to potential depositors and borrowing clients. The bank would be free to invest funds deposited in any manner countenanced by the terms of the investment account contract and would naturally be incentivised to find the most profitable investment opportunities available. Banks, in depending upon the profitability of their fund-using clients, would be encouraged to maintain a close business relationship with them. The bankrupting of a struggling business client in order to retrieve liquidity would almost certainly be a rarer occurrence.

Deposit guarantees for investment accounts are incompatible with the system described above. A guarantee to return 100% of the funds invested contravenes the principles established under mudarabah and musharakah, since a loss for the investor could not then arise even if the funds had been invested by the bank in an unprofitable manner. However, with regard to the current accounts, we have seen that the deposit-taker is responsible for the item deposited where a fee is charged. It would not seem to be outside the scope of Islamic law to implement a deposit guarantee on these current accounts, enacted perhaps through a suitable (i.e. charitably constituted) industry-wide mutual insurance contract. Muhammad Siddiqi, Irhad Ahmad and Ahmad Najjar all support a deposit insurance scheme for current accounts, operated under the aegis of the central bank. However, where a 100% reserve system operates, it is difficult to see what events could trigger a payout under current account deposit insurance, other than loss through fire or theft perhaps.

Otherwise, our previous arguments leave us with little choice but to view deposit insurance as a child of the fractional reserve banking system. When depositors are told that their deposits are available for withdrawal in the short term, but those deposits are simultaneously lent out under long term loans, the familiar liquidity problems can begin. The United States Savings and Loan crisis is a case in point. Alan and Gale point out in The London School of Economics Discussion Paper No. 191, July 1994:

The Savings and Loan crisis of the 1980's illustrates some of the limitations of the US financial system in terms of its intergenerational risk sharing capabilities. The S&L's had made long term loans at low interest rates which were funded with short term deposits. When market rates rose, depositors withdrew their funds and put them in instruments such as money market mutual funds. As a result many S&L's became insolvent and had to be rescued by the government. The transfers from taxpayers that were required are a form of intergenerational transfer since they were funded by government debt which will have to be borne by future generations. Thus government insurance of bank deposits can be regarded as a form of intergenerational risk sharing.

The Japanese banking system has in recent times shown quite clearly the scale of the problems that deposit insurance would have to cope with in the event of large scale bank failures in the conventional system. Given the scale by which bank money dwarfs state money in the modern economy, no amount of private insurance could fund the requests for withdrawal of cash in a large scale banking collapse. Writing in *The Independent* in August 1995, Helen Dunne and Robert Guest comment:

Panic-stricken depositors in Japan yesterday rushed to withdraw more than 100 billion Yen (£650 million) from Kizu Shinyo Kumiai, the country's largest credit association, after the authorities suspended its operations and announced a restructuring of the Hyogo Bank, the 38th largest.

Kizu's collapse was the fourth collapse of the year, loaded with bad debts exceeding 600 billion Yen (£3.9 billion) largely in the form of non-performing property loans. Meanwhile, Hyogo bank had collapsed with more than 1.5 trillion Yen (almost £10 billion) in bad debts, forcing a financial rescue on the part of the Japanese government.

Such options were not however available to Argentina during 2001. Argentina had achieved the semblance of monetary stability for several years by borrowing dollars from foreign lenders in order to support its otherwise overvalued exchange rate on the international markets. With a "currency peg" to the US dollar in place, arbitrageurs borrowed dollars abroad at low interest rates in order to convert them to pesos and lend to Argentine borrowers at higher interest rates. When confidence in the currency peg became weak, the process reversed as arbitrageurs sought to convert their peso loans back into US dollars before the peso was devalued on the foreign exchanges. Successive IMF loans were made to the Argentine government, but the dollars thus borrowed were quickly used to meet interest repayments on the country's growing foreign debt or used on the foreign exchanges an attempt to defend the currency peg. The beneficiaries of this exercise were often foreign investors who were spared the cost of a currency loss on their peso loans, or the costs of a default on loan repayments. Unsurprisingly, the IMF loans were therefore seen in many quarters as a crude bail out for the financial community. The cost of the bail out, however, will ultimately be borne by the Argentine people who now have to repay the massive dollar debt in the face of recession and social chaos. (Mr. Mahatir is one of the few leaders not to have been trapped in this manner.)

It is alien to the Islamic principles proposed here that risk should be shared by those who have no potential to benefit from the taking of that risk. Alan and Gale see no need to cure the monetary illness and argue that future generations would be willing to pay a price in order to inherit a stable financial system instead of a collapsed one. Only twisted logic can provide us with such a selfish conclusion. Should we really expect our children to pay the price of our own unnecessary failures?

In the Islamic banking model, depositors seeking withdrawal from current accounts could be repaid fully, immediately, with no reason for panicky bank-runs and without the support of the central bank or a deposit insurance scheme. Meanwhile, deposits in Islamic investment accounts would be invested with entrepreneurs under profit-sharing or rental contracts, not on a fixed-interest basis. Investors would know this, and could take the risk or leave it. There might be no pre-agreed time scale for redemption of investment accounts as this would depend wholly upon the liquidity of the bank's portfolio. If users of funds were not in a position to repay the bank, the bank would not be in a position to repay the investment account holders. (Hence the importance placed by many commentators upon providing securitised financial products to the Islamic banking sector. With tradable investment certificates forming a substantial part of an Islamic bank's asset portfolio, such investments could quickly be sold on a stock exchange to raise cash. Investment account holders wishing to withdraw their funds could then quickly be repaid).

In structuring an investment account, an Islamic banking institution would most usually manage the funds received without showing them as an item on its own balance sheet. The principle is that the funds do not belong to the Islamic institution itself, but are simply managed by it on behalf of depositors. These funds are therefore held 'off-balance-sheet', appearing merely as a note to the Islamic bank's main accounts. Where investment accounts are concerned, Islamic banks can therefore be seen as having more in common with investment companies than conventional banks.

The reluctance of the Bank of England, for example, to issue banking licences for Islamic banks immediately becomes clear. A bank cannot fulfil the requirements of the UK Banking Act 1987 to repay deposits at 100% of the original amount deposited, or above, (i.e. to offer 'capital-certain' accounts) if those funds are simultaneously invested on a profit-sharing basis. Profit-sharing implies the possibility of loss-sharing, and guarantees against investment losses contravene the injunctions of Islamic investment techniques. The difficulty in establishing an Islamic bank in the UK and other western countries has revolved partly around this conflict with existing regulations.

A marketing campaign to attract deposits into an Islamic investment account could of course meet a sceptical response from those depositors who are accustomed to placing funds in conventional banks. After all, deposits in a conventional bank are not supposed to be at risk of falling in value. And of course an Islamic current account that pays no return at all is at a commercial disadvantage when compared with a conventional current account that pays interest. Muslims depositing their cash into an Islamic bank current account will have to be reminded that if they expect their funds to be kept safe in the bank, then the bank cannot simultaneously be investing them and therefore there cannot be a gain for the depositor. This of course is the marketing hoop through which the conventional bankers jumped all those centuries ago. They told depositors that their funds were safe in the bank and available for immediate withdrawal, and at the same time they told borrowers that loans were being made out of depositors funds. Both statements could not be true at the same time.

As we have seen in Chapter Six, Islamic banks tend to invest their depositors' funds into BBA and murabahah where investment periods are short, returns are fixed and competitive with market interest rates. For example, in its 1994 accounts, the Faysal Islamic Bank of Bahrain had total assets of US$ 439 million of which US$ 235 million was due to mature in less than three months and a further US$ 81 million nine months afterwards. In reality, profit-sharing contracts such as mudarabah and musharakah do not remotely match the volumes of murabahah and BBA transactions.

I have discussed in some detail, in Chapter Four, why it is that lenders on a fixed interest basis usually require a cushion of collateral from the borrower before proceeding with a loan. Under the Islamic alternative, collateral is also quite permissible, but not as security for a pre-defined repayment schedule. Instead, if a project makes a loss, the investor's stake will diminish in value but collateral can still be used to secure this now reduced amount.

As a result of implementing the banking structures described so far, I propose that there would be a far weaker tendency for Islamic banks to base financing decisions on the existence of collateral. Since funds advanced would provide a return that depended upon the project's profitability, banks will be less keen to advance funds on the basis of existing collateral. This is because collateral seizure would no longer be an option whereby a pre-defined rate of return could be achieved. In contrast to the lending policy of conventional banks that was highlighted in Chapters Two and Four, finance would be made available more on the basis of potential profitability and less on the basis of the amount of collateral on offer. With the institution of zakat in place, a banking system of this type would ensure to a much greater degree that wealth did not circulate simply among the rich of the community.

Under an Islamic banking system it should now be clear that the 'cost of funds' disappears from the liability side of a bank's balance sheet. (If Islamic bankers talk about the 'cost of funds', then one can be reasonably sure that they have not escaped from the mentality of interest). A cost of funds could however be calculated in retrospect, this being a cost that reflected business profitability from an accounting perspective. In the Islamic economy, it would be the real sector that determined the rate of return to the financial sector.

Siddiqi maintains that creation of bank money (he refers to the process using the standard terminology of 'credit creation') can still feature under an Islamic banking system, but that it would be controlled and directed to useful purposes:

In the absence of interest ... bank advances would be made only for the purpose of productive enterprise. Credit would be created only to the extent there exist genuine possibilities of creating additional social wealth through productive enterprise. ... Credit created on the basis of profit-sharing would not be inflationary in the long run. Demand for profit-sharing advances will be limited by the extent of the available resources and banks' ability to create credit will be called into action only to the extent of this demand, subject to the constraint imposed by profit expectations that satisfy the banks. Supply in this case would not be able to create its own demand as it does at present.

Siddiqi, M. N., *Issues in Islamic Banking* (1983) p. 55

I differ with Siddiqi on this last point. There are often no limits upon the demand for bank credit, as any property speculator will tell you during a boom. And since banks can create huge amounts of credit at no cost, the supply side often has little to restrain it either. Of course, there is nothing wrong with credit per se, rather the problem has arisen because of a confusion between the words 'credit' and 'money'. The businessman who sells goods to a customer for payment within thirty days has advanced credit ('non-bank credit' to be precise) but has not created money in the process. Hence, while I am in disagreement with his view on money supply expansion, I would agree that:

The institution of credit and bank money has been another object of scrutiny by the Islamic economists. Early writers saw something morally wrong in it. Some doubted its need and ascribed its proliferation to the vested interests of the banks. More recently it has been realised that interest is the villain of the peace. Abolition of interest will, to a large extent, curtail the harmful features of the creation of credit by banks.

Siddiqi, M. N., *Issues in Islamic Banking* (1983) p. 19

Without the ability to charge interest, the banks would find no profit in creating money. In aggregate, profit and loss sharing investment involves the re-distribution of an existing pool of money, not a growth in that pool. Here, if the economy holds $500 of money supply at the beginning of an investment period, then it is not necessary that more than $500 exists in order for profit-sharing investors to be repaid at the end of that period. But where the $500 of money supply is constituted as bank money, loaned to businesses at 10% interest for one year, then $550 is required to repay the loan at the end of the year. In the long run, therefore, there is little point in creating money if one cannot also charge interest. Why create $500 for lending today, if there will only be $500 tomorrow from which to make repayment? This one fact exposes the fallacy of an Islamic banking system that, like its conventional counterpart, creates money out of nothing yet pretends to be based upon the principle of profit-sharing.

Having identified monetary fluctuations as the most important cause of inflation and deflation in the modern economies, it should also be made clear that an economy operating upon Islamic principles would not itself be excluded from specific forms of asset price increase or decrease. (Note that an asset price increase is not necessarily evidence of inflation because inflation is the term given to a general rise in the level of prices across an economy and not to a price rise in a specific sector.) For example, an increase in demand for air travel might result in an increase in ticket prices. However, if this occurred at the expense of demand for coach travel, then the general level of prices would tend to remain stable because coach ticket prices would decline. Where there is no monetary expansion, general rises in expenditure across the economy tend not to occur (although inflation may increase despite a stable money supply if the velocity of circulation of money increases). The point here is that Islam does not wage war on specific forms of price movement. In fact price flexibility is a vital component of a healthy economy since, without the operation of a price signal, demand cannot so easily be satisfied when and where required.

It is often asserted that a booming economy must bring with it inflationary pressures. The reason that conventional economists make such assertions is that economic booms are often the consequence of a substantial money supply expansion. The boom comes first and the inflation later. But in the Islamic economy envisaged in this work, production would normally increase without money supply expansion as the prime cause. Real factors, improvements in technology and a better educated workforce for example, would achieve this result. Production would increase in a gradual fashion since genuine human endeavour does not often bring results overnight, and certainly does not do so with the immediacy of money manufacture.

The argument that money supply needs to grow in order to facilitate increased trade is by no means proven. For example, in the absence of money supply expansion, an abundance of new goods might result in the general level of prices declining. This outcome has been modelled by Robert Barro in his well regarded 1979 paper (see: *Barro, R., Money and the Price Level Under the Gold Standard, The Economic Journal, March 1979*). The impact of long term price decreases accompanied by growth in productive output is so contrary to the theories and experience of the interest-based economy that its probable impact upon society as a whole can only be guessed at. It is worth mentioning that a society in which prices were expected to fall over time might not value present consumption more highly than future consumption. Why buy a car today when waiting a year will get you a cheaper price and perhaps a better quality car? Patience would be rewarded and consumerism discouraged in the Islamic economy.

An interest-free Money Supply

Whenever the suggestion is made that society should return to the use of gold and silver as a monetary medium, critics tend to provide one or more of the objections that were reviewed and rejected in Chapter Three. From a purely technical perspective, many of those arguments were seen as naive. However, when revealed knowledge is taken into account by a Muslim, some of those arguments become still less acceptable. Among them is the idea that Islamic injunctions are now old fashioned and should be somehow updated. Of course 'old fashioned' does not mean 'no longer relevant'. The Qur'an and Sunnah are old but they will be relevant for the rest of time. That is why there is no need for further revelation. Therefore, a Muslim should never say that it is wrong to use gold and silver as currency. If the Prophet s.a.w. used them, it cannot be wrong.

I envisage a monetary system in which everyone has the right to produce money, not just the banks and the state. At its most basic, all the people need do under this new monetary system is 'go out and dig for it'. Then, if the amount of gold obtained by digging is more than the amount of gold spent in doing the digging, the people will produce money. This is the simple, market-driven mechanism for the supply of money that was held by the early Classical economists of England. It is a system that tends towards price stability, that has nothing to do with interest, nor with the arbitrary creation of money for no effort. And if people want to dig for platinum, let them. Or if one man feels that another will accept oil as payment, let him produce oil. The role of the State under such a system would be to verify weights and measures, and to ensure compliance with accepted standards.

When the people have true freedom in their choice of money, when there is no law of legal tender to force their choice and no system of usury to create an artificial demand for bank money, then history shows that the people will tend to choose gold and silver as money. This is because Allah has created man with a love for these two commodities:
Alluring to men is the love of things they covet - women, sons, hoarded treasures of gold and silver, highly bred horses, cattle and land.
Qur'an 3 : 14

Allah has created everything for a purpose, and for ibn Khaldun the purpose of gold and silver is to act as money.
God created the two mineral stones gold and silver as the measure of value for all capital accumulations. Gold and silver are what the inhabitants of this world, by preference, consider treasure and property to consist of. Even if, under certain circumstances, other things are acquired, it is only for the purpose of ultimately obtaining gold and silver. All other things are subject to market fluctuations, from which gold and silver are exempt. They are the basis of profit, property and treasure.
Ibn Khaldun, *The Muqaddimah* (1967) p. 313

The banker economists would like us to believe that money is a development of later times, to believe that when man became more advanced he likewise invented a more advanced monetary system. If society accepts this story, it will be that much easier for banks to invent the monetary system that fits their profit motive, a system based on any token piece of paper or electronic data they care to create. Just like all good secularists, they promote a man-made system in place of the God-given one. According to an athar of Kab (quoted by ibn Abu Shayba in *al-Musanaf* and referred to by As-Suyuti in *Al-Fatawi al-Hawi: Kitab al-Buyu*), it was Adam a.s. who minted the first gold dinar. If this is true, then money is not at all an invention of later times.

The Companions were well acquainted with the defined weights of the dinar and dirham. When coins were used as payment they would be weighed *not* counted, because the weight of metal constituted the value of the payment, *not* the number of coins.

We have seen in Chapter Three how the English pound came to be debased and how the people came to pay for goods and services with a token of value instead of value itself. By their debasements, the Kings began the crucial transition from money as a commodity exchanged under free subjective valuation, to money as a token imposed by force of law.

With the advent of modern banking, the transition was completed. The bankers produced something of no intrinsic value, a piece of paper, and gave it the name "one pound". They encouraged the people to use this valueless thing, for in so doing they could profit immensely by lending at interest money that they had produced at almost no cost. But the people have always preferred gold and silver to paper. So the bankers demeaned the state's metallic money and promoted their own paper in its place.

Today they spend millions in promoting 'direct debit', encouraging us by this means to use bank money instead of state money, in turn reducing the level of cash reserves necessary to operate safely, and thus achieving ever more profitable deposit multipliers. In the UK, it was illegal for a private individual to purchase gold bullion for much of the twentieth century. Similarly so in the United States following Roosevelt's devaluation of the dollar in 1934. Such prohibitions of what Allah has allowed, like allowances of what He has prohibited, should alert the knowledgeable Muslim that something in the system has gone badly wrong.

Some time after the death of the Prophet Muhammad s.a.w., the monetary standard of the Muslims came to comprise a dinar weighing some 4.25 grams of gold and a dirham weighing some 2.98 grams of silver. At the prices of early October 2002 we can value a dinar at approximately US$50 and a dirham at approximately US$0.50. This valuation exercise provides one useful but often neglected context against which ahadith can be read. If gold and silver were used as a measure, the prices of Makkah and Madinah 1400 years ago would not be far out of place today. I am grateful to Dr. Yasin Dutton for bringing to my attention one of the more striking of these monetary comparisons, the first among others that I have gathered below.

`Urwa related that the Prophet gave him one Dinar so as to buy a sheep for him. 'Urwa bought two sheep for him with the money. Then he sold one of the sheep for one Dinar, and brought one Dinar and a sheep to the Prophet. On that, the Prophet invoked Allah to bless him in his deals. So 'Urwa used to gain (from any deal) even if he bought dust.
Hadith: al-Bukhari, 4. 836

In the United Kingdom today, a sheep can still be purchased for the equivalent of one dinar in Sterling and, if one searches long enough, it is sometimes possible to purchase two sheep at such a price. No form of paper money has ever held its value so well (the reader may wish to revisit the statistics on page 76).

Narrated by Aiman "I went to 'Aisha and she was wearing a coarse dress costing five Dirhams ...
Hadith: al-Bukhari, 3.796

... Then that camel surpassed the others thenceforth. The Prophet said, "Sell it to me." I replied, "It is (a gift) for you, O Allah's Apostle." He said, "Sell it to me. I have bought it for four Dinars and you can keep on riding it till Madinah ...
Hadith: al-Bukhari, 3.504

... giving them [the two dirhams] to the Ansari, He (s.a.w.) said: Buy food with one of them and hand it to your family, and buy an axe and bring it to me ...
Hadith: Abu Daud, 1637

... Some men said, "If one wants to buy a house for 20,000 Dirhams ...
Hadith: al-Bukhari, 9.109

At first, the early Muslims adopted Sassanian silver coins but in 79AH a native silver dirham was issued that was to be used throughout the Umayyad period. Prior to this, in 77AH, a gold dinar based on the common Byzantine mithqal was issued. A key function of the state was to provide quality assurance on the purity and weight of minted coins.

In al-Maqrizi's *Risalatu fi'l-Nuqud al-Islamiyyah* (Book on Islamic Money), it is argued that Islam never countenanced the use of copper money, *fulus*, as a medium of exchange. Copper did not, according to al-Maqrizi, bear the required features of a true monetary unit. In *Ighathah* Al-Maqrizi blames the substantial increase in the circulation of token copper coinage (the *dirham of account*) under the Mamluk sultans in Egypt for the rise in prices of agricultural commodities. He contrasts this state of affairs with previous periods of high prices that were caused by poor harvests (in other words, by 'real' rather than 'monetary' factors). The excessive issue of the dirham of account is clearly evidenced by the fall in its exchange value against the gold dinar, from 38:1 in 803 AH, to 150:1 in 808 AH (1406 CE). Al-Maqrizi summarises:

Know - May God grant you eternal happiness and felicity - that the currency that has become commonly accepted in Egypt is the fulus ... This is an innovation and a calamity of recent origin. It has no root among any community that believes in a revealed religion, nor any legal foundation for its implementation. Therefore its innovator cannot claim that he is imitating the practice of any bygone people, nor can he draw upon the utterance of any human being. He can only cite the resultant disappearance of the joy of life and the vanishing of its gaiety; the ruination of wealth and the annihilation of its embellishments; the reduction of the entire population to privation and the prevalence of poverty and humiliation ...The price of one irdab of wheat reached 450 dirhams of account ... a watermelon in season sold for 20 dirhams of account ... one chicken egg [for] 2 dirhams of account ... one ratl of pears [for] over 50 dirhams of account ... Anyone who considers these prices in the light of the rate of gold and silver will realize that they have increased only slightly, but if he considers them in relation to the abundance of the fulus that has afflicted the people, he will find that this is a frightening abomination that is too odious to mention.

al-Maqrizi, Ahmad ibn Ali, *Ighathah*, tr. Adel Allouche, (1994) p. 77 - 79

Al-Maqrizi's description of the impact of a monetary illness upon the economic and social environment of his time could easily be applied today, when a similar monetary illness afflicts us. What gaiety is there for a society that is forced to focus so much of its effort on the repayment of debt, or on protecting itself against the repeated ravages of inflation and deflation?

Whilst copper fulus may not be as 'alluring to men' as gold coins, I believe that the most important condition to be fulfilled if it is to be used as money is that a token value should not be given to it. Rather, every coinage should be allowed to find its own value in the marketplace through the exchange of goods and services. In other words, if Person A agrees with Person B to exchange ten ounces of copper for a chicken, no mechanism should be allowed to interfere with this exchange transaction. Certainly, a piece of copper weighing one ounce should not legally be imposed as a medium for that transaction. Though such an imposition may initially seem far-fetched, it is the very mechanism that turned an English pound of silver into a piece of paper with the word "one pound" printed upon it. Ibn-Taimiyah would concur here. He too was concerned that the expansion of the fulus circulation was unjust and advocates the establishment of value for copper coinage according to a 'fair' value in exchange, rather than by means of a fiat value imposed by the state :
He [ibn-Taimiyah] asked the Sultan to check erosion of the value of money which caused such a disturbance in the economy. He opposes debasement in the currency and over-production of money. He says 'the authority should mint the coins (other than gold and silver) according to the just value of peoples' transactions, without any injustice to them'.
Islahi, A. A., *Economic Concepts of Ibn-Taimiyah* (1988) p. 141

Ibn-Khaldun's idea that money is equated with wealth and that economic activity is largely directed at the accumulation of gold and silver, rather than the accumulation of goods, appeared later in history as a key feature of the mercantilist tradition. Under mercantilism, the selling of goods abroad was prioritised since it led to just such an accumulation of precious metal wealth. In this world view, the importing of goods was therefore deemed economically undesirable since it could only lead to a diminution of the precious metal stock in the domestic economy. Among others from the age of mercantilism, Misselden in *Free Trade, or the Meanes to Make Trade Flourish* (1662) and Thomas Mun in *A Discourse of Trade From England to the East Indies* (1621) portray the same ideas in one form or another.

While gold and silver may be considered by men as 'treasure', it is a rather stronger statement to suggest that the accumulation of this treasure is the objective of economic activity. To go still further and make such accumulation the objective of life, as seems to be the case in many quarters nowadays, certainly contradicts the Islamic view. In Islam, money is a means to an end, not an end in itself. Yet because of the artificial shortage of money that has been created by the commercial banks' core activity, it is quite understandable why so many people have come to focus so persistently on 'making money'. What other reaction would one expect in a society where total money supply is insufficient to repay existing debt?

Debasement is unambiguously condemned, and both al-Maqrizi and ibn-Taimiyah predate Gresham on the topic:
Moreover, if the intrinsic value of coins are different it will become a source of profit for the wicked to collect the small (bad) coins and exchange them (for good money) and then they will take them to another country and shift the small (bad) money of that country (to this country).
Ibn-Taimiyah, *Majmu Fatawa Shaikh al-Islam* in Economic Concepts of ibn-Taimiyah (1988) p. 143

Naturally, counterfeiting is also prohibited:
It is an oppression on the public to use counterfeit coins. The first man to use such coins will get the sins of every person who subsequently transfers them to other persons.
al-Ghazali, *The Revivification of the Sciences of Religion*, Vol 2 p. 63

In adopting two precious metals as the monetary medium, the rulers of the Islamic empire became familiar with the problems of bimetallism. The mistake of employing fixed bimetallic ratios had noticeable consequences during the reign of al-Muiz. Once more the hand of the state replaces the force of the market in determining the exchange value of coinage, fiat value arises, and the familiar problems begin. Al-Maqrizi's account of the events of this period is reproduced by Aidit Ghazali:
The value of the dirham to the dinar fell again ... This created some disturbance among the people. The state then acted upon the matter by dispatching twenty trunks full of new dirham. An order was decreed prohibiting transactions using the old dirham. A three day grace period was given for the exchange of old dirhams for new ones. The old ones then had to be surrendered to the Dar al-Dabi, the department for the printing of money. Exchange rate was fixed at 1 new dirham = 4 old dirhams, and the exchange rate between the new dirham and the dinar was set at 1 dinar = 18 dirhams.
Ghazali, A., *Islamic Thinkers on Economics, Administration and Transactions* (1991)

A rather different, but vital, aspect of the currency debate has been dealt with by Siddiqi when he reflects upon the importance of zakat:
Liquidity premium is not the cause but the effect of interest ... To discourage hoarding and bring money on a par with other assets (commodities) it should be subjected to a carrying cost besides being divested of liquidity premium by abolition of interest. ... The key to a solution lies in subjecting money to the natural law of depreciation over time to which all other commodities are subjected. This is the Islamic principle of Zakat which makes all forms of private wealth 'depreciate' from the viewpoint of the private owner by about 2.5% per annum. This will discourage hoarding and make all money circulate.

Siddiqi, M. N., *Issues in Islamic Banking* (1983) p. 16

Siddiqi's argument might have found favour with Silvio Gesell, whose proposal during the 1920's for a date-stamped money attracted the attention of Keynes:
[Gesell] points out that the rate of interest is a purely monetary phenomenon and that the peculiarity of money lies in the fact that its ownership as a means of storing wealth involves the holder in negligible carrying charges, and that stocks of wealth, such as stocks of commodities which do involve carrying charges, in fact yield a return because of the standard set by money. ... He argues that the growth of real capital is held back by the money rate of interest, and that if this brake were removed the growth of real capital would be, in the modern world, so rapid that a zero money rate of interest would probably be justified, not indeed forthwith, but within a comparatively short period of time. Thus the prime necessity is to reduce the money rate of interest, and this, he pointed out, can be effected by causing money to incur carrying costs just like other stocks of barren goods. This led him to the famous prescription of stamped money with which his name is chiefly associated and which has received the blessing of Professor Irving Fisher. According to this proposal, currency notes (though it would clearly need to apply as well to some forms at least of bank-money) would only retain their value by being stamped each month ... with stamps purchased at a post office. The cost of the stamps could, of course, be fixed at any appropriate figure. The idea behind stamped money is sound. It is indeed possible that means might be found to apply it in practice on a modest scale. But there are many difficulties which Gesell did not face. In particular, he was not aware that money is not unique in having a liquidity premium attached to it, but differed only in degree from other articles, deriving its importance from having a greater liquidity premium than any other article. Thus if currency notes were to be deprived of their liquidity premium by the stamping system, a long series of substitutes would step into their shoes, bank money, debts at call, foreign money and the precious metals.

Keynes, J. M., *The General Theory of Employment Interest and Money* (1936) p. 355-358

Since money can be lent at a nominal 'money-rate' of interest, the choice between lending money at interest and employing physical wealth in a productive process would always be in favour of lending money unless physical wealth could be used in a productive process to yield at least as attractive a rate of return. The marginal rate of return on such physical investments as are undertaken, Keynes's Marginal Efficiency of Capital (or MEC), must then be above the rate of interest on borrowed funds in order for the businessman to make profit. Where this expectation is not held, the businessman will choose not to invest borrowed money into physical capital goods.

In order to encourage greater investment into physical capital goods, Gesell advocates the imposition of a cost of carry to money, achieved through the date-stamping mechanism described above. Gesell suggests 5.2% per year as the price of the date-stamps in terms of face value. Keynes meanwhile, argues that 5.2% per annum would have been too much for the circumstances of his time but both essentially agree that the system would effect the taxation of idle money, and that since invested money would yield a return, the incentive to invest would be substantially encouraged. The stamped money proposition is not simply a form of remedy to stimulate investment against the impact of interest. It is an encouragement to invest whether interest exists or not and, as Siddiqi points out, it allows our financial conventions to more closely describe the physical world in which we live.

In giving his qualified support to Gesell's proposal, Keynes points out that a long line of substitutes would exist to fill the shoes of stamped currency notes once people rejected them as being too expensive to hold as a form of wealth. He criticises Gesell for not realising this to be the case. All other forms of money-like wealth would have to be taxed too, argues Keynes, for example bank deposits, jewellery and precious metals. What then would Keynes have thought of the zakat wealth tax? Since zakat impacts upon money and money-like wealth at 2.5% year, whatever form that wealth takes, would it not achieve precisely what he, Gesell and Fisher were in favour of?

Under the Islamic banking and monetary system described in this work, the accounting identity between money supply and debt would cease to exist. Since investments would no longer be made as interest bearing loans of newly created money, but rather as profit and loss sharing investments of existing money, money supply would no longer be forced to grow in sympathy with a pre-defined interest rate. This fundamental difference between the performance of the two alternative monetary systems has yet to be widely recognised.

The state would act to validate the authenticity and enforce standards of quality on producers of intrinsic money, money that has value irrespective of the force of law, money that is given its value by the free choices of the people. Whether such money is a commodity, or a basket of commodities such as Bernard Lietaer's "Terra", freedom of valuation and absence of usury remain two crucial principles in its adoption.

It is only by jumping over a series of legal and practical hurdles, for example by expanding the law of legal tender and by making interest a tax deductible expense, that the banking establishment has managed to force its monetary system upon society. If we turn to this establishment for solutions to the debt and monetary crises of our age, we will be provided with solutions that are not cures, cough medicine when what is required is that the patient gives up smoking. Except that in this case the one who prescribes the cough medicine will also be the one who manufactures the cigarettes. We will see wonderful announcements, monetary unions, "fresh starts" and all manner of slogans, but the one thing we will not see is genuine change. For that, we need to appoint an entirely different doctor, one who is independent of the illness, and we need to have the confidence to listen to his advice in the face of open hostility from the usury lobby.

IN CONCLUSION

I have argued that the original and most important reason for the growth of commercial banking was the profit that arose in the process of manufacturing money for lending at interest. Banking was the industry, money the product. In the modern world the same motive drives commercial banking in a highly sophisticated way. An individual can be arrested for 'manufacturing' money in his own home but the commercial banking system is given the full protection of the law in doing what amounts to the same thing. There is no justice in this.

Every year the United States government pays hundreds of thousands of millions of dollars in interest on its national debt. Other 'rich' nations are paying similarly huge amounts of interest on their own national debt. Yet this debt need not exist in the first place and the interest payments on it are therefore incurred unnecessarily. The Third World countries have been entrapped with more obviously vicious results. They cannot manufacture Western money out of nothing in order to get by. For them, the only method of economic survival is to export their resources en masse to the developed world or to go still deeper into debt.

The commercial banking system in its current form inflicts a cost upon the whole of society, even those few whose finances are removed from the world of banking and debt. Fractional reserve banking is a major cause of inflation in the modern world, and the lending criteria on which it operates encourage speculative booms and large inequalities in wealth.

Society has always lived with the risk that events in the real world may prove harmful to its wealth. In most cases, it has responded by designing an infrastructure that minimises these risks. Yet where our monetary arrangements are concerned we find ourselves saddled with an infrastructure that is inherently unstable, that actually increases the amount of risk society must bear. The ill effects of real world events can be magnified out of all proportion by the workings this flawed monetary system. Indeed, the system itself has now become a source of risk to society.

Knowing what dangers lurk within the modern world of banking and finance, the politicians are obliged to battle for its stability. They call this battle 'monetary policy'. It is a policy in which I do not believe. I argue for a currency of intrinsic value that cannot be manufactured by a monopoly of bankers or at the whim of the state. Real factors may change the purchasing power of money but the decisions of the financial establishment surely should not do so.

Keynes said of Gesell that 'he displayed more passion than is decent in a scientist'. But even scientists may find their passions rising when confronted by the tinkering irrelevance of modern economics. Whilst the practice of fractional reserve banking goes largely unchallenged, Ormerod informs us that the academic establishment is debating 'upper hemicontinuity at the continuum limit' and 'the hypothesis that agents' relative risk aversion coefficients are smaller than one'. Intellectual self-abuse and attempts to describe the intricacies of modern life with complex formulae mistake the purpose of economics entirely. Ultimately, economists are here to advise on ways of improving the economic system, not to understand better how an unjust system operates. Let us waste less time predicting the future of the world on a computer model or extrapolating trends and selling the results as informed analysis. Let us sit down and be normative.

Nowadays, economic growth is heralded as the ultimate goal of most governments. It is a goal forced upon society as it struggles to meet the interest charges on its debt. Whilst debt grows at compound interest towards infinity, in the physical world everything depreciates towards zero. I propose that the price we shall eventually pay for running this unwinnable race against compound interest is a polluted and depleted world.

In the absence of interest, our economic efforts would be directed away from wealth transfer and towards wealth creation. The entrepreneur would share his profit with the financier according to mutual good fortune, not an arbitrary rate of interest. The practice of leverage would largely disappear and with it the speculative mentality of our time. Business would be encouraged to preserve our environment, not to discount it into oblivion. Small scale enterprise would flourish and debt leveraged monoliths would gradually wither.

In my private nightmare, the high street in every town offers nothing but the anonymous facades of giant banking institutions, paid for by the profits of fractional reserve banking. Perhaps it is symbolic of the end that awaits us, the final victory of banking over human industry. It is an end that both Cobbett and Soddy foresaw. For Cobbett the road of truth led to prison, for Soddy to the humiliating conclusion of an illustrious career. Their enemies were powerful and had no reason to let their advantage slip. In the decades since, their grip has tightened, their political influence has deepened, and their literature has overwhelmed our academic institutions.

With so many opinions to choose from in the field of economics, politicians have little chance of identifying the most worthy alternatives. Surrounded by the cronies of the orthodox establishment, they are subjected to a continuous bombardment of conventional theory, which they then parrot to the public before moving on to their next appointment. In this manner, the safe ideas of consensus economics are perpetuated, of interest rate and monetary policy, of selfish economic man and value-free economics.

Islamic finance is not a product to be offered to a niche market. It is part of the whole that we call Islamic society, a system that must work together with other systems in order to function correctly. The Islamic monetary system is one such system and it cannot be established by the private sector alone. A lead is required from the State, since there is a need to redefine the meaning of the words 'legal tender'. We must somehow overturn the monetary system as it is. We need a payment transmission system, a safekeeping service, and investment advisory services. To all these things, yes. To money creation for the sake of profit, no.

BIBLIOGRAPHY

The Qur'an
(Translations from Arabic by Ali, Y. and Asad, M.)

The Revised English Bible
OUP, CUP (1989)

Chambers Science and Technology Dictionary
(W & R Chambers Ltd., CUP 1988)

Ahmad, K. (Editor)	*Studies in Islamic Economics* International Centre for Research in Islamic Economics and The Islamic Foundation (1976)
al-Mawardi, Abu'l-Hasan	*The Laws of Islamic Governance* (English translation by Dr. Asadullah Yate Phd) Ta-Ha Publishers Ltd. (1996)
Al-Maqrizi, Ahmad ibn Ali	*Ighathah* (English translation by Adel Allouche) University of Utah Press (1994)
al-Qaradawi, Y.	*Islamic Awakening Between Rejection and Extremism* International Islamic Publishing House, The International Institute of Islamic Thought (1995)
Alwani, T. J.	*Ijtihad* International Institute of Islamic Thought (1993)
Angell, James W.	*The 100 Per Cent Reserve Plan* Quarterly Journal of Economics, Vol 50, Issue 1, p. 1-35 (November 1935)
Asad, M.	*The Principles of State and Government in Islam* Dar al-Andalous (1980)
Bain, A. D.	*The Economics of the Financial System* Blackwell Publishers Limited (1981)
Bank of England	*Statistical Abstract Part 2* Bank of England (1993)
Bank of England	*Quarterly Bulletin September* Bank of England (1981)

Bank of England — *The Transmission Mechanism of Monetary Policy*
Monetary Policy Committee (2001)

Barro, R. — *Money and the Price Level Under the Gold Standard*
The Economic Journal, 89 (March 1979)

Belchamber, C. — *The U.K. Government Bond Market*
Credit Suisse First Boston Limited (1988)

Bingham, R. D. and Hill, E. W. and White, S. B. (Editors) — *Financing Economic Development*
Sage Publications (1990)

Böhm-Bawerk, E. — *Positive Theorie des Kapitales*
Universitäts-Buchhandlung, Innsbruck, (1889)

Brealey, R. A. and Myers, S. C. — *Principles of Corporate Finance*
McGraw Hill Book Company (1988)

Brittan, S. — *The Role and Limits of Government : Essays in Political Economy*
Wildwood House Limited (1987)

Cappie, F. H., & Wood, G. E. — *Monetary Problems, Monetary Solutions and the Role of Gold*, Research Study No. 25, World Gold Council (April 2001)

Chown, J. F. — *A History of Money*
Routledge, The Institute of Economic Affairs (1993)

Clapham, Sir J. — *The Bank of England: A History* Cambridge University Press (1944)

Clarke, G. M. and Cooke, D. — *A Basic Course in Statistics*
Edward Arnold (1992)

Cline, W. R. — *The Economics of Global Warming*
Institute for International Economics (1992)

Cobbett, W. M. — *Paper Against Gold*
W. M. Cobbett, 183 Fleet Street, London (1812)

Connolly, B. — *The Rotten Heart of Europe*
Faber and Faber (1995)

Cox, J. C., Rubinstein, M. — *Options Markets*
Prentice-Hall (1985)

Das, Satyajit	*Swaps And Financial Derivatives* IFR Books (1994)
Deane, M. and Pringle, R.	*The Central Banks* Hamish Hamilton (1994)
Doi, A. R. I.	*Shari'ah: The Islamic Law* Ta-Ha Publishers Ltd. (1984)
Fabozzi, F. J. and Pollack, I.M.	*The Handbook of Fixed Income Securities* Dow Jones Irwin (1983)
Fage, P. and Hannigan, T.	*The Deutsche Mark Bond Markets* Credit Suisse First Boston (1988)
Feaveryear, A. E.	*The Pound Sterling, A History of English Money* Oxford at the Clarendon Press, 1931
Fisher, I.	*100% Money* Adelphi, New York (1935)
Fitzgerald, M. D.	*Financial Futures* Euromoney Publications (1983) *Financial Options* Euromoney Publications (1987)
Francis, J. C.	*Investments* McGraw-Hill Book Company (1986)
Galbraith, K.	*The Affluent Society* Penguin Books (1984) *The Nature of Mass Poverty* Penguin Books (1979) *Economics in Perspective* Houghton Mifflin Company (1987)
Gale, D.	*Money in Disequilibrium* James Nisbet and Company Ltd., Press Syndicate University of Cambridge (1983) *Money in Equilibrium* CUP (1982)
Georgescu-Roegen, N.	*The Entropy Law and the Economic Process* HUP, Massachusetts (1971)
Goodhart, C. A. E.	*Monetary Theory and Practice* Macmillan Education Limited (1984)

Graham, Frank D.   *Partial Reserve Money and the 100 Per Cent Proposal*
American Economic Review, Vol 26, Issue 3, p. 428-440 (September 1936)

Green, T.   *Central Bank Gold Reserves*, Research Study No. 23, World Gold Council (November 1999)

Haneef, M. A.   *Contemporary Islamic Economic Thought*
Ikraq, Kuala Lumpur (1995)

Hargreaves Heap, S. P. and Varoufakis, Y.   *Game Theory*
Routledge (1995)

Harmston, S.   *Gold as a Store of Value*, Research Study No. 22, World Gold Council (November 1998)

Hawking, S. W.   *A Brief History of Time*
Bantam Books (1988)

Haykal, M. H.   *The Life of Muhammad*
(8th. Edition English translation by Faruqi, I.)
The Islamic Book Trust (1993)

Henry, S. G. B.   *Elementary Mathematical Economics*
Routledge, Kegan Paul Ltd. (1969)

Holt, P. M. and Lambton, A. K. S. and Lewis, B.   *The Cambridge History of Islam*
CUP (1970)

Homer, S. & Sylla, R.   *A History of Interest Rates, 3rd. Ed.*
Rutgers, The State University (1996)

Howells, P. G. A. and Bain, K.   *Financial Markets and Institutions*
Longman Group UK Ltd. (1994)

HSBC Holdings plc   *Annual Report and Accounts 1997*

Hull, J.   *Options, Futures and Other Derivative Securities*
Prentice-Hall International Inc. (1993)

Hutton, W.   *The State We're In*
Jonathan Cape (1995)

ibn Kathir   *Tafsir ibn Kathir*
(abridged by Ar-Rafa'i, M. N.)
al-Firdous Ltd. (1996)

Ibn Khaldun	*The Muqaddimah* (abridged edition, tr. Rosenthal, F.) New York, Princeton University Press (1967)
ibn Taimiyah	*Public Duties in Islam, The Institution of the Hisba* (English translation by Muhtar Holland) The Islamic Foundation (1985)
Imam an-Nawawi	*Riyadh-us-Saleheen* (English translation by Abbasi, S. M.) Dar al-Arabia, Beirut (1983)
Imam Ghazali	*Ihya Ulum-id-din* (English translation by Karim M. F.) Kitab Bhavan, New Delhi (1982)
Imam Malik	*al-Muwatta'* (English translation by Rahimuddin, Prof. M.) Sh. Muhammad Ashraf, Lahore (1985)
Imam Muslim	*Sahih Muslim* (revised English translation by Matraji, Dr. M.) Dar al-Fiker, Beirut (1993)
International Institute of Islamic Thought	*Islamization of Knowledge* International Institute of Islamic Thought (1989)
Islahi, A. A.	*Economic Concepts of Ibn Taimiyah* The Islamic Foundation (1988)
Islamic Council of Europe	*The Muslim World and the Future Economic Order* The Islamic Council of Europe (1979)
Islamic Research and Training Institute	*Developing a System of Financial Instruments* Islamic Research and Training Institute & Islamic Development Bank (1990)
Kamali, M. H.	*Principles of Islamic Jurisprudence* Pelanduk Publications, Selangor (1989)
Kauffman, G. B. (Editor)	*Frederick Soddy* D. Reidel Publishing Company, Holland (1986)
Keynes, J. M.	*The General Theory of Employment, Interest and Money* Macmillan & CUP (1936)
Khan, M. A.	*Glossary of Islamic Economics* The Islamic Foundation (1990)

Khan, M. F.	*Essays in Islamic Economics* The Islamic Foundation (1995)
Kirzner, I. M. (Editor)	*Classics in Austrian Economics* William Pickering (1995)
Landau, R.	*Islam and the Arabs* George Allen and Unwin Ltd.(1958)
Macleod, H. D.	*Bimetalism* Longmans, Green and Company, New York (1894)
Mannan, M. A.	*Economic Development and Social Peace in Islam* Ta-Ha Publishers Ltd. (1989)
McCormick, B., Kitchin, P., ...	*Introducing Economics* Penguin Books (1983)
McKenna, R.	*Post-war Banking Policy* William Heinemann Ltd., London (1928)
Miller, M.,	*Debt and the Environment: Converging Crises* United Nations (1991)
Mishkin, F. S.	*Money, Banking and Financial Markets* Harper Collins Publishers, New York (1992)
Mubarakpuri, Sheikh S.	*The Sealed Nectar* Maktaba Dar-us-Salam, Riyadh (1996)
An-Nabhani, Taqiuddin	*The Economic System in Islam, 4th edition* Al-Khilafah Publications, London (1997)
Nasr, S. H.	*Islam and the Plight of Modern Man* Longman Group Ltd. (1975)
Nevitt, P. K. and Fabozzi, F.	*Project Financing, 6th Edition* Euromoney Publications (1995)
Noonan, J.	*The Scholastic Inquiry Into Usury* Harvard University Press (1957)
Ormerod, P.	*The Death of Economics* Faber and Faber Limited (1994)
Pepper, G.	*Money, Credit and Asset Prices* St. Martins Press Inc., New York (1994)

Philips, Abu Ameenah Bilal	*The Evolution of Fiqh* International Islamic Publishing House, Riyadh (1995)
Price, C.	*Time, Discounting and Value* Blackwell Publishers (1993)
Quigley, C.	*Tragedy and Hope: A History of the World in Our Time* Macmillan, New York (1966)
Ramadan, S.	*Islamic Law* P. R. Macmillan Limited (1970)
Roll, E.	*A History of Economic Thought* Faber and Faber Limited (1992)
Rowbotham, M.	*The Grip of Death* Jon Carpenter Publishing (1998)
Sabiq, As-Sayyid	*Fiqh us-Sunnah* (English translation by Dabas, Zarabozo J. M.) American Trust Publications, Indiana (1991)
Sarnoff, P.	*Trading in Financial Futures* Woodhead-Faulkner Limited (1985)
Shelton, J.	*Money Meltdown* The Free Press, New York (1994)
Siddiqi, M. N.	*Banking Without Interest* The Islamic Foundation (1988) *Issues in Islamic Banking* The Islamic Foundation (1983)
Siddiqi, M. Z.	*Hadith Literature* The Islamic Texts Society (1993)
Soddy, F.	*The Role of Money* George Routledge And Sons (1934)
Stewart, M.	*Keynes and After* Penguin Books (1986)
Stigum, M.	*The Money Market* Dow Jones Irwin (1983)

Taylor, A. J. P.	*English History 1914-1945* Penguin Books (1975)
Thomas, A. S.	*What is Permissible Now!?* The Muslim Converts' Association of Singapore (1995)
Thomas, H.	*An Unfinished History of the World* Hamish Hamilton (1979)
Thomas, Rollin G.	*100 Per Cent Money: The Present Status of the 100 Per Cent Plan* American Economic Review, Vol 30, Issue 2, p. 315-323 (Jun 1940)
Trevelyan, G. M.	*A Shortened History of England* Penguin Books (1942)
Umari, A. D.	*Madinan Society at the Time of the Prophet* (English translation by Khattab, H.) International Islamic Publishing House & International Institute of Islamic Thought (1992)
United Nations Development Programme	*Human Development Report* (1996, 1997, 1998)
ur-Rahim, A.	*Jesus Prophet of Islam* Tahrike Tarsile Qur'an Inc., New York (1991)
Vadillo, 'Umar.	*The End of Economics* Madina Press, Granada (1991)
Wells, H. G.	*A Short History of the World* Penguin Books (1965)
Yusuf, S. M.	*Economic Justice in Islam* Kitab Bhavan, New Delhi (1988)
Zaman, S. M. H.	*Economic Functions of an Islamic State* The Islamic Foundation (1981)

INDEX

100% reserve ratio, 73

added-value, 100, 102, 106, 109, 111, 112, 117
agent as representative, 144
ahadith, 125, 140, 145
Ahmad, I., 177
akhlaq, 126
al-aqd, 144
al-Ghazali, 144, 145, 155
allocation of resources, 107, 116, 130
al-Maqrizi, 187, 188
amana, 158
aqidah, 126, 128
Arabic, 135, 156
arbitrage, 84, 88
asset sale compared to debt sale, 152
asset trading, 152
astronomy, 122
auction in Islam, 147
automatic stabiliser, 81
average earnings, 116

balance sheet, 47, 48, 64, 179, 181
bank balance sheet, 47
bank balance sheet, 47
Bank Charter Act 1844, 45
bank collapse, at Hyogo Bank, 178
bank credit, 79
bank money, 35

Bank of England, 41, 42, 43, 45, 46, 51, 63, 64, 67, 80, 86, 87, 88, 89, 90, 91, 179
bank runs, 37, 45, 49
bank statements, 46
Banking Act 1987 (UK), 179
bay, 145
bay al-dayn, 151, 152
bay al-salam, 145, 150
bay al-urban, 148
bay bithamin ajil, 149, 160, 162, 163, 166, 180
bay mu'ajjal, 149, 159
bay muzayadah, 147
bearer notes, 36, 42
Bentham, 119
bil kalam, 144
bil kitabah, 144
bimetallism, 188
Bischof, R., 65
Boltzman, L., 4
bond, 42, 62, 105, 166, 167
Bretton Woods, 91, 92, 93, 94, 95, 96
Brussels Agreement, 96
Bucaille, M., 122
Bukhari, 125, 146

calling in of loans, 52
capital stock, 21, 99
Carnot, S., 4
central bank, 48, 49, 50, 51, 52, 56, 59, 62, 63, 75, 93, 94, 95, 103, 177
central bank directives, 63

central bank reserves, 88, 90, 91, 93, 94, 95
charity, 154
cheque, 35, 46, 48, 49, 50, 87
Chown, D., 23, 45, 87
Churchill, W., 90, 93
Cobbett, W., 44, 73
coins, 84
collapse of Kizu Shinyo Kumiai, 178
collateral, 41, 99, 107, 108, 110, 111, 112, 113, 117, 151, 160, 166, 171, 180, 181
commercial bank reserves, 36, 37, 43, 45, 48, 49, 50, 52, 57, 70, 71, 72
commercial contracts in Islam, 145
company shares, 157
competition, 102, 133
compound interest, 8
Congdon, T., 65
consensus economics, ix
contract, 144
contract (options in Islamic law), 148
contracts (basic conditions in Islam), 144
contracts (deferred exchange in Islam), 146
contracts (exchange of ownership in Islam), 145
contracts (no short selling in Islam), 146
contracts (offer and acceptance in Islam), 144
contracts (permissible subject matter in Islam), 146
contracts of charity, 145

contracts of exchange, 145
contracts of investment, 145
contracts with non-Muslims, 145
contractum trinius, 23, 147
convenience, 130
Copernicus, ix, 123
corset, 63
Council of Nicea, 23
countervalue, 76, 105, 139, 145, 151
country banks, 45
coupon, 166, 167

daman, 159
daruriat, 129
debasement, 85, 187
debt, 8, 12, 13, 46, 53, 56, 62, 72, 73, 88, 91, 107, 108, 109, 110, 112, 133, 152, 167, 168, 170, 172, 177, 191, 192
debt deflation, 114
deception, 143
deductive, 123
deflation, 69, 113, 114, 116
deforestation, 12, 13
denomination, 43, 82, 83
deposit multiplier, 47
deposit-taking institutions, 47
destabilisation, 105
devaluation, 92, 94, 108
dicount houses, 51
diminishing musharakah, 155
dinar, 186, 188
dirham, 186, 188
discount, 14, 15, 18, 20, 21, 22, 29, 50, 51, 52, 63
discount market, 50, 51

discount rate, 14, 15, 18, 20, 21, 22, 29, 51
discount rate (financial market usage), 51
discount rate compared with interest rate, 51
discounted cash-flow analysis, 13
discounting, 16, 17, 19, 20, 21, 22, 111, 112, 117, 192
Discounting, 29
discounting of financial instruments, 50
dividend, 110, 114, 170
Doane, R., 131
ducats, 84

Earl of Liverpool, 43
Earth, ix, 3, 5, 7, 11, 12, 19, 22, 31, 32, 122, 123, 127, 129, 132
education, 99, 109
Edward I, 84
eligible bills, 51
eligible liabilities, 63
endogenous utility, 120
energy, 1, 2, 3, 5, 6, 11, 32, 106
eurobonds, 95
eurodollars, 95
exchange rate, 75, 82, 88, 89, 90, 91, 92, 93, 94, 96, 97, 102, 103, 188
exogenous utility, 120
expectation, 114, 181
export, 12, 84
exports, 65
externalities, 6

farthings, 84
Faysal Islamic Bank, 180

Federal Reserve, 56, 94, 95, 97
fiat money, 52, 53, 79
finance leases, 151
fiqh, 125
Fiqh Academy, 153
fixed exchange rates, 92, 94
floating exchange rates, 96, 97
Florence, 84
flow concepts, 3
forward, 159
fourthings, 84
fractional reserve banking, 38
Friedman, M., 62
fulus, 187
fungible, 150
future value, 10, 105
futures market, 104, 105

GDP, 12, 20, 88, 89, 99, 100
gearing, 170, 172
Gestetner, 104
gharar, 135, 145
Ghazali, A., 188
Gibsons Greetings, 104
gift, 154
gifts, 154
global warming, 5, 19, 20
God, 5, 25, 122, 124, 125, 126, 127, 128, 129, 132, 133, 140, 141, 163, 185
gold, 35, 36, 37, 38, 43, 44, 45, 46, 50, 53, 76, 77, 79, 80, 81, 82, 83, 84, 85, 86, 87, 88, 89, 90, 91, 92, 93, 94, 95, 96, 97, 104, 120, 132, 138, 169, 184, 185, 186, 187
gold standard, 76, 80, 81, 82, 86, 87, 88, 90, 91, 92, 93, 95, 97
Gold Standard, 75, 82

government bills, 50
government bonds, 42
government borrowing, 42
greenhouse effect, 19
Gresham's Law, 86
growth, 21, 29, 56, 62, 63, 65, 66, 67, 68, 79, 100, 170, 183, 189, 192

hadith, 125
hajiat, 129
halal, 128
halfpennies, 84
Hanbal, 145, 146
Hanifa, 146, 148, 155
haram, 127, 154
Hayek, F, 73
Henry III, 84
Henry VIII, 85
hiba, 154
high powered money, 56
hikma, 125
Hizb ut-Tahrir, 157
hoarding, 189
house prices, 66, 115, 116
housing, 64, 66, 108, 116
hukm, 125
human reproduction, 122
Hutton, W., 68

ibadat, 126
ibn-Khaldun, 187
ibn-Rushd, 156
ibn-Taimiyah, 152
ijara, 150, 151, 169
ijara wa iqtina, 151
ijma, 125
ijtihad, 125
illa, 125

IMF, ix, 92, 93, 94
imports, 67, 94
inductive, 123, 124
industry, 6, 21, 32, 65, 168, 177
inflation, ix, x, 17, 25, 26, 61, 64, 65, 66, 67, 68, 69, 85, 86, 92, 94, 97, 114, 182, 183, 191
injustice, 141, 170, 187
inter-bank cheque clearing, 50
interest rate, ix, 10, 13, 16, 20, 25, 27, 28, 29, 46, 51, 56, 64, 65, 66, 67, 68, 89, 90, 91, 92, 94, 95, 97, 102, 109, 110, 113, 162, 177, 180
interest spread, 46
interest-based loan, 151
IOU, 53
IPCC, 19
isentropic state, 4
Islam, vii, xi, 25, 122, 123, 124, 126, 127, 128, 129, 132, 133, 141, 144, 152, 159, 162, 163, 168, 172, 175, 183, 184, 187, 188, 195, 198, 199, 200, 202
Islamic bank, 160, 161, 180
Islamic banks, 149, 153, 159, 160, 161, 162, 179, 180, 181
istisna, 151, 159

Jefferson, T., 73, 87
jizhya, 132
judgement, 119, 125, 126

Kahf, M,, 175
Kamali, Prof., 146, 152
Keynes, J., 25, 30, 93, 189, 190, 192
Keynesian, 96
khalifa, 129

Khan, F., 130, 172, 173
kharaj, 132
khiyar, 148
King William III, 41
Knight, F., 62, 73

labour, 21, 79
Lawson, N., 64, 65, 66
lease payments, 150, 151
lender of last resort, 49
lessee, 151
lessor, 150
leverage, 105, 112, 113, 170, 172, 192
Lipton, M., 13, 16
liquidity, 30, 52, 63, 90, 103, 111, 112, 114, 117, 176, 177, 179, 189
liquidity preference, 30
loan losses, 41
Lord Hanson, 22
Louvre Accord, 97
Lucca, 84
luxury, 120

MacDonald, R., 91
maisir, 135, 141, 145
mal, 156
Malik, 146, 155, 163
margin, 42, 104
marginal productivity of capital, 20
marginal utility, 120
Marshall, A., 4
maslahah, 129, 130
Maslow, 129
means testing, 132
Menger, 120
Metallgesellschaft, 104

minting of coins, 45, 53, 83, 84, 187
Mishkin, F., 56
monetarists, 65, 67
monetary aggregate, 66
monetary base, 56, 62
monetisation, 73
money at call, 52
money supply, 42, 48, 52, 54, 56, 57, 60, 61, 62, 63, 64, 65, 67, 68, 69, 71, 72, 75, 77, 79, 81, 85, 87, 88, 91, 92, 93, 94, 96, 97, 110, 113, 114, 182, 183
money supply (narrow measure), 59
money supply (wide measure), 59
money supply and neo-classicists, 61
mortgage, 66, 67, 116
muamalat, 126, 127, 128
mudarabah, 156, 172, 176, 177, 180
mudarib, 156
multiple deposit expansion, 48
mumayyiz, 144
Mun, T., 187
murabahah, 148, 149, 159, 160, 162, 163, 169, 180
murahanah, 141
musharakah, 155, 169, 172, 176, 177, 180
Muslim, xi, 122, 124, 126, 128, 132, 142, 160, 163, 168, 169, 172
Muslim (Imam), 125, 137, 138

narrow money, 62
Nasai, 147

national debt, 43, 44, 72, 191
NDP, 99
necessity, 120, 127
need, 7, 30, 32, 42, 100, 105, 115, 116, 123, 129, 130, 131, 132
nisab, 126, 132
Nixon, R., 94, 96
nominal interest rate, 26
non-operational deposits, 50
normative economics, xi, 119, 120, 192

open market operations, 56
operating lease, 150
operational deposits, 49
option, 50
Ormerod, C., 99, 100, 192
overnight money, 52

paper money, 43, 44, 45, 53, 76, 77, 79, 81, 85, 86, 87, 88, 93
par, 189
parallel market, 50
Parliament, 121, 133
Pasteur, L., ix
payee bank, 49
paying bank, 49
Peel,, 45, 87
performance bond, 150
permanent musharakah, 155
physical world systems, 16, 28, 31, 32, 190, 192
Plaza Accord, 97
pledge, 158
Plender, J., 62
pollution, x, 6, 16, 100
positive economics, xi, 119, 120, 124

poverty, 106, 128, 129
present value, 10, 13, 17
price of money, 29
Price, C., 16, 22, 27, 29, 30
product substitution, 32
production, 11, 21, 43, 44, 53, 60, 79, 81, 106, 107, 113, 120, 150, 151, 169, 183, 187
profit, x, 13, 16, 37, 42, 62, 64, 65, 68, 71, 98, 100, 105, 106, 107, 108, 109, 114, 115, 119, 137, 141, 143, 152, 155, 160, 162, 164, 167, 169, 170, 172, 176, 179, 180, 181, 185, 188, 190, 192
profit-sharing, 145, 156, 160, 172, 176, 179, 181
Profit-sharing, 179
promissory note, 42, 43, 45
Prophet Muhammad s.a.w., 125, 127, 140, 145, 186
Protector Somerset, 85
prudent banking, 37

qard hasan, 153
qiyas, 125
Qur'an, 25, 122, 123, 129, 140, 141, 163, 169, 184
Qur'an, 146

Rahimuddin, Prof., 163
rahn, 158
real rate of interest, 26
receipt, 36, 161
recession, 68, 80
recoinages, 85
rent on money, 30

reserve ratio, 36, 37, 38, 43, 47, 48, 52, 57, 63, 73, 97, 175
reserves shortage, 45
resources, 3, 5, 6, 11, 13, 16, 30, 62, 65, 76, 101, 103, 107, 109, 115, 129, 130, 131, 132, 181
returns on assets, 171
returns on equity investments, 171
revealed knowledge, 121, 123
Revised English Bible, 23
riba, 135, 137, 138, 139, 140, 141, 145, 169
riba al-buyu, 137
riba al-nasia, 137, 164
Ricardo, D., 119
Riley, B., 68
risk, 17, 25, 27, 28, 42, 82, 101, 108, 109, 110, 111, 112, 142, 149, 164, 170, 171, 172, 173, 176, 177, 178, 180, 191, 192
risk premium, 27
Rogaly, J., 102
Rosly, S., 172

S&L's, 177
sadaqa, 132
Saint Augustine, 122
Sarakhsi, 156
saving, 113
science and religion, 122
SDR, 94
securitisation, 166
security, 107, 111, 112, 145, 158, 160, 180
seignorage, 52, 85
Shafi'i, 146, 155, 163
shareholders, 157
Shariah, 126, 130, 147, 152

sharikat al-abdan, 156
sharikat al-inan, 155
sharikat al-mufawada, 156
sharikat al-wujuh, 156
Shelton, J., 81, 82
shock therapy, ix
Siddiqi, N., 176, 177, 181, 189, 190
sight deposit, 175
Sihah Sitta, 125
silver, 44, 83, 84, 85, 86, 87, 132, 138, 184, 185, 186, 187
Simons, H., 73
simple interest, 8
Smith, A., 119
Smithsonian Agreement, 96
Soddy, F., 1, 8, 9, 31, 53, 54, 62, 73
sovereigns, 45, 86, 88
special deposit, 63
speculation, 30, 75, 81, 91, 97, 102, 103, 104, 113, 116, 117, 169
spot market, 105
spot transactions, 105, 146, 148
SRTP, 20, 21
state money, 35
statistical thermodynamics, 4
Sterling, 63, 67, 75, 89, 90, 91, 96
subjective valuation, 120
Sun, 3, 122
sunnah, 125
Suspension of Payments, 43, 86

Tantawi, Sheikh, 137
tasiniat, 130

tax, 28, 91, 92, 95, 101, 102, 108, 109, 119, 132, 133, 172, 190
term deposit, 71, 177
Thatcher, M., 93
thermodynamics, 1, 2, 4, 8
Third World, 62
tijara, 169
time preference, 22, 25, 30
Tirmidhi, 146, 147
Torah, 23
trade, 44, 62, 67, 80, 81, 87, 89, 97, 98, 102, 104, 105, 145, 149, 150, 152, 163, 169
trade deficit, 80
trading of debt, 151
treasure trove, 132
trust, 158
Tudor inflation, 86

uncertainty, x, 81, 104, 142, 143, 144
unemployment, 65, 80, 91
use value, 6, 30
usufruct, 150
usury, 23, 24, 25, 127, 135, 140, 163, 168, 169, 181
utility, 21, 22, 25, 28, 29, 30, 31, 119, 120, 130

value judgement, 119, 120, 121, 124, 126, 128, 133
Venice, 84
virtual wealth, 53
Volker, P., 97, 103
von Mises, L., 82
von Weizsacker, R., 65

wadia, 158, 175
wages, 79, 120
Walras, L., 120
want, 6, 120, 129, 130, 131
waqf, 154
waste, 3, 5
wealth, x, 1, 5, 6, 7, 8, 16, 28, 53, 85, 99, 100, 101, 103, 104, 106, 107, 108, 109, 110, 112, 119, 120, 127, 128, 129, 130, 132, 133, 141, 181, 187, 189, 190, 191, 192
wealth creation, 117
wealth distribution, 133
welfare, 129, 130, 132, 133
World Bank, 92

Yusuf, S., 175

zakat, 132, 133, 135, 181, 190